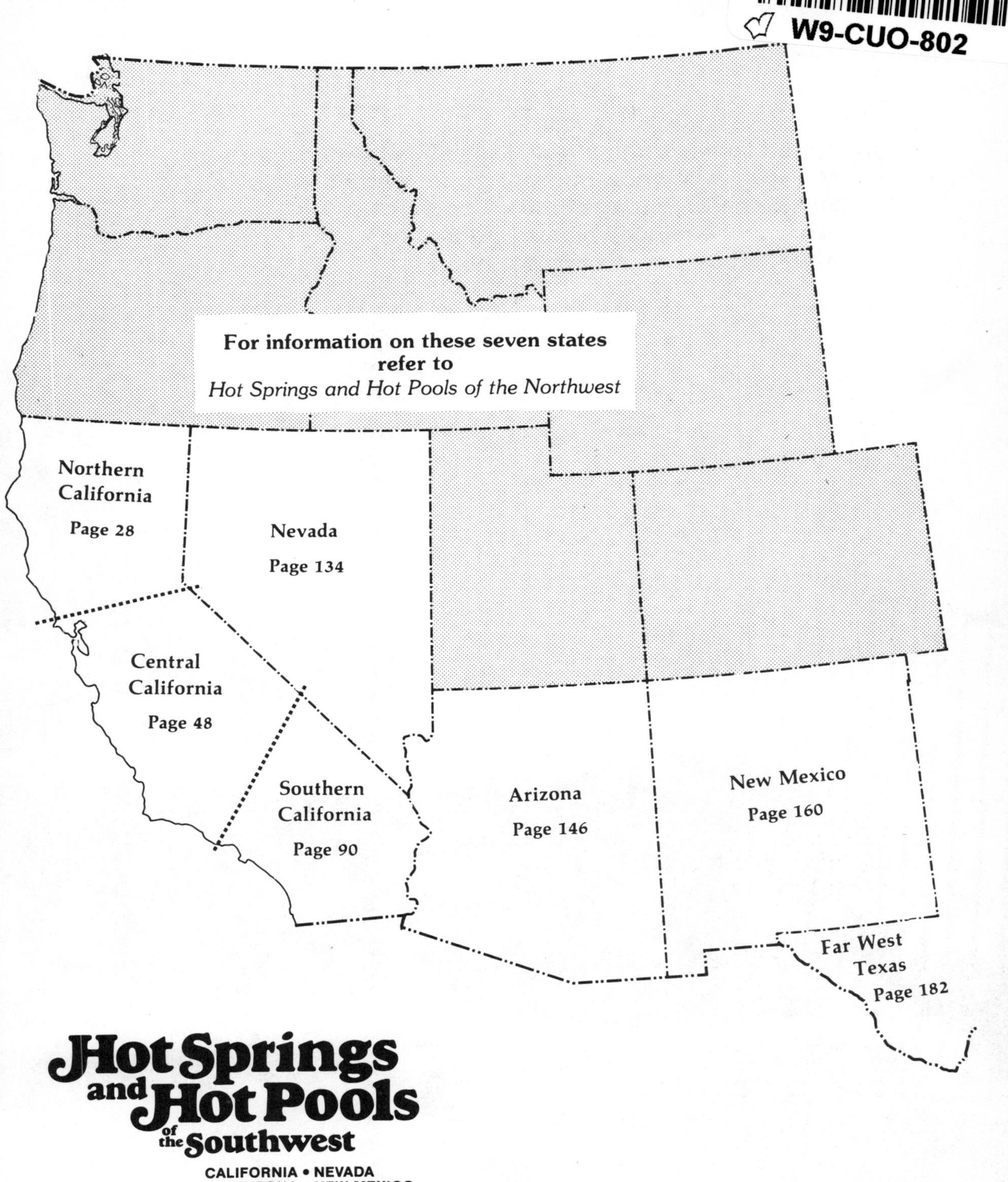

Hot Springs and Hot Pools of the Southwest

CALIFORNIA • NEVADA
ARIZONA • NEW MEXICO

Jayson Loam's original guide to mineral water resorts and spas, wilderness hot springs, flowing hot wells and RV parks with geothermal pools, plus hydropool-equipped motels and private space hot tubs for rent by the hour.

Hot Springs and Hot Pools of the Southwest

CALIFORNIA • NEVADA
ARIZONA • NEW MEXICO

JAYSON LOAM
AND GARY SOHLER

Wilderness Press
Berkeley

Grateful Acknowledgements to:

My son and co-author, Gary Sohler, for taking the initiative by braving the wilds of West Texas and New Mexico before being lured away to Maui; my daughter, Melanie Sohler, for advice and extra hours of work on design, typesetting and map production; Paul Grim, co-author of the NOAA *Thermal Spring List For The United States,* for sending me a personal copy of my primary research tool; National Forest, National Park and Bureau of Land Management personnel for their patient courtesy and generous cooperation; the hot-spring soakers who agreed to be in the photographs; the resort owners for their hospitality; and to Tom Winnett, my publisher, for an uncommon degree of tolerance and understanding as we learned how to combine our respective skills in an efficient manner.

Art Direction by Haaga Design Studio
Maps by Jayson Loam

Library of Congress
Card Catalogue Number 84-51377
ISBN 0-89997-045-01

Manufactured in United States of America
Published by Wilderness Press
2440 Bancroft Way
Berkeley, CA 94704
Write for free catalog

Front cover:		
	Tub Hot Spring	Page 67
Back cover:		
Top left	Glen Ivy Hot Springs	Page 122
Top right	Spence Hot Springs	Page 166
Center right	Boquillas Hot Springs	Page 184
Bottom right	Ten Thousand Waves	Page 171
Bottom left	Best Western Ponce De Leon Hotel	Page 109

DEDICATION

To a gentle nudge, an expert logician, an enthusiastic traveling companion, a willing photographer an understanding literary critic and a truly warm personal friend, Marjorie Gersh, known to me as "Sugah".

Photo Credits:

Kathy Thormud (Esalen Institue), pages 2, 3, 81. Gary Sohler, pages 6, 14, 15, 23, 120, 126 center right, 162, 165 top right and bottom left, 166, 167 top right, 168 top right and bottom center, 169 top left and bottom center, 171 top right, 174, 175, 183, 184, 185, back cover top right, center right and center. Marjorie Gersh, page 27, 159 center left. Tom Winnett, page 60. J.C. Jenkins, page 61. Lupin Lodge, page 76. Alive Polarity, page 105 bottom left and top right. Splash, The Relaxation Spa, pages 128, 129. Hot Tub Fever, pages 130, 131. L.A. Waterworks, page 132 top right and bottom ceter. Ten Thousand Waves, page 170 center top and center bottom, 171 center left, back cover bottom right. Vic Topmiller, page 179. Jayson Loam, front cover, back cover top left and bottom left, and all others.

Contents

1. Put Your Body In The Water

This is a personal book, not an objective report on geothermal phenomena. For me there is a special joy and contentment which comes from soaking in a sandy-bottom pool of flowing natural mineral water, accompanied by good friends and surrounded by the peaceful quiet of a remote primitive setting. At such an idyllic moment it is hard to get overly concerned about geology, history or chemistry. In this book it is my intent to be of service to others who also like to soak in peace, and who need some help finding just the right place.

The cataclysmic folding and faulting of the earth's crust over millions of years is a fascinating subject, especially where geologic forces have combined just the right amount of underground water with just the right amount of deep magma to produce a hot surface flow that goes on for centuries. It would probably be fun to research and write about all this, including new material on geothermal power sources, but that is not what this book is about.

Many hot springs have long histories of special status with Indian tribes which revered the healing and peace-making powers of the magic waters. Those histories often include bloody battles with white men over hot-spring ownership, and there are colorful legends about Indian curses that had dire effects for decades on a whole series of ill-fated owners who tried to deny Indians their traditional access to a sacred tribal spring. That, too, would be an interesting theme for a book someday, but not this book.

In the 19th century it was legal and often quite profitable, to claim that mineral water from a famous spa would cure an impressive list of

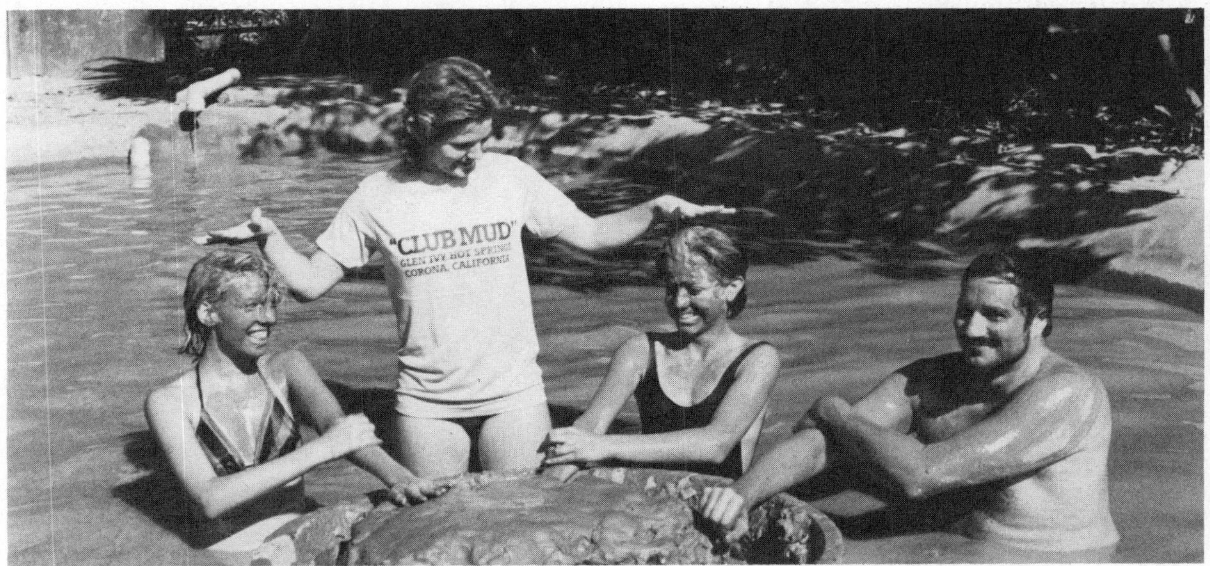

A do-it-yourself beauty treatment of mineral water and red clay at *Glen Ivy Hot Springs.*

ailments. Such advertising is no longer legal, and modern medicine does not include mineral water soaks, or drinks, in its list of treatments, but quite a few people still have an intuitive feeling that, somehow, spending time in natural mineral water is beneficial. I agree with the conclusion that it is "good for you," but it would take an entire book to explore all the scientific and the anecdotal material which attempt to explain *why*. Someone else will have to write that book.

This book simply accepts the facts that hot springs do exist, that they have a history, and that soaking the human body in geothermal water does indeed contribute to a feeling of well-being. That still leaves one very very large practical question: "Where can I go to legally put my body in hot water, how do I get there, and what will I find when I arrive?" To answer that question is the purpose of this book.

One nice thing about creating a new book is the freedom to be arbitrary and to establish personal limits and policies. In my opinion water isn't hot enough to soak in unless it is over 85°, so in this book I simply ignore all those warm springs with lower temperatures. Again, I wanted my readers to keep a whole skin while they are soaking so I do not provide directions to fenced, posted or closed hot springs where they might get arrested or shot for trespassing. I do

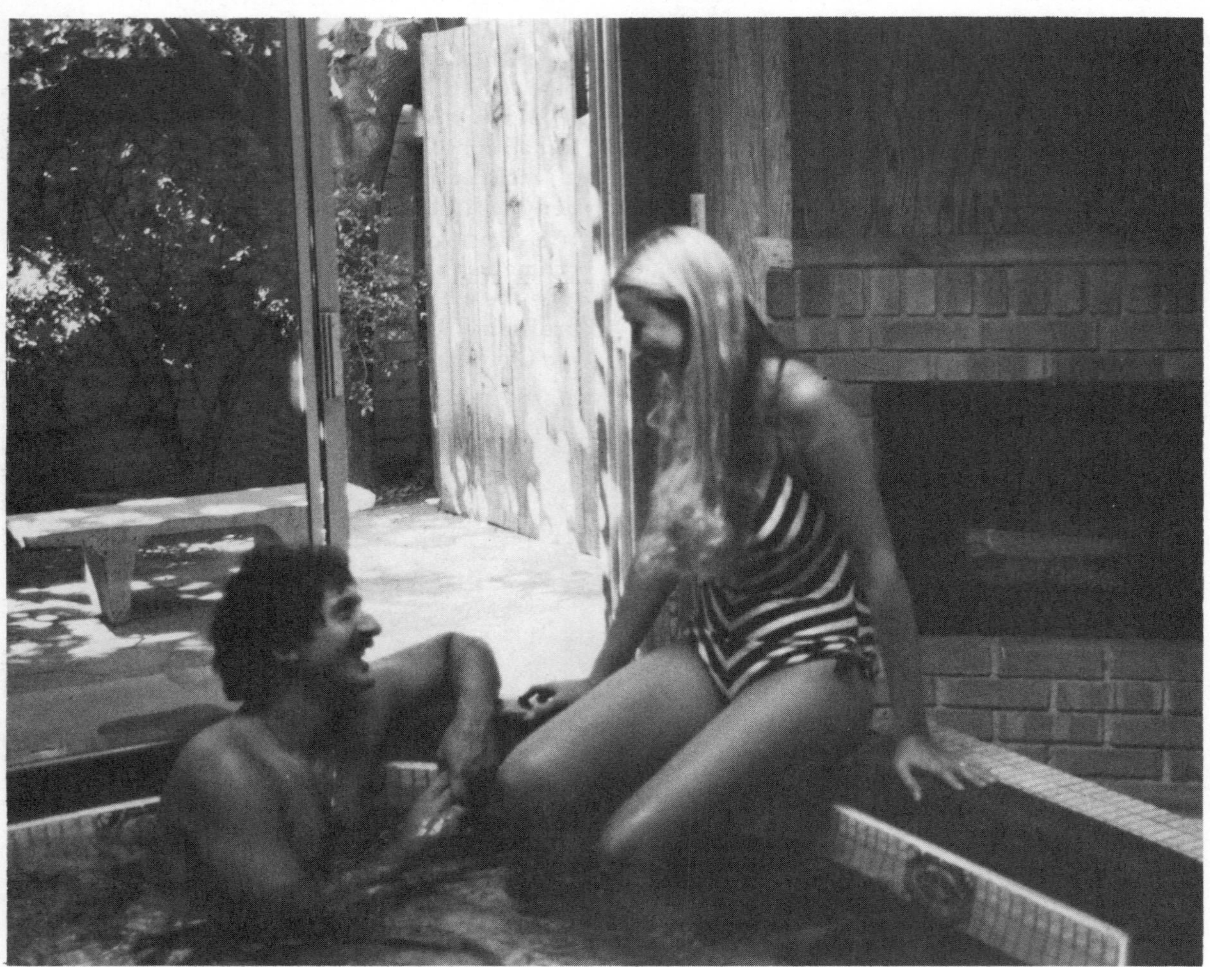

This private tub space, at *Oasis Hot Tubs*, is ten minutes from downtown Tucson.

include the names of many such springs in the master index but describe them only as being NUBP (Not Usable By the Public).

The first two words in the title of my book are *Hot Springs,* within which I choose to include all artesian and pump-operated wells that emit geothermal mineral water. I have also chosen to include *Hot Pools,* which are filled with gas-heated tap water, simply because there are now so many of them accessible to the public. What's more, they have been built in convenient locations, in or near population centers. Just as there is no one "typical" hot springs, so there is no one "typical" hot-spring enthusiast. Some readers will have a whole summer vacation to trek from one remote, primitive hot spring to another. Others will be trying to make the most of a two-week vacation, or a long week-end, or a Saturday, or a few hours after a hard day's work. Some readers will have a self-contained RV, while others will have only a family car, and still others must depend on flying in to an airport to be picked up. Some readers will be skinnydippers wanting to know where they will be welcome, and other readers will want to know how to avoid skinnydippers.

Whatever your schedule, transportation and modesty needs, this book is intended to help you make an informed choice, and then to help you get to the location(s) you have chosen.

A wilderness permit, and a five-hour hike, are needed to reach *The Meadows Hot Springs.*

2. Hot Springs Belong To Everyone

In 1980 the National Oceanic and Atmospheric Administration (NOAA) published the *Thermal Springs List for the United States,* containing over 1,700 entries, nearly all of them in the western states. Latitude, longitude, water temperature and the name of the applicable USGS topographic quadrangle are given for each entry. There is also a big map of the area sprinkled with colorful location dots.

This impressive package of official information, prepared by the Environmental Data and Information Service office of NOAA, has prompted more than one desk-bound writer to reproduce or recommend this list, implying that there is a publicly owned, freely available, idyllic hot spring under every dot: just pick your spot, buy the appropriate USGS map and go for it.

After many weeks and thousands of miles of field research, I can report that the real world of geothermal water is not quite that wonderful. The NOAA Springs List contains 752 entries in the states of California, Nevada, Arizona and New Mexico. I eliminated nearly a third of these because they were multiple listings at essentially

A geothermal creek flows through the grounds of privately owned *Warm Springs Resort.*

the same location, or failed to meet my minimum of 85°. Out of the remainder I found just 81 locations (11%) which are usable by the public, of which only 41 (5%) are publicly owned and freely available.

Space does not permit listing all the reasons why various NOAA-list springs are not usable by the public. One of the reasons is that some of the NOAA data is 50 to 100 years old, and in the meantime many springs have simply ceased to flow, especially after an earthquake or heavy irrigation pumping in the area. Some springs have long since been drowned under new lakes created by storage dams, and others have been capped and 100% of the flow piped into a water-district supply system.

The largest single group of NUBP springs are those on private property. Under our public-liability laws a hot-spring owner must either operate a commercial establishment at the spring or post the property with NO TRESPASSING signs. Several owners who have graciously permitted free public use of a spring for years have had a user hurt himself on the property, file suit against the owner, and collect damages. An owner's only defense against such suits is to post the property, then show that the person injured was trespassing and therefore not legally entitled to blame the owner for anything. One of the most depressing sights is a once-flourishing but long-closed hot-spring resort decaying into rubble while the once-cherished magic water is wasted into a drainage ditch. Here again, the owner must keep the property posted to protect himself.

Owners whose hot-spring property adjoins national forest land have an additional risk. If a fire starts on that property and spreads into the national forest, the proprety owner can be sued by the Forest Service for the cost of fighting the fire, no matter how big it gets. A cattle rancher with an attractive hot spring also faces extra

The Orange County Parks Department leases *Capistrano Hot Springs* to a private firm which paid for improvements, including redwood hot tubs for rent to the public.

risks if he permits public access: he can expect to lose some livestock when thoughtless users leave gates open.

I wish it were otherwise, but I certainly can't blame those hot-springs owners who feel they must restrict the use of their property to invited personal guests. All of which leaves only a few dozen freely usable publicly owned hot springs out of all those dots on the NOAA map. But I am happy to say that there are a few beauties among them.

The crystal-clear 105° water in *Spence Hot Spring* overflows through a pipe to create a spectacular shower in the lower pool. On almost any rating scale this national forest primitive spring belongs in the top ten for the entire west.

3. Outdoor Tips for City Slickers

Most of the hot-spring resorts have efficient trash systems, and some of the national-forest springs have adjoining parking areas equipped with handy garbage cans. However, the moment you hike a few yards beyond the range of trash pick-up trucks , the whole situation changes. There are no litter bags, and no one to carry trash away, except you, the person who was there before you, and the person who will come along after you.

If you intend to visit a hot spring which involves any amount of hiking to reach always take along your own personal litterbag, even if you aren't camping overnight. It pleases me to report that nearly all hot springs located more than 1/4 mile from the nearest parking area are lovingly cared for by those who are willing to take the trouble to hike that far. They routinely take out their trash plus some extra to make up for the last person who brought city habits into a primitive environment. Please help maintain that tradition.

For those who plan more extensive trips into backcountry and wilderness areas, here are the recommendations of the Southwestern Region, U.S. Forest Servce:

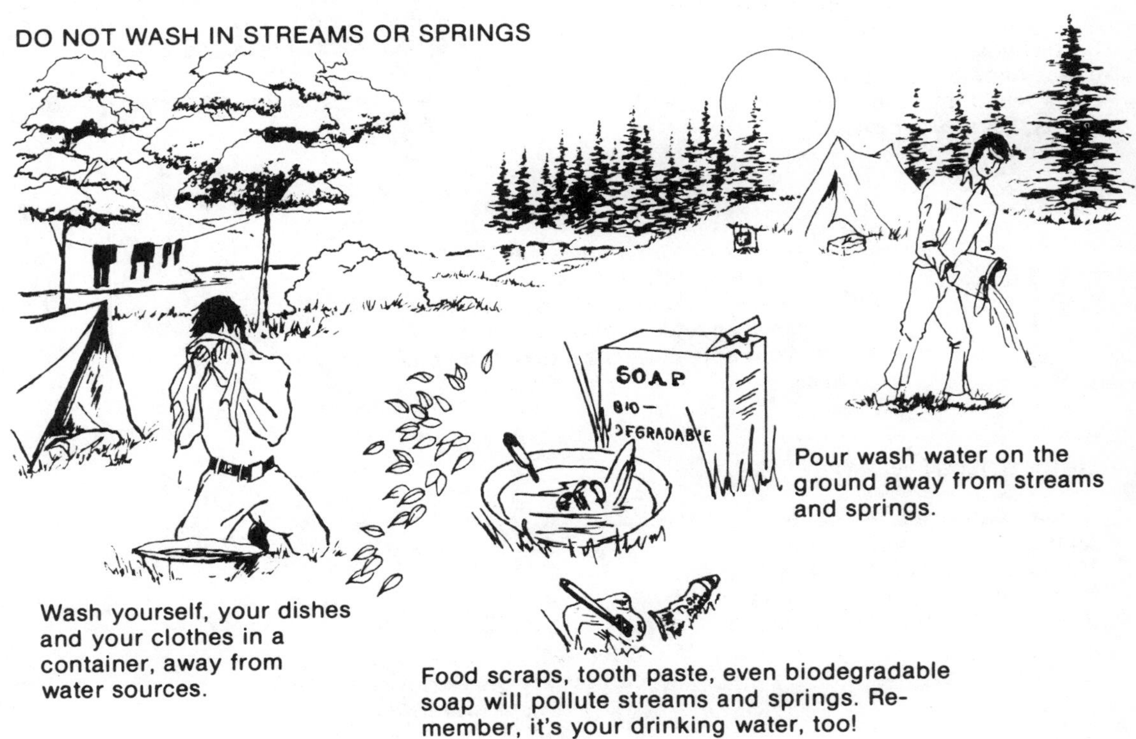

DO NOT WASH IN STREAMS OR SPRINGS
SOAP
BIO-
DEGRADABLE
Pour wash water on the ground away from streams and springs.
Wash yourself, your dishes and your clothes in a container, away from water sources.
Food scraps, tooth paste, even biodegradable soap will pollute streams and springs. Remember, it's your drinking water, too!

Times are changing. More and more people are taking to the trails. Poor camping practices can destroy the natural character of the backcountry. We must all learn to use the backcountry wisely, or be faced with more restrictions if heavy use and resource damage increases.

When planning and starting your backcountry trip:

- Check at a Forest Service office for wilderness permit, if necessary; weather, fire and water conditions; size of group; camping locations; maps; and other useful information.
- Keep your party small. Group size may be limited.
- Take a gas stove to help conserve firewood.
- Bring sacks to carry out your trash.
- Take a light shovel or trowel to help with personal sanitation.
- Carry a light basin or collapsible bucket for washing.
- If you take horses or mules, pack plenty of processed feed for them.

SETTING UP CAMP

Avoid camping in meadows; you'll trample the grass.

Pick a campsite where you won't need to clear away vegetation or level a tent site. Do not trench around tents.

Use an existing campsite, if available.

Camp 300 feet from streams, springs, or trails. State law prohibits camping within ¼ mile of an only available water source (for wildlife and livestock).

Before leaving camp, naturalize the area. Replace rocks and wood used; scatter needles, leaves and twigs on the campsite.

Do not cut trees, limbs or brush to make camp improvements. Carry your own tent poles.

Scout the area to be sure you've left nothing behind. Everything you packed into your camp should be packed out. Try to make it appear as if no one had been there.

BURY HUMAN WASTE

When nature calls, select a suitable spot at least 100 feet from open water, campsites and trails. Dig a hole 4 to 6 inches deep. Try to keep the sod intact.

After use, fill in the hole completely burying waste and TP: then tramp in the sod.

The natural beauty of *Delonegha Hot Springs* is only 20 yards from a main highway, so broken glass and thoughtless party litter is all too abundant in the surrounding space.

CAMPFIRES

Use gas stoves when possible to conserve dwindliing supplies of firewood.

Use only fallen timber for firewood. Even standing dead trees are part of the beauty of wilderness, and are important to wildlife.

If you need to build a fire, use an existing campfire site if available.

Clear a circle of all burnable materials.

Dig a shallow pit for the fire.

Keep the sod intact.

If you need to clear a new fire site, select a safe spot away from rock ledges that would be blackened by smoke; away from meadows where it would destroy grass and leave a scar; away from dense brush, trees and duff where it would be a fire hazard. Keep fires small.

Never leave a fire unattended.

Put your fire COLD OUT before leaving, by mixing the coals with dirt & water. Feel it with your hand. If it's cold out, cover the ashes in the pit with dirt, replace the sod, and naturalize the disturbed area. Rockfire rings, if needed or used, should be scattered before leaving.

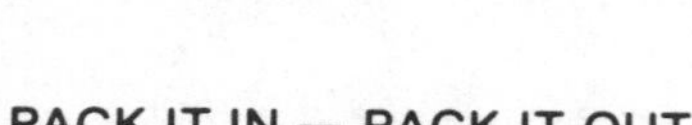

PACK IT IN — PACK IT OUT

Bring trash bags to carry out all trash that cannot be completely burned.

Aluminum foil and aluminum lined packages won't burn up in your fire. Compact it and put it in your trash bag.

Cigarette butts, pull-tabs and gum wrappers are litter, too.

They can spoil a campsite.

DON'T BURY TRASH!

Animals dig it up.

Try to pack out trash left by others. Your good example may catch on!

The debris of an old burned-out resort usually invites more trash , but *Verde Hot Springs* is kept clean by volunteers who must wade across the river to and from the parking area.

4. To Bare Or Not To Bare

Robert's Rule of Relative Indecency
I cannot be prudish
About things that are nudish
For I'm very broad minded, you see.
But the real stupid moron
Is the jerk who has more on,
or less on, than broad minded me.

In our culture it is generally all right to be nude in the privacy of your own bathtub or shower, but is not all right to be nude in the presence of others. That's all very well as long as people don't bathe together in a group, but the widespread popularity of personal hot tubs has confronted many people with a difficult problem. When a couple with a new secluded patio hot tub discover the comfort of soaking together without bathing suits, they have to decide what to say, and do, when friends drop in to share a soak. Then the friends have to decide what to say, and do, in response.

Similar, but more complex, circumstances are to be found at various hot-spring and hot-pool locations. The intent of this section—and this whole book—is to help you select those places that are the most compatible with your beliefs and attitudes about the nude human body, including your own.

Start with the basic rule, "The person who owns or is in charge of the property gets to call the shots." As might be expected, all the conventional hotel/motels, hot-spring resorts and RV/mobile parks require bathing suits in and around their pools, and most of the rent-a-tub establishments require clothing except in the private tub rooms. On the other hand, there are a few unconventional hot-spring resorts

Bathing suits are a local custom, at least during daylight hours, at *Boquillas Hot Springs,* on the Rio Grande River.

where clothing is generally optional and is prohibited in the pools, and a few rent-a-tub locations that follow the same policy. All naturist and nudist parks prohibit clothing in pools and a few of them prohibit clothing everywhere, weather permitting. In all of the above cases, there is a person in charge who can answer your questions, listen to your complaints and take action if necessary when there is an infraction of the local rules.

When you get out in the boondocks there may not be anyone nearby to take charge. Most of the remote, primitive hot springs are on federal land administered by the Bureau of Land Management, the U.S. Forest Service or the National Park Service. No federal regulations prohibit nudity per se, so you do not risk a citation if a ranger simply observes you soaking nude by yourself or with like-minded friends. Even if some other citizen complains to a ranger that he is offended by your nudity, you still do not risk an immediate citation. The complaining person first has to agree that he will go before a magistrate and sign a written complaint, then the ranger has to advise you of the complaint and give you an opportunity to put on your clothes. Only if you refuse to dress at that point do you become liable for a citation . There are very few hikers who will take the trouble to go find a ranger just to force a skinnydipper to dress. It is more likely that arriving hikers will simply join you in the pool, wearing as little or as much as they individually choose.

Misunderstandings about nudity most often occur around unsupervised hot springs that can be easily reached by automobile or camper. If skinnydippers are the first arrivals, followed by a family that feels offended by the nudity, that family can easily drive off to find a ranger, and agree to sign a complaint. Then the skinnydippers will have to dress in order that the family can use the hot spring their way.

The skinnydippers were there first, and they believe they should not have their skinnydipping disturbed. The family believes that the ranger should have prevented the nudity before the family arrived, and the ranger believes that he could be doing more useful tasks. All of the

The clothing optional policy at *Harbin Hot Springs* offers freedom of choice and this young boy has chosen to wear a swim suit.

above people may get very emotional.

At some easily reached hot springs, complaints have become so numerous that the rangers have erected NO NUDE BATHING signs, which the regulations permit them to do. The first few arrivals may agree to ignore such a sign—at the risk of being cited by a ranger or a county sheriff, without any need for a complaining citizen in person. Just remember that the person in charge of the property has the last word.

Insofar as I could determine local clothing customs, or infer customs from the visibility or remoteness of a hot spring or hot well, that information is part of the data given for each location. However, the actual custom at any given moment is whatever the people present at that spring are doing, so don't try to convince them otherwise by quoting my book at them. Even if you are the first arrival and choose to skinnydip, it would be prudent for you to ask each new arrival if your nudity is offensive, and if you get a yes answer, be as gracious as you can while you dress.

If you are a skinnydipper, I want this book to help you find others. If you are not a skinnydipper, I want this book to help you avoid them. If both of you happen to meet at an unposted, unsupervised hot spring, it is my hope that you will find a way to soak in peaceful coexistence.

In this Arizona *(Ringbolt) Hot Spring* pool a group of clothed hikers were invited to join a skinnydipper birthday party. All joined the party but not all skinnydipped.

THE AUTHOR'S PAGE

A wise man once told me,
"The only sin in the whole world is doing anything other than what you love to do."

I love my work.

Jayson Loam

If you are not the owner of the copy you are reading, and would like to have a copy of your own, here are several suggestions:

1. Use the key maps in this book to look up the nearest hot-spring resort or rent-a-tub facility and write down the phone number. Call them and ask if they have a copy of this book in stock. If they do, reserve yourself a copy, and while you are at it, make a reservation to take a soak when you go to pick it up. If they don't have it in stock, ask them to order it for you directly from the publisher.

2. Phone your nearest book store, or hiking and camping store, and ask them if they have a copy in stock, or if they are willing to order it for you. Most of these retailers already carry the Wilderness Press line of books so they should be able to give you fast service.

3. If all else fails, send your prepaid order directly to the publisher. Make your check or money order payable to Wilderness Press. Prices including postage are:

Southwest (192 pages) -$13.95
Northwest (160 pages) -$10.95

Wilderness Press
2440 Bancroft Way
Berkeley, CA 94704

At least one of my readers is going to find a mistake in this book. If I knew where it was I would fix it, but I need your help to find it and tell me about it. It is O.K. to write me a nasty letter giving me a bad time for being wrong, but don't forget to include the right information. I may squirm a little, but it is more important that I make the correction in the next revision.

As the months roll by, several readers are going to notice that the conditions at this location or that location have changed since my book was published. I don't really want a nasty letter about such a change, but I would appreciate your letting me know about it.

I don't expect very many brand new hot springs to start flowing, but some closed springs may reopen, and I'm sure that more rent-a-tub establishments will be built. If you find out about any kind of a new place to put your body in hot water, please write to let me know about it. Thank you very large.

You don't even have to send me any information. It is O.K. to just write and say something nice, if that is how you feel.

Jayson Loam
c/o Wilderness Press
2440 Bancroft Way
Berkeley, CA 94704

Northern California

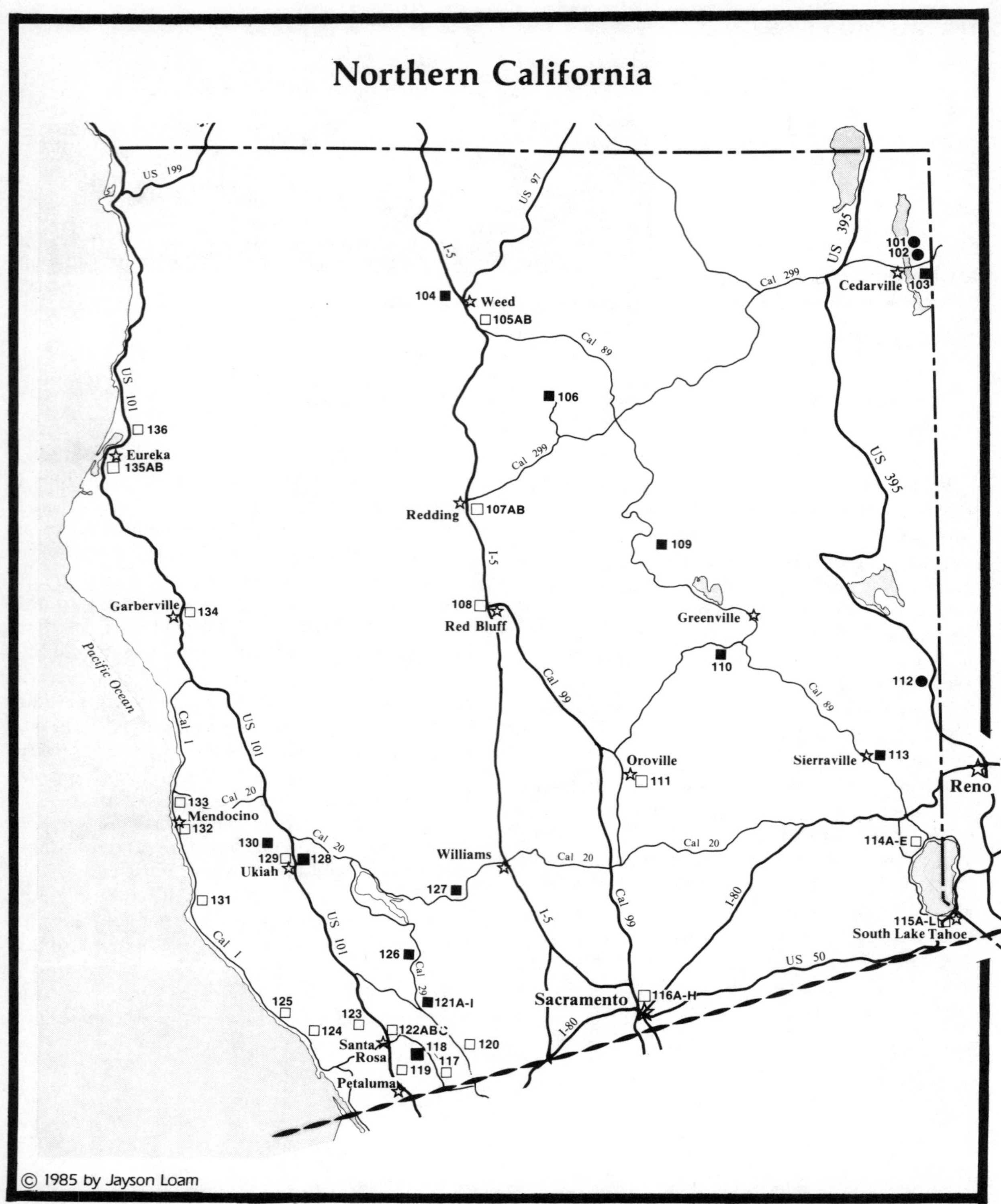

MAP AND DIRECTORY SYMBOLS

- ● **Unimproved natural mineral water pool**
- ■ **Improved natural mineral water pool**
- □ Gas-heated tap or well water pool

- ——— Paved highway
- – – – Unpaved road
- ······ Hiking route

PR = Tubs or pools for rent by hour, day or treatment

MH = Rooms, cabins or dormitory spaces for rent by day, week or month

CRV = Camping or vehicle parking spaces, some with hookups, for rent by day, week, month or year

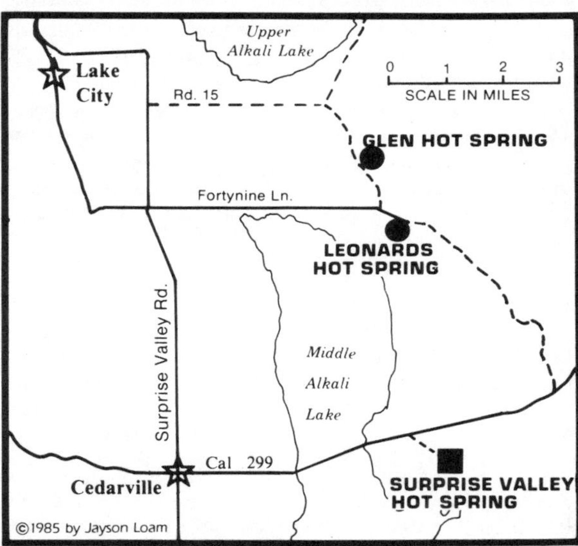

Leonard's Hot Spring: Abandoned resorts are prime targets for vandals. The buildings in this 1980 photo are now totally flattened.

#101 GLEN HOT SPRING (see map)

● **Near the town of Cedarville**

non-commercial

Undeveloped cluster of hot springs on a barren slope along the east side of Upper Alkali Lake. Elevation 4,600 ft. Open all year.

Natural mineral water flows out of several springs at 150°, and cools as it runs toward the lake. Volunteers have built shallow soaking pools where the water has cooled to approximately 100°. The apparent local custom is clothing optional.

No services are available on the premises. There is a limited amount of unmarked open space on which overnight parking is not prohibited. It is ten miles to a service station and all other services.

Source map: USGS *Cedarville.*

#102 LEONARD'S HOT SPRING (see map)

● **Near the town of Cedarville**

non-commercial

Abandoned and deteriorated old resort on a barren slope along the east side of Middle Alkali Lake. Elevation 4,500 ft. Open all year.

Natural mineral water flows out of the ground from several springs at a temperature of 150°, and cools as it runs toward the lake. A diversion ditch used to carry this water to the resort, but it now flows through a winding ditch fifty yards southeast of the old swimming pool. Volunteers have built shallow soaking pools in the ditch where the water has cooled to approximately 100°. The apparent local custom is clothing optional.

No services are available on the premises. There is an abundance of unmarked level space on which overnight parking is not prohibited. It is nine miles to a service station and all other services.

Source map: USGS *Cedarville.*

#103 SURPRISE VALLEY HOT SPRING

■ **P.O. Box 407** **(see map)**
Cedarville, CA 96104

A recently active resort, closed for reorganization and remodeling. Write for information on re-opening. Elevation 4,500 ft.

Natural mineral water flows out of two artesian wells at boiling temperatures.

Stewart Mineral Springs: A rustic covered bridge conveys the peace of this resort.

#104 STEWART MINERAL SPRINGS

■ **2222 Stewart Springs Road (916) 938-2222**
Weed, CA 96094 PR + MH + CRV

A well-kept rustic retreat with expansion plans, offering group seminars as well as individual wellness programs. Located on a mountain stream in a green canyon northwest of Mt. Shasta. Elevation 3,900 ft. Open all year.

Natural mineral water is pumped from a well at 40° and propane heated as needed. There are twelve individual bathtubs and larger tubs in private rooms. Water temperature in each tub is controlled as desired by mixing cold and hot mineral water. Tubs are drained and refilled after each use, so no chemical water treatment is necessary. The outdoor hydropool is filled with creek water, filtered, chlorinated and heated to 102°. Bathing suits are required in public areas.

Facilities include rooms, restaurant, bar (beer and wine), camping spaces and partial hook-up RV spaces. Visa and MasterCard are accepted. Massage, and summer seminars, conducted by *Meeting of the Ways,* are available to the public. It is seven miles to a store, service station and public bus. Special pickup at the bus depot and at the Weed airport is available by arrangement.

Directions: From I-5, north of Weed, take the Edgewood exit, and follow signs four miles north on Stewart Springs Road to the resort.

#105A MOUNTAIN AIR LODGE
□ 1121 S. Mt. Shasta Blvd. (916) 926-3411
Mt. Shasta, CA 96067 Hydropool MH

#105B ALPINE LODGE MOTEL
□ 908 S. Mt. Shasta Blvd. (916) 926-3145
Mt. Shasta, CA 96067 Hydropool MH

#106 BIG BEND PREVENTORIUM HOT SPRINGS

■ **196 Hot Springs Row (916) 337-6680**
Big Bend, CA 96011 PR + MH + CRV

The remains of a historical resort, being improved and operated by a cooperative Essene Community. Located 50 miles northeast of Redding on the tree-shaded south bank of the Pit River. Elevation 2,000 ft. Open all year.

Natural mineral water flows from three springs at 180°:

(1) Indian Springs. Located ten feet above the level of the nearby Pit River, the flow from this spring cools as it meanders through a series of shallow pools created by volunteers from riverbed rocks. Bathing suits are optional in this area and in the adjoining river.

(2) Main spring. Located on a plateau fifty feet above the river level, this major controlled flow supplies a greenhouse and a bath house containing three bathtubs in separate rooms, plus a steambath room. Just outside the bath house is a large fiberglass tub with a view of the river. Bathing suits are optional in these tubs.

(3) Minor spring. Located on the edge of a plateau fifty feet above the Pit River, this smaller flow runs continuously into three interconnected natural stone/cement pools, each large enough for six persons. Faucet-controlled cold creek water is admitted into each pool to produce whatever temperature is desired by occupants. Each pool has seating at various depths and all of them have a superb view of the river. Bathing suits are required until 4 PM, after which they are optional.

Massage, cabins, RV spaces and overnight camping are available on the premises. Seminar programs are also open to the public. No credit cards are accepted. It is ¼ mile to a cafe, store and service station.

Directions: From I-5 in Redding, go 35 miles east on Cal 299, then turn north 15 miles to the town of Big Bend, which is at the end of the pavement. Look for Big Bend Hot Springs sign 200 yards south of Big Bend store.

Big Bend Hot Springs: This creative series of adjustable-temperature hot pools has a sweeping view of the Pit River.

One of the *Big Bend* source springs feeds these rock pools in the Pit River bed.

#107A	MARINA RV PARK on Park Marina Dr. Redding, CA 96001	(916) 241-4396 Hydropool CRV
☐		
#107B	WONDERLAND RV PARK on Wonderland Rd. Redding, CA 96001	(916) 275-1281 Hydropool CRV
☐		
#108	RIO VISTA MOBILE ESTATES on West Ave. Red Bluff, CA 96080	(916) 527-2793 Hydropool CRV
☐		

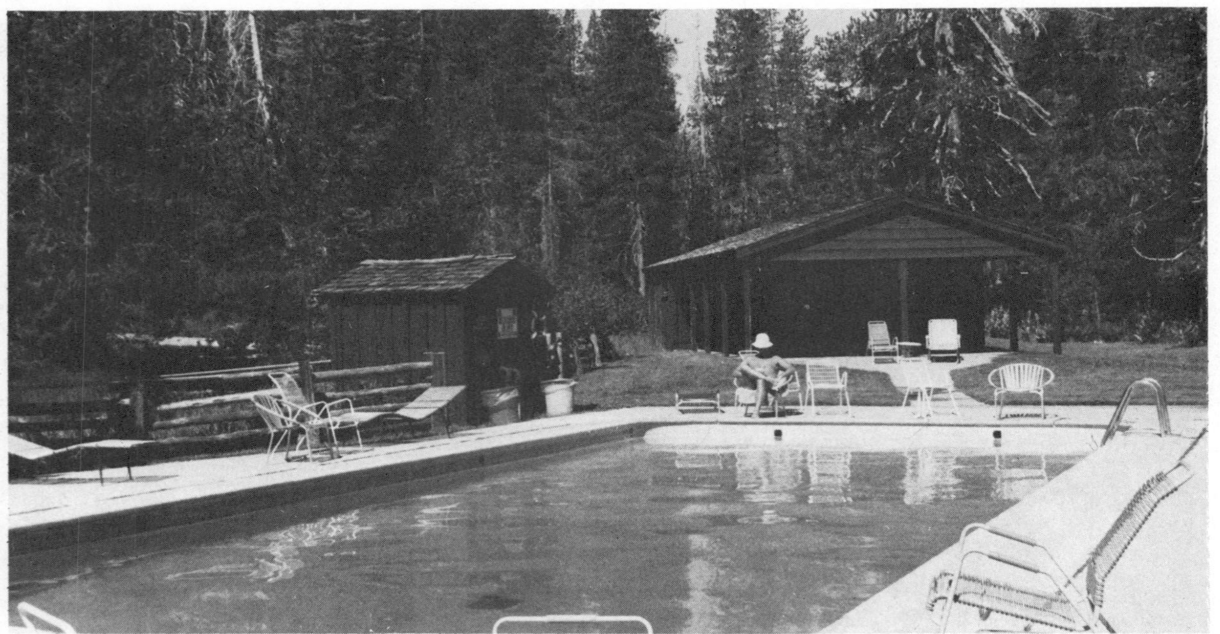

Drakesbad Guest Ranch: This beautiful alpine valley is blessed with an abundance of geothermal water (foreground).

Drakesbad offers a peaceful vacation in the pines plus the unusual extras of a hot mineral water pool and bath-house tubs.

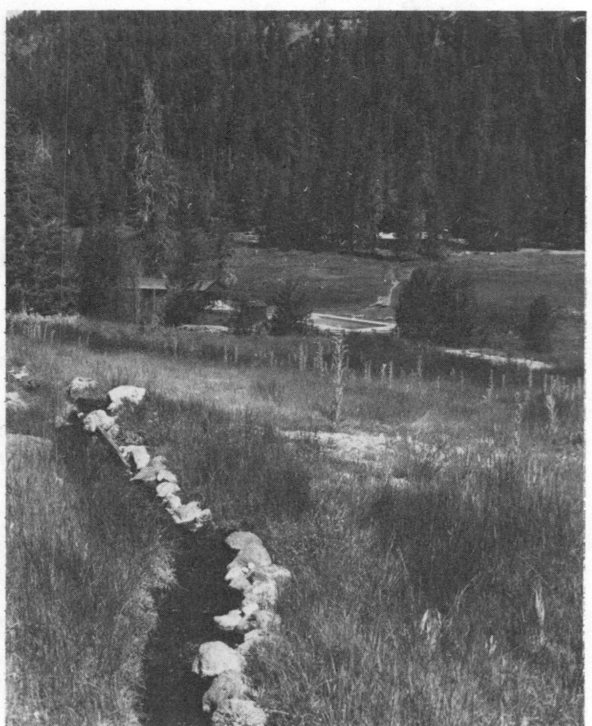

#109 DRAKESBAD GUEST RANCH

c/o California Guest Services
2150 Main Street #7 **(916) 529-1512**
Red Bluff, CA 96080 **MH**

A rustic mountain ranch/resort, with a mineral water swimming pool, plus horses and guides for riding and hiking. Located in a superb mountain meadow within the boundaries of Lassen Volcanic National Park. Elevation 5,700 ft. Open June 16-September 16.

Natural mineral water flows out of two springs at temperatures of 85° and 125° and is piped to the pool and to four private-room bathtubs. The swimming pool temperature is maintained in the 80's during the day and over 100° at night by mixing the two hot water flows. Pool flow is shut off after midnight, and chlorine added to control algae growth, but chlorine content reduces rapidly when flow-through is resumed the following day. Bathing suits are required, except in private bathtub rooms. Pools and bathtubs are available to registered guests only. No day use is permitted.

Facilities include lodge, rooms, cabins, and dining room (all kerosene lit). Saddle horses and guides are available for rent. Visa and MasterCard accepted. It is 20 miles to RV spaces, store, and service station. Telephone for reservations.

Directions: From Cal 36 in the town of Chester take Warner Valley Road northwest to resort, which is at the end of the road.

Woody's Feather River Hot Springs: Located 30 yards from a highway and a tavern, this is a place for informal fun.

#110 WOODY'S FEATHER RIVER HOT SPRINGS

P.O. Box 7 **(916) 283-4115**
Twain, CA 95984 **PR + MH + CRV**

Primarily a fishing and hunting resort, this site does have two small soaking pools on the north bank of the Feather River, where you can also pan for gold. It is located in the tree-covered upper Feather River Canyon. Elevation 2,700 ft. Open all year.

Natural mineral water flows directly into two cement pools at 99° and 102°. No chemical treatment is added. Clothing is optional in the pools and in the adjoining river.

Facilities include motel rooms, RV spaces, restaurant and bar. No credit cards are accepted. It is 3 miles to a store and 15 miles to a service station.

Directions: on Cal Route 70, go four miles west from the Quincy-Greenville "Y".

#111 CAMPOTEL
on Hwy 162 (916) 534-1133
Oroville, CA 95965 Hydropool CRV

#112 ZAMBONI HOT SPRINGS (see map)

Near the intersection of US 395 and Cal 70
non-commercial

Small undeveloped hot spring, under a railroad trestle, in high desert country. Elevation 4,500 ft. Open: all year.

Natural mineral water flows out of the ground at 103°. Volunteers have built a shallow rock and mud pool, large enough for two, in which the water temperature is approximately 102°. The apparent local custom is clothing optional.

There are no services on the premises. There is a small amount of unmarked space, fifty yards away, on which overnight parking is not prohibited. It is ten miles to a store and service station, and thirty miles to all other services.

Source map: USGS *Constantia*.

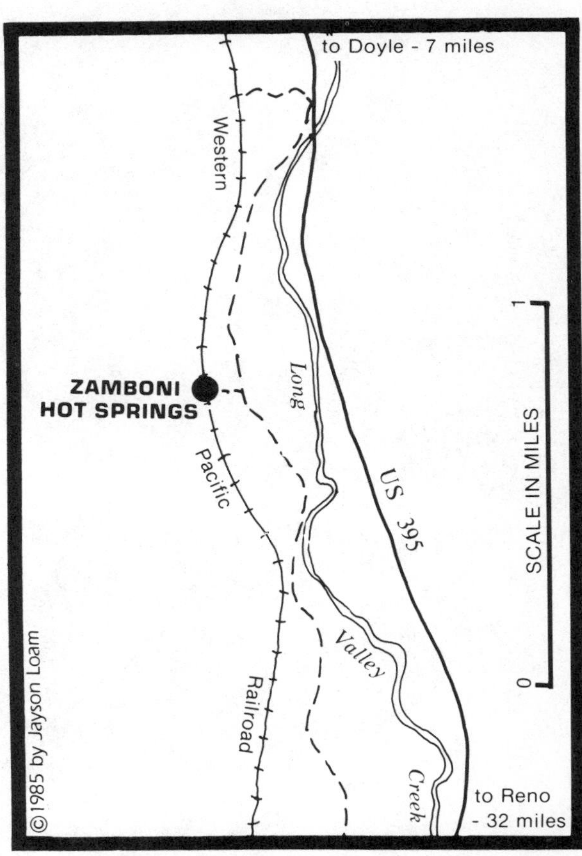

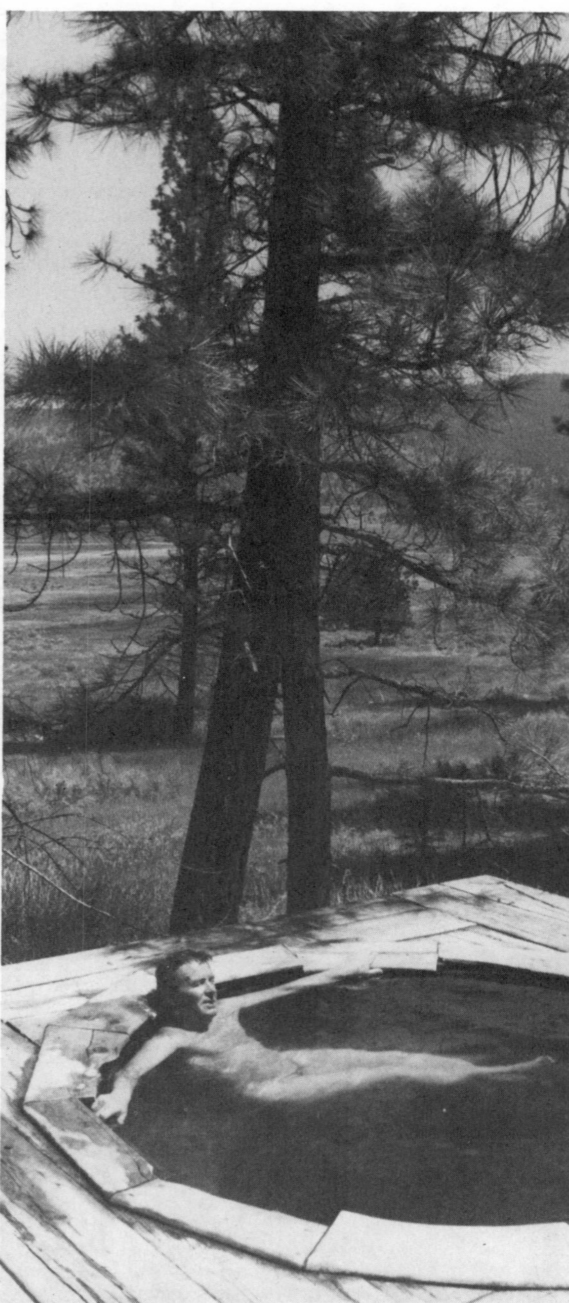

#113 CAMPBELL HOT SPRINGS

P.O. Box 234 **(916) 994-8984**
Sierraville, CA 96104 **PR + MH + CRV**

A 700 acre older resort purchased by the leader of the Theta Seminars organization, and operated by a self-administering group of members. It is primarily used for Rebirthing Training and Group Seminars, but public use of the facilities is welcome on a space-available basis. Elevation 6,000 ft. Open all year.

Natural mineral water flows out of several springs at temperatures up to 115°. The outdoor swimming pool is maintained at approximately 80°, without chemical treatment. On a nearby wooded slope there are a variety of tubs and temperatures, using flow-through mineral water without chemical treatment: (a) three cement soaking pools, 110°, 106°, 102°, (b) two white bathtubs, 102°, and (c) one redwood hot tub, 102°. There is also a bath house with six private room tubs, in which the temperature is controllable up to 105°. One quarter mile away is a 95° mud bath pit. Clothing is optional in all pool areas.

Massage, rooms, meals, overnight RV spaces and camping spaces are available on the premises. No credit cards are accepted. It is two miles to a store and service stations.

Directions: From the intersection of Cal 89 and Cal 49 in Sierraville, follow Cal 49 east to Lemon Canyon Road, which runs along the north edge of the airport, then turn right on the road which runs along the east edge of the airport, into the foothills, and to the main lodge.

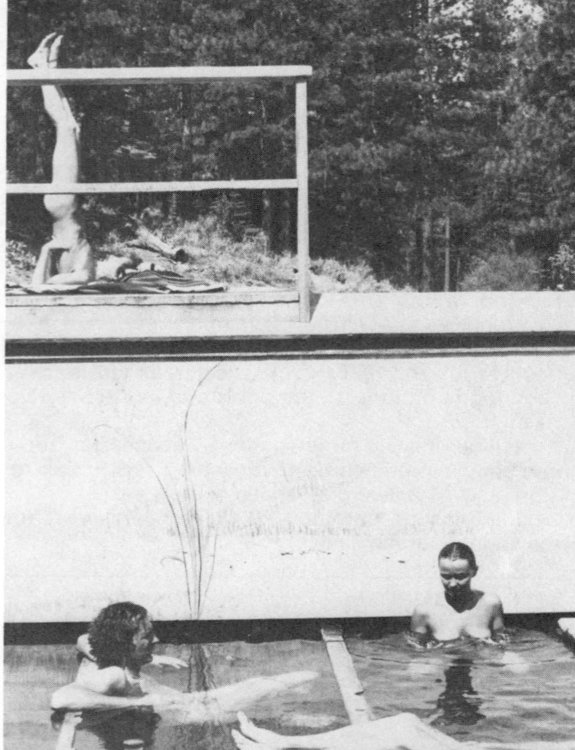

▲ *Campbell Hot Springs:* The rustic setting offers a wide variety of soaking pool options, including a redwood tub with sun ► deck (above) and multiple cement pools with different temperatures (right).

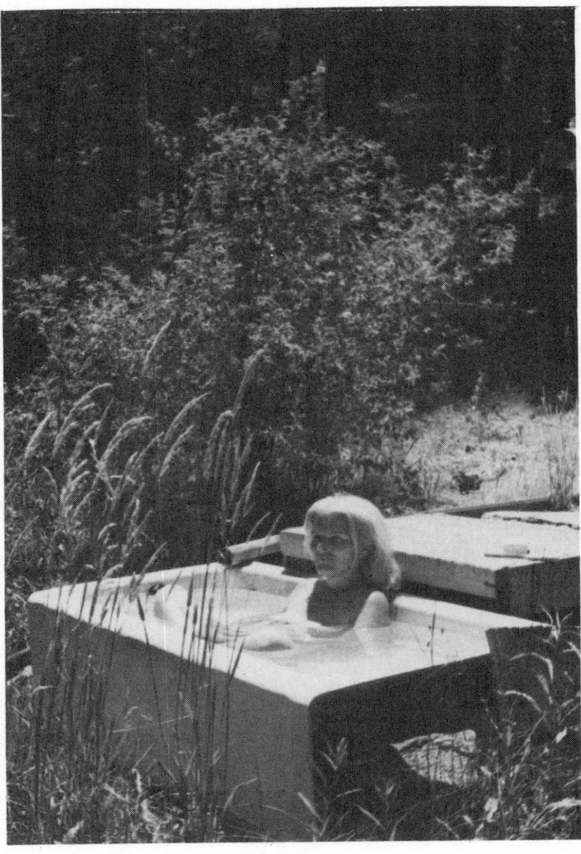

This bathtub-in-the-grass at *Campbell Hot Springs* has a continuous flow of 102° water and is designated for use with shampoo.

#114A GRANLIBAKKEN SKI & RACQUET RESORT
P.O. Box 6329 (916) 583-4242
☐ Tahoe City, CA 95730 Hydropool MH

#114B NORTHSTAR-AT-TAHOE RESORT
P.O. Box 2499 (916) 562-1113
☐ Tahoe City, CA 95730 Hydropool MH

#114C CHARMEY CHALET MOTEL
P.O. Box 316 (916) 546-2529
☐ Tahoe Vista, CA 95732 Hydropool MH

#114D SILVER SANDS RESORT
P.O. Box 109 (916) 546-2592
☐ Tahoe Vista, CA 95732 Hydropool MH

#114E NORTH LAKE LODGE
8716 N. Lake Blvd. (916) 546-2731
☐ Kings Beach, CA 95719 Hydropool MH

Nephele: Bar service to private outdoor hot pools is available day and night, including during the snow season.

#115A NEPHELE
1169 Ski Run Blvd. (916) 544-8130
☐ So. Lake Tahoe, CA 95729 PR

Combination bar, restaurant and rent-a-tub establishment, located between the lake and a ski run.

Pools for rent to the public, using gas-heated tap water, treated with chlorine.

Four private outdoor enclosures, rented by the hour. Water temp: 102°.

Special features: dinner-and-soak combination discounts.

Other facilities: bar and restaurant.

Services available: bar service (but not food service) available at poolside.

Credit cards accepted: Visa, MasterCard and American Express.

Phone for rates, reservations and directions.

#115B PACIFICA LODGE

☐ 931 Park Ave. (916) 544-4131
So. Lake Tahoe, CA 95729 MH/P

Large motel with some special rooms containing fiberglass hydropools. Located a few blocks from the beach and from the Nevada state line.

Gas-heated tap water is used in six in-room pools which may be rented overnight or longer for private use. These pools are drained and refilled after each check-out, so no chemical water treatment is necessary.

The outdoor communal swimming pool is maintained at 80°. Both use gas-heated tap water treated with chlorine and are reserved for registered guests only.

Visa, MasterCard and American Express credit cards are accepted. Phone for information about rates, reservations, and directions.

#115C TAHOE HACIENDA MOTEL

☐ 3820 Hwy 50 (916) 541-3805
So. Lake Tahoe, CA 95705 MH/P

Major motel with a dozen rooms containing hydropools. Located on the south side of Hwy 50.

Gas-heated tap water is used in 12 fiberglass pools, in rooms which may be rented overnight or longer for private use. These pools are drained and refilled after each check-out, so no chemical water treatment is needed. Temperature in each pool is adjustable to the guest's preference.

The outdoor communal swimming pool (78-80°) is open June through September, and the outdoor communal hydropool (102-104°) is open all year. Both outdoor pools require chlorination. Bathing suits are required in outdoor pools, optional in private rooms.

Visa, MasterCard, American Express, Carte Blanche and Diners Club credit cards are accepted. Phone for information about rates, reservations and directions.

#115D CHATEAU L'AMOUR

☐ 3620 Hwy 50 (916) 544-6969
So. Lake Tahoe, CA 95706 MH/P

Specialized motel, with in-room spas, adult movies and appropriate decor, located on the south side of Hwy 50.

Gas-heated tap water is used in fiberglass pools in rooms which may be rented overnight or longer for private use. These pools are drained and refilled after each check-out, so no chemical water treatment is needed. Water temperature in each pool is adjustable to the guest's preference. There are no outdoor communal pools.

Visa, MasterCard, American Express, Carte Blanche and Diners Club credit cards are accepted. Phone for information about rates, reservations and directions.

115E PINEWOOD LODGE

☐ 3818 Hwy 50 (916) 544-3319
So. Lake Tahoe, CA 95729 MH + PR

Small motel with one separate room containing a hot tub, sauna and shower. Located on the south side of Hwy 50.

Gas-heated tap water, treated with chlorine, is used in the redwood tub, and water temperature is maintained at 100°. This tub/sauna room may be rented by the hour or may be negotiated in connection with regular motel room registration.

Visa, MasterCard and American Express credit cards are accepted. Phone for information about rates, reservations and directions.

#115F BEST WESTERN STATION HOUSE INN

☐ P.O. Box 4009 (916) 542-1101
So.Lake Tahoe, CA 95729 Hydropool
MH

#115G FLAMINGO LODGE

☐ 3961 Hwy 50 (916) 544-5288
So. Lake Tahoe, CA 95729 Hydropool
MH

#115H FOREST INN

☐ 1100 Park Ave. (916) 541-6655
So. Lake Tahoe, CA 95729 Hydropool
MH

#115I LAKELAND VILLAGE

☐ P.O. Drawer A (916) 541-7711
So. Lake Tahoe, CA 95705 Hydropool
MH

#115J SIERRA HOUSE INN

☐ P.O. Box 6499 (916) 541-4801
So. Lake Tahoe, CA 95729 Hydropool
MH

#115K THE WAYSTATION RESORT HOTEL

☐ P.O. Drawer 1267 (916) 541-6220
So. Lake Tahoe, CA 95705 Hydropool
MH

#115L TAHOE STYLE

☐ 3742 Hwy 50 (916) 544-2847
So. Lake Tahoe, CA 95729 Hydropool
MH

#115M BIG 7 MOTEL

☐ 3790 Hwy 50 (916) 544-7696
So. Lake Tahoe, CA 95729 Hydropool
MH

 *Tubs for Two:* Jet controls are handy.

#116A TUBS FOR TWO
1250 Howe Ave. (916) 920-8827
☐ Sacramento, CA 95825 PR

Basic private room rent-a-tub-with-sauna facility, located in a suburban shopping center.

Pools for rent to the public, using gas-heated tap water, treated with chlorine.

22 private rooms, rented by the hour. Water temp. 98-103°. Sauna included.

Credit cards accepted: Visa, MasterCard and Capitol Express.

Phone for rates, reservations and directions.

#116B SPIRIT OF HEALTH
3530 Auburn Blvd. (916) 971-1660
☐ Sacramento, CA 95821 PR

Recreation-oriented private room rent-a-tub establishment located in a suburban shopping center.

Pools for rent to the public, using gas-heated tap water, treated with chlorine.

Nine private rooms, rented by the hour. Water temp. 102-103°. Sauna included.

Special features: Each room is elaborately decorated with a different world-wide theme.

Other facilities: Sun tan lounge, environmental habitat and float tank.

Credit cards accepted: Visa, MasterCard and American Express.

Phone for rates, reservations and directions.

#116C FUN TUBS
5948 Auburn Blvd. (916) 344-2972
☐ Citrus Heights, CA 95621 PR

Basic private room rent-a-tub facility located in a suburban shopping center.

Pools for rent to the public, using gas-heated tap water, treated with chlorine.

Six private rooms, rented by the hour. Water temp. 100-104°.

Special features: Each room has a different decorating theme.

Credit cards accepted: Visa and MasterCard.

Phone for rates, reservations and directions.

#116D HOLIDAY INN—NORTHEAST
5321 Date Ave. (916) 338-5800
☐ Sacramento, CA 95841 Hydropool MH

#116E BEST WESTERN SANDMAN MOTEL
236 Jibboom St. (916) 443-6515
☐ Sacramento, CA 95814 Hydropool MH

#116F AMBASSADOR INN
2030 Arden Way (916) 929-5600
☐ Sacramento, CA 95825 Hydropool MH

#116G BEST WESTERN HARBOR MOTOR INN
1250 Halyard Dr. (916) 371-2100
☐ West Sacramento, CA 95691 Hydropool MH

#116H EL RANCHO HOTEL
1029 W. Capitol Ave. (916) 371-6731
☐ West Sacramento, CA 95691 Health Club MH

#117 SONOMA MISSION INN
18140 Sonoma Hwy (707) 996-1041
☐ Boyes Hot Springs, CA 95416 Hydropool MH

#118 AGUA CALIENTE MINERAL SPRINGS
17350 Valietti Drive (707) 996-6822
■ **Sonoma, CA 95476 PR**

A summertime plunge and picnic grounds in the middle of the Sonoma Valley. Elevation 100 ft. Open summer months only.

Natural mineral water is pumped from a well at 96° and piped to a swimming pool which averages 86°, and to a hydropool which averages 95°. The adjoining diving pool and wading pool are filled with unheated tap water averaging 70°. All pools are treated with chlorine. Bathing suits are required.

A seasonal snack bar is available on the premises. No credit cards are accepted. It is less than one mile to a store, service station, etc.

Directions: From the city of Sonoma, go three miles north on Cal 12 and watch for Agua Caliente signs.

#119 KOA SAN FRANCISCO NORTH/PETALUMA
on Rainsville Rd. (707) 763-1492
☐ Petaluma, CA 94952 Hydropool CRV

#120 BEST WESTERN NAPA VALLEY LODGE
Hwy 29 at Madison St. (707) 944-2468
☐ Yountville, CA 94599 Hydropool MH

CALISTOGA SPAS

All eight of the following locations are in or near the town of Calistoga, which is on Cal 29, 40 miles north of Vallejo. Elevation 400 ft. All of them are open all year, and are one to ten blocks from a store, cafe, service station, public bus and the RV campground operated by Napa County at the Fairgrounds.

All of them have their own hot wells, and offer soaking and swimming pools containing natural mineral water treated with chlorine. Resorts with pool facilities offer them for day use unless otherwise noted. Bathing suits are required everywhere except in men's and women's bath houses.

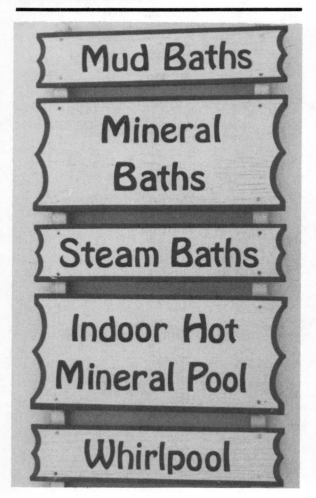

#121A LE SPA FRANCAIS

1880 Lincoln Ave. (707) 942-4636
Calistoga, CA 94515 PR + MH

Outdoor swimming pool, 80-85°, and wading pool, 90-95°. Enclosed hydropool, 100-105°. Indoor men's and women's bath houses, each containing two hydrotherapy tubs, two mud baths, two steam cabinets and a sauna. One co-ed gymnasium.

Massage, facials, herbal bath, salt scrub, sweat wrap and fitness classes are available on the premises. Facilities include rooms, restaurant, bar (beer and wine) and conference meeting rooms. Visa and MasterCard are accepted.

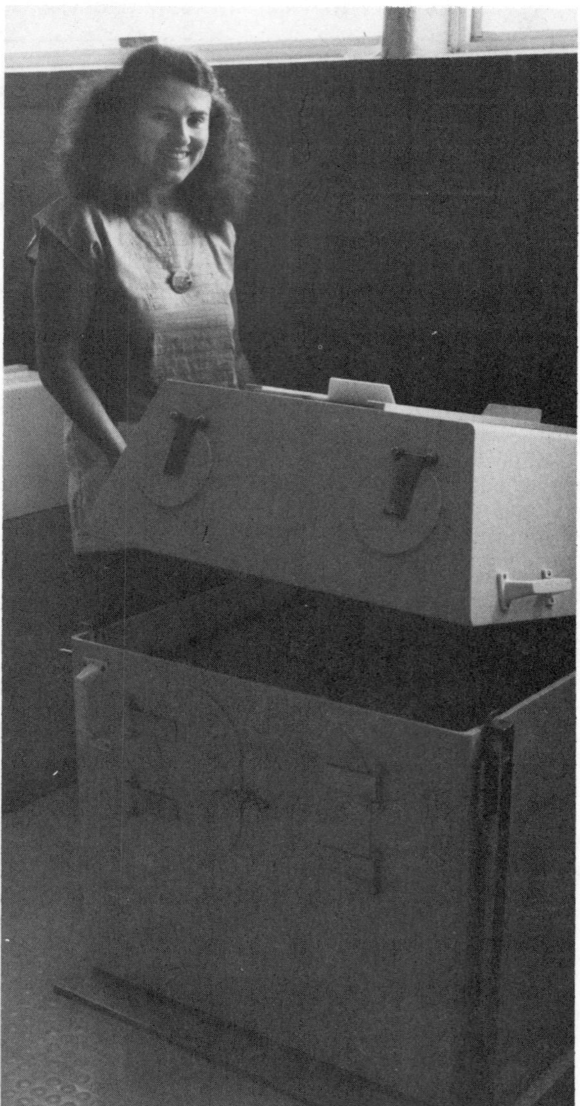

#121B CALISTOGA HOT SPRINGS

■ **1712 Lincoln Ave.** **(707) 942-5589**
Calistoga, CA 94515 **PR + MH**

Outdoor swimming pool, 90° (open April 1 to November 1). Indoor men's and women's bath houses, each containing five individual tubs, four mud baths and two steam baths.

Rooms and massage are available on the premises. Visa and MasterCard are accepted.

#121C NANCE'S HOT SPRINGS

■ **1614 Lincoln Ave.** **(707) 942-6211**
Calistoga, CA 94515 **PR + MH**

Indoor hydropool, 103°. Indoor men's and women's bath houses, each containing four individual tubs (up to 110°), three mud baths and two steam baths.

Rooms and massage are available on the premises. Visa, MasterCard and American Express are accepted. Glider rentals are available at the adjoining airport.

#121D DR. WILKINSON'S HOT SPRINGS

■ **1507 Lincoln Ave.** **(707) 942-4102**
Calistoga, CA 94515 **PR + MH**

Outdoor swimming pool, 82°. Indoor hydropool, 103°. Indoor men's and women's bath houses, each containing four individual tubs, two mud baths and a steam bath.

Rooms, massage, and physical therapy by a Registered Physical Therapist are available on the premises. Visa and MasterCard are accepted.

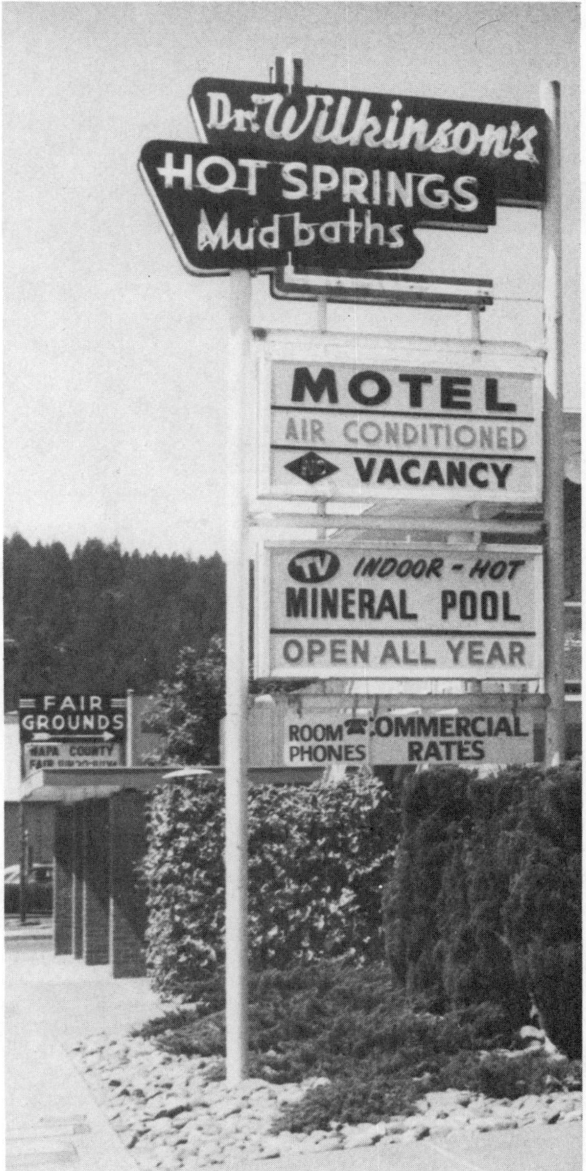

#121E CALISTOGA SPA

■ **1006 Washington St.** **(707) 942-6269**
Calistoga, CA 94515 **PR + MH**

Outdoor soaking pool, 100°. Covered hydropool, 105°. Indoor men's and women's bath houses, each containing four individual tubs, two mud baths and three steam baths.

Rooms, and massage are available on the premises. Visa and MasterCard are accepted.

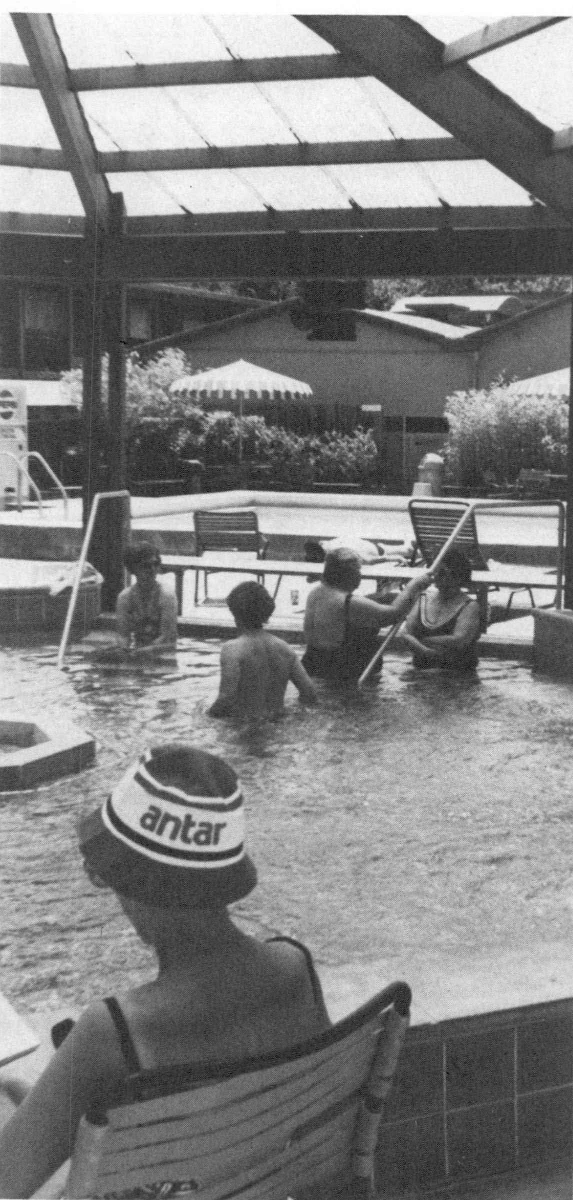

#121F ROMAN SPA

■ **1300 Washington St.** **(707) 942-4441**
Calistoga, CA 94515 **PR + MH**

Outdoor swimming pool, 90° and hydropool, 104°. Indoor hydropool, 100°. Motel rooms available. Visa and MasterCard accepted.

International Spa, under separate management, offers massage, reflexology, acupressure, co-ed mud baths, mineral baths, herbal blanket wrap and herbal facials. No credit cards.

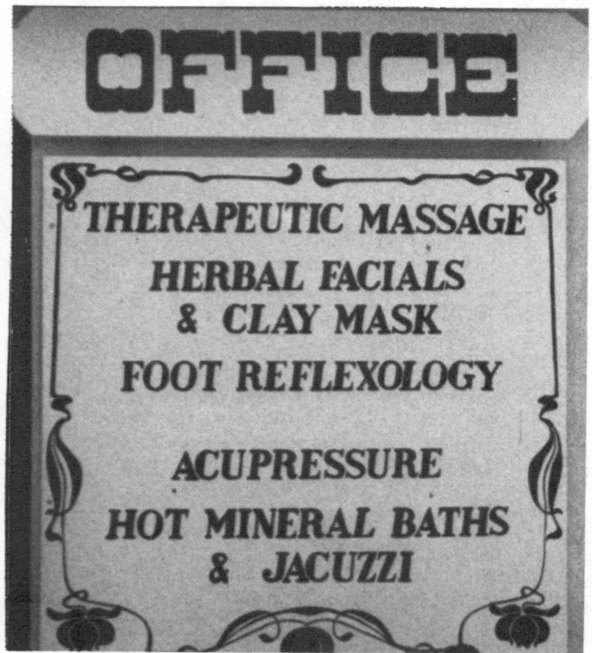

#121G GOLDEN HAVEN HOT SPRINGS

■ **1713 Lake St.** **(707) 942-6793**
Calistoga, CA 94515 **PR + MH**

Outdoor redwood hot tub, 103°. Enclosed swimming pool, 80°. Covered hydropool, 100°. Two indoor roman baths, large enough for two persons, are available for separate private rental during the week.

Rooms, massage, facials and reflexology are available on the premises. Visa and MasterCard are accepted.

#121H HIDEAWAY COTTAGES

■ **1412 Fairway** **(707) 942-4108**
Calistoga, CA 94515 **MH**

Outdoor swimming pool, 82°, and hydropool, 104°. Reserved for registered guests; no day use.

Cottages are available. Visa and MasterCard are accepted.

#121I OLD FAITHFUL GEYSER OF CALIFORNIA

OF CALIFORNIA does not have a pool in which you can soak or swim, but it is a symbol of this geothermal community. It has been known to behave erratically before earthquakes, as well as afterward.

#122A JUST FOR THE HEALTH OF IT

☐ Corner 5th and Davis (707) 544-4510
Santa Rosa, CA 95402 PR

Recreation oriented rent-a-tub establishment with redwood tubs, located a few blocks from the city center.

Pools for rent to the public, using gas-heated tap water, treated with bromine.

17 private rooms, rented by the hour. Water temp. 102-105°. Sauna included.

Other facilities: tanning suite, Kohler environment.

Services available: juice bar.

Credit cards accepted: Visa and MasterCard.

Phone for rates, reservations and directions.

#122B LOS ROBLES LODGE

☐ 925 Edwards Ave. (707) 545-6330
Santa Rosa, CA 95401 Hydropool MH

#122C EL RANCHO TROPICANA MOTOR HOTEL

☐ 2200 Santa Rosa Ave. (707) 542-3655
Santa Rosa, CA 95401 Hydropool MH

#123 THE LODGE AT FORESTVILLE

☐ 7871 River Rd. (707) 887-1556
Forestville, CA 95354 PR + MH

Newly remodeled resort, featuring hot water pools, located along the Russian River, northwest of Santa Rosa.

Pools for rent to the public, using gas-heated tap water, treated with chlorine.

Four private rooms, rented by the hour. Water temp. 102-105°. Sauna included.

12 private outdoor enclosures, rented by the hour. Water temp. 102-105°.

Eight private motel suites, rented by the night. Water temp. controllable by customer. No chlorine; drained and refilled after each check-out.

One unheated swimming pool for registered guests only.

Special features: pools in motel suites have outdoor views.

Bathing suits: optional in private rooms; required elsewhere.

Other facilities: restaurant and bar.

Services available: massage.

Credit cards accepted: Visa, MasterCard and American Express.

Phone for rates, reservations and directions.

#124 TIMBER COVE INN

☐ North Coast Hwy 1 (707) 847-3231
Jenner, CA 95450 In-room hydropools MH

#125 TIMBER COVE BOAT LANDING

☐ on Hwy 1 (707) 847-3278
Fort Ross, CA Hydropool MH

#126 HARBIN HOT SPRINGS (see map)

■ **P.O. Box 782 (707) 987-2477**
Middletown, CA 95461 PR + MH + CRV

Large historical resort being restored and expanded by a non-profit organization with a major residential program. Located in a rugged foothill canyon south of Clear Lake. Elevation 1,500 ft. Open all year.

Natural mineral water, with mild mineral content, flows out of the ground at 120°, and is piped to several soaking pools and a swimming pool. An enclosed cement pool has an average temperature of 110-115°. The adjoining cement pool has an average temperature of 100-104°, and the swimming pool ranges from 60-70°. All pools operate on a frequent cleaning and flow-through basis, so no chemical treatment is needed. Clothing is optional everywhere within the grounds.

Facilities include day use of pools, rooms, camping and RV spaces, a large new conference center, and a restaurant where vegetarian meals are optional. Massage, and massage training in a state-accredited school, are available on the premises. No credit cards are accepted. It is four miles to a store and service station.

Phone for rates, reservations and directions.

Harbin Hot Springs: Harold Dull, one of the directors of *Harbin's* massage school, demonstrates Watsu, a form of Shiatsu which makes use of the warm-water pool.

Harbin's residential community includes some families with small children.

Clothing is customary in the dining room and on the adjoining deck, which commands a view of *Harbin's* vegetable gardens.

#127 WILBUR HOT SPRINGS

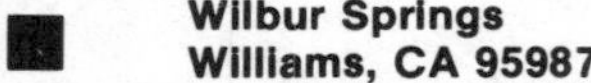

Wilbur Springs **(916) 473-2306**
Williams, CA 95987 **PR + MH**

A self-styled "Health Sanctuary", 22 miles from the nearest town, with an abundance of hot mineral water, and no electricity. The large, multi-temperature soaking pools, the sundecks, and the restored turn-of-the-century hotel are located in the treeless foothills of the western Sacramento valley. Elevation 1350 ft. Open all year.

Natural mineral water flows out of several springs at 120°, through a series of large concrete soaking pools under an A-frame structure, and into an outdoor swimming pool. Soaking pool temperatures are approximately 115°, 105° and 95°, with the swimming pool kept warm in the winter and cool in the summer. The water is not chemically treated. Bathing suits are optional in pool areas only; required elsewhere.

Massage, rooms, dormitory and communal kitchen are available on the premises. Visa and MasterCard are accepted. It is 22 miles to a restaurant, store and service station.

Directions: From Interstate 5 in Williams, go west on Cal 20 to the intersection with Cal 16. A few yards west of that intersection, take gravel road heading north and west for appoximately five miles, and follow signs.

Please no drop-in visitors. Phone first for reservations and confirmation of any services or uses.

Wilbur Hot Springs: The soaking pools under the A-frame have been likened to "oversize horse troughs" which are just deep enough to sit comfortably on the bottom, and wide enough to stretch out your legs. While soaking in these pools the open ends of the A-frame provide a dramatic view of the nearby hills.

#128 VICHY SPRINGS

2605 Vichy Springs Road **(707) 462-9515**
Ukiah, CA 95842

Historical resort, with naturally carbonated water, temporarily closed for rebuilding and remodeling. Located a few miles east of Ukiah in rolling foothills. Elevation 700 ft.

Natural mineral water flows from several springs and soaking pools for day use, private hot-pool enclosures, motel rooms and family residence suites with private hydropools. Camping and RV spaces will also be available. Phone or write for information on reopening plans and facilities.

#129 LU-ANN MOTEL
1340 N. State St. (707) 462-8873
Ukiah, CA 95482 Hydropools MH

Bath House - Healing Room
Circ. 1850
Natural Sulphur Mineral Springs
95° to 110° F
A Peacefull Healthful Place
where we ask there be
NO... Smoking, Glass or Soap
Please scrub and plug bathtubs
after using.
ENJOY
OM TAO

Orr Hot Springs: Soaking in the magic geothermal waters has been a tradition for more than a century, but a general clothing optional policy on the grounds has emerged in the last few decades.

#130 ORR HOT SPRINGS

■ **13201 Orr Springs Road** **(707) 462-6227**
Ukiah, CA 95482 **PR + MH + CRV**

A small older resort, being gradually improved by an active residential community, offering friendly informality and colorful flowerbeds. It is located on a wooded creek, 35 miles inland from the ocean. Elevation 800 ft. Open all year, on Friday, Saturday, Sunday and Monday only.

Natural mineral water flows out of several springs at 100°, and is piped to a swimming pool, an indoor soaking pool, and to four bathtubs in private rooms. The swimming pool averages 70 to 80°. Some of the water is heated to 105° and pumped to an enclosed redwood tub, and to an adjoining outdoor soaking pool. All pools operate on a flow-through basis so no chemical treatment is added. Clothing is optional everywhere on the grounds.

Facilities include a sauna, communal kitchen, rooms, cabins, dormitory and tent spaces along the creek. Massage is available by reservation. Space is limited, so telephone first for any use of the facilities. No credit cards are accepted. It is 13 miles of steep and winding roads to a restaurant, store, and service station.

Directions: From Route 101 in Ukiah, take the North State Street exit, go several hundred yards north to Orr Springs Road, and turn west for 13 miles to the resort.

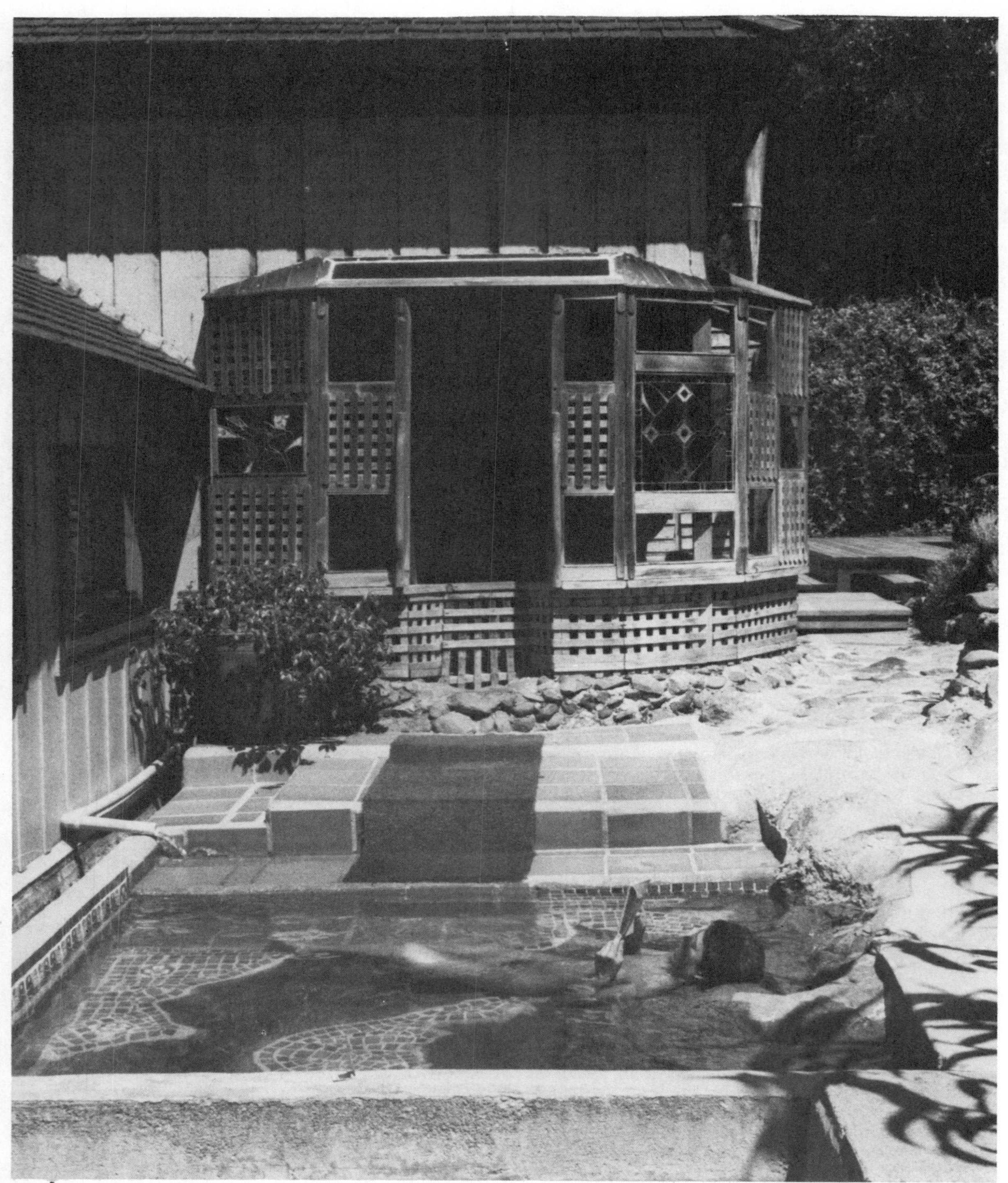

Orr Springs has a redwood tub behind the stained glass, plus an outdoor soaking pool.

#131 KOA—MANCHESTER BEACH
☐ on Kinney Rd. (707) 882-2375
Manchester, CA 95459 Hydropool CRV

#132 SWEETWATER GARDENS
☐ 955 Ukiah St. (707) 937-4140
Mendocino, CA 95460 PR + MH

Newer rent-a-tub establishment featuring natural wood tubs, walls and decking, with hanging greenery. Located on the coast of Northern California.

Pools for rent to the public, using gas-heated tap water, treated with chlorine.

One private enclosure, rented by the hour. Water temp. 104-106°, will adjust on request.

One private suite, rented by the hour and also by the night. Water temp. 104-106°, will adjust on request. Sauna included.

One communal hydropool, day rate charge. Water temp. 104-106°.

Special features: There is a private room above the communal pools available for overnight rental.

Bathing suits: optional everywhere.

Services available: massage.

Credit cards accepted: none.

Phone for rates, reservations and directions.

#133 CASPAR TUBBS
☐ P.O. Box 43 (707) 964-6668
Caspar, CA 95420 PR

Pioneer rent-a-tub establishment in a small town near Mendocino. Elevation 50 ft. Open all year.

Gas-heated well water is used in three open-roof redwood hot-tub enclosures, which may be rented by the hour. Water temperature is maintained in the range of 104-108°, and automatically chlorinated. Each unit includes a sauna and a shower. MasterCard and Visa are accepted.

Directions: From Cal 1, turn west on Caspar Street, which ends at Main Street (old Hwy 1). Turn north on Main Street ½ mile to Pacifica, then west to Caspar Tubbs sign.

#134 TRAILER LIFE'S BENBOW VALLEY RESORT
☐ on Benbow Dr. (707) 923-2777
Garberville, CA 95440 Hydropool RV

#135A EUREKA INN
☐ 7th & F St. (707) 442-6441
Eureka, CA 95501 Hydropool MH

#135B BEST WESTERN THUNDERBIRD LODGE
☐ 5th & Broadway (707) 443-2234
Eureka, CA 95501 Hydropool MH

#136 RAMADA INN—ARCATA/EUREKA
☐ 4975 Valley Blvd. (707) 822-4861
Arcata, CA 95521 Hydropool MH

COMMUNAL TUB
RINSE BEFORE ENTERING

Sweetwater Gardens: The rough-hewn wood and clothing-optional policy are typical of Mendocino coast rustic informality

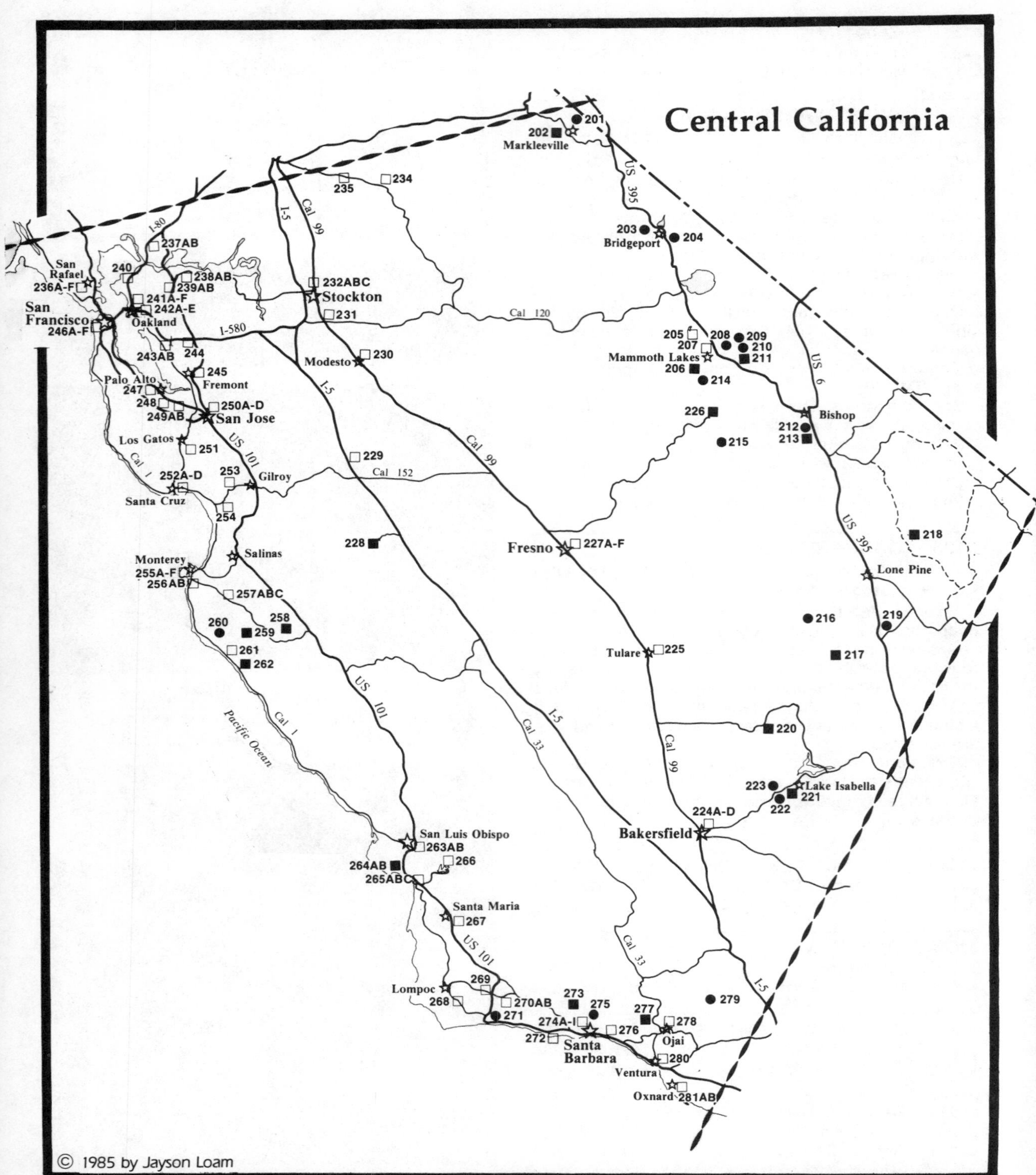

Central California
Markleeville
Bridgeport
Mammoth Lakes
Bishop
Lone Pine
Lake Isabella
Bakersfield
Tulare
Fresno
Modesto
Stockton
San Rafael
San Francisco
Oakland
Fremont
Palo Alto
San Jose
Los Gatos
Santa Cruz
Gilroy
Salinas
Monterey
San Luis Obispo
Santa Maria
Lompoc
Santa Barbara
Ojai
Ventura
Oxnard
Pacific Ocean
US 395
US 6
Cal 120
I-580
I-80
I-5
Cal 99
US 101
Cal 1
Cal 152
Cal 33
© 1985 by Jayson Loam

MAP AND DIRECTORY SYMBOLS

● **Unimproved natural mineral water pool**
■ **Improved natural mineral water pool**
□ Gas-heated tap or well water pool

Paved highway
Unpaved road
Hiking route

PR = Tubs or pools for rent by hour, day or treatment
MH = Rooms, cabins or dormitory spaces for rent by day, week or month
CRV = Camping or vehicle parking spaces, some with hookups, for rent by day, week, month or year

East Carson River Hot Springs: One of the raft-trip guides demonstrates how to get a hot shower while wearing a life jacket. Warming up is fun after a cold paddle.

#201 EAST CARSON RIVER HOT SPRINGS

near the town of Markleeville

non- commercial

Two undeveloped hot springs along a remote section of the East Carson River in Toiyabe National Forest. The only access is by raft or kayak. Elevation 5,000 ft. Open during rafting season which is approximately May, June and July.

Natural mineral water emerges from several springs at various temperatures and cools as it flows to the river. Riverside Hot Springs flows at approximately 104° as it drops eight feet onto shoreline rocks. Hot Showerbath, 200 yards upcanyon from the river, flows at approximately 95° as it drops ten feet into a shallow, volunteer-built pool. Clothing optional is the probable custom in this remote location.

There are no services available on the premises. One and two day raft trips (Class II rapids), conducted by experienced guides, are available locally. For information and/or pre-trip meals and lodging, contact Sorenson's Resort, (916) 694-2203.

These springs are not shown on any Forest Service or USGS map but are well known to raft trip guides.

Grover Hot Springs: When attendance is at capacity, a line forms at the gate.

These hot pools make adjoining *Grover State Campground* an especially popular site for a family vacation in the mountains.

#202 GROVER HOT SPRINGS

Box 188 **(916) 694-2248**
Markleeville, CA 96120 **PR + RV**

Conventional swimming pool and soaking pool next to major state campground and picnic area, located in a wooded mountain valley. Elevation 6,000 ft. Open all year; not accessible by road in winter.

Natural mineral water flows out of several springs at 147° into a holding pond, from which it is piped to the pool area. The soaking pool is maintained at 102-105°, using natural mineral water treated with bromine. The swimming pool is maintained at 70-80°, using creek water treated with chlorine. A heat exchanger is used to simultaneously cool down the mineral water and warm up the creek water. Admission is on a first-come, first-served basis, and the official capacity limit of 50 persons is reached early every day during the summer. Bathing suits are required.

Campground spaces are available by prior reservation as with all other California State parks. Cross-country skiers are encouraged to camp in the picnic area during the winter, and to ski in to use the soaking pool. It is five miles to the nearest restaurant, motel and service station.

Location: On Alpine County Road E4, 4½ miles west of Markleeville. Follow signs.

Source map: USGS *Markleeville.*

#203 BUCKEYE HOT SPRING (see map)

Near the town of Bridgeport

non-commercial

Unimproved hot spring on north bank of Buckeye Creek in Toiyabe National Forest. A superb natural setting. Elevation 6,900 ft. Open all year; not accessible by road in winter.

Natural mineral water flows out of the ground at 135° and runs over a large mineral deposit before its final drop into the creek. Volunteers have built a loose rock pool along the edge of the creek below the hot waterfall. The pool temperature is controlled by admitting more or less cold water from the creek. The apparent local custom is clothing optional.

There are no services on the premises. Three hundred yards upstream are several acres of unmarked open space on which overnight parking is not prohibited. It is one mile to a Forest Service Campground, and nine miles to a restaurant, motel, store and service station.

Source maps: *Toiyabe National Forest.* USGS *Matterhorn Peak.*

Buckeye Hot Spring: In the upper pool hot mineral water cascades in from the bank while cold creek water seeps in around the rocks. A person lying in the middle can experience a 30° temperature difference.

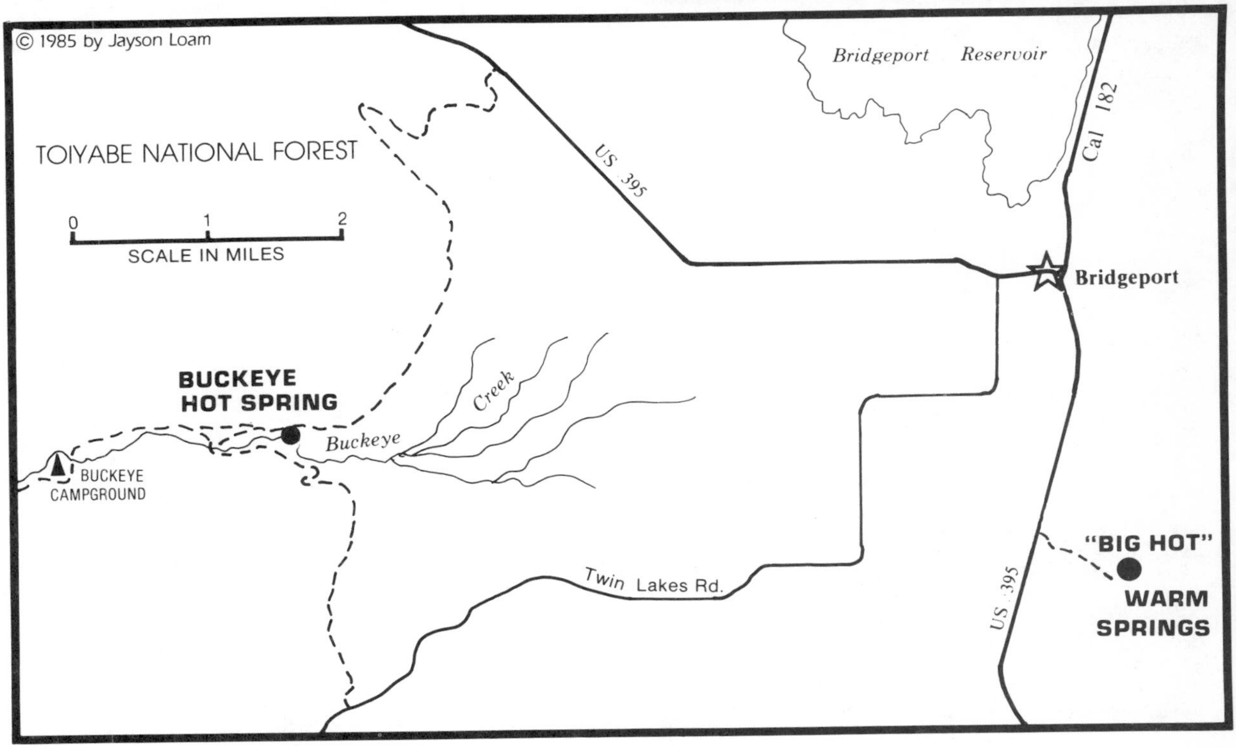

Bridgeport Reservoir

Cal 182

TOIYABE NATIONAL FOREST

US 395

0 1 2

SCALE IN MILES

Bridgeport

BUCKEYE HOT SPRING

Creek

Buckeye

BUCKEYE CAMPGROUND

"BIG HOT"

WARM SPRINGS

Twin Lakes Rd.

US 395

See map — page 51

#204 "BIG HOT" WARM SPRINGS

Near the town of Bridgeport

non-commercial

Unimproved warm springs on a hillside at the end of a rough dirt road, with a great view of the Sierra. Elevation 7,000 ft. Open all year; not accessible by road in winter.

Natural mineral water flows up from many seeps and holes at various temperatures up to 93°. Air temperatures and wind conditions affect the average pool temperatures. The largest pool is big enough for two dozen persons and is more than ten feet deep in the center. The apparent local custom is clothing optional.

There are no services on the premises. There is a substantial amount of unmarked open space on which overnight parking is not prohibited. The final 200 yards of road goes up a steep bank suitable only for walking or a 4WD vehicle. It is four miles to the nearest store, restaurant, motel and service station.

Source map: USGS *Bodie.*

"Big Hot" Warm Springs: Although the water is only lukewarm, this large natural tufa formation pool has spectacular view.

#205 BOULDER LODGE
P.O. Box 68 (619) 648-7533
June Lake, CA 93539 Hydropool MH

#206 RED'S MEADOW HOT SPRINGS

In Red's Meadow Campground near Devil's Postpile National Monument **RV + MH**

Tin roof shed with six cement tubs in six small private rooms, on the edge of a mountain meadow campground. Elevation 7,000 ft. Open approximately Memorial Day to September 20.

Natural mineral water flows out of the ground at 110° into a storage tank, and then by pipe into the bath house. Depending on the rate of use, water temperature out of the shower heads will vary from 95 to 105°. No charge is made for the use of the tubs, which are available on a first-come, first-served basis.

A Forest Service Campground adjoins the hot spring. A restaurant, store, gas station and motel rooms are available at a nearby pack station, which is a stop on the shuttle bus service to Mammoth Lakes. No credit cards are accepted. It is 13 miles to a full RV hookups.

Directions: From the town of Mammoth Lakes, take Cal 203 west to end, then follow signs to Devil's Postpile National Monument, and to Reds Meadow Camground.

Source Maps: *Inyo National Forest.* USGS *Devil's Postpile.*

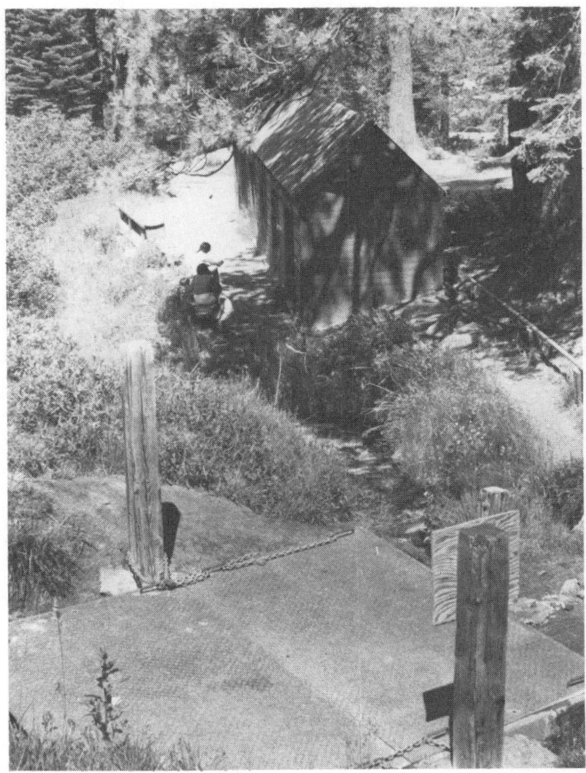

Red's Meadow Hot Springs; The source spring is chained shut. Soak only in the bath house.

#207A MAMMOTH TRAVELODGE
P.O. Box 360 (714) 934-8576
Mammoth Lakes, CA 93546 Hydropool MH

#207B INTERNATIONAL INN
P.O. Box 1089 (714) 934-6855
Mammoth Lakes, CA 93546 Hydropool MH

#207C BEST WESTERN WILDWOOD INN
P.O. Box 568 (714) 934-6855
Mammoth Lakes, CA 93546 Hydropool MH

#207D ALPINE LODGE
P.O. Box 359 (714) 934-8526
Mammoth Lakes, CA 93546 Hydropool MH

#207E SIERRA NEVADA INN
P.O. Box 918 (714) 934-2515
Mammoth Lakes, CA 93546 Hydropool MH

Hot Creek: Numerous Forest Service signs remind visitors of the dangers and restrictions on the use of this area.

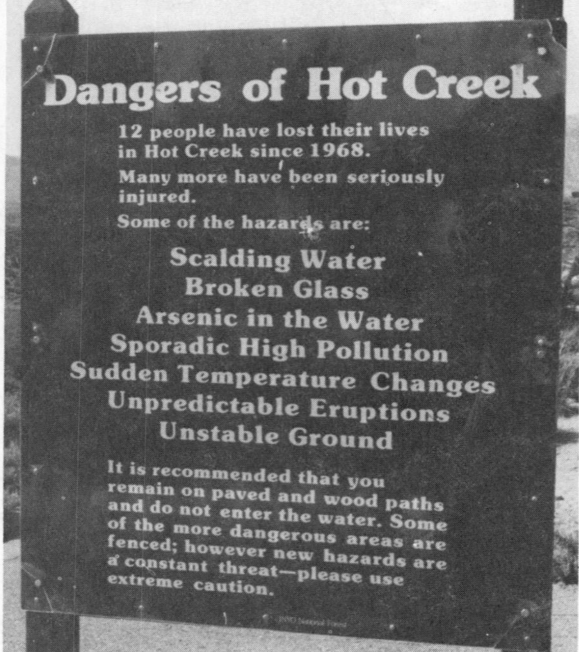

Despite the warning dozens of people gather in that part of the creek where boiling water flowing up from the creek bottom makes a tolerable mix with the ice-cold creek water.

#208 HOT CREEK (see map)

Near the town of Mammoth Lakes

non-commercial

Primarily a geologic observation and interpretive site with some limited use by bathers. Located in the foothills east of a popular skiing area. Elevation 7,000 ft. Open daylight hours only.

Natural mineral water emerges from many fissures as steam or boiling water and several danger areas have been fenced off for safety. A bend in the creek provides a natural eddy in which the mixing of hot and cold water stays within a range of 50° to 110°. Those who venture into the creek encounter vivid thermal skin effects and some danger. Bathing suits are required.

Night use of the location has resulted in many injuries and some fatalities so the Forest Service closes the area at night. During the winter, when snow blocks the access road, skiers and hikers are still admitted during daylight hours.

Men's and women's dressing rooms are available in the parking lot but no other services are available, and overnight parking is prohibited. It is eight miles to a store, cafe, service station and campground

Directions: On US 395, from the Mammoth Lakes interchange, go 3.0 miles southeast, then turn northeast on gravel road toward the fish hatchery. Go 1.5 miles beyond hatchery to Hot Creek parking lot.

Source maps: *Inyo National Forest.* USGS *Mt. Morrison.*

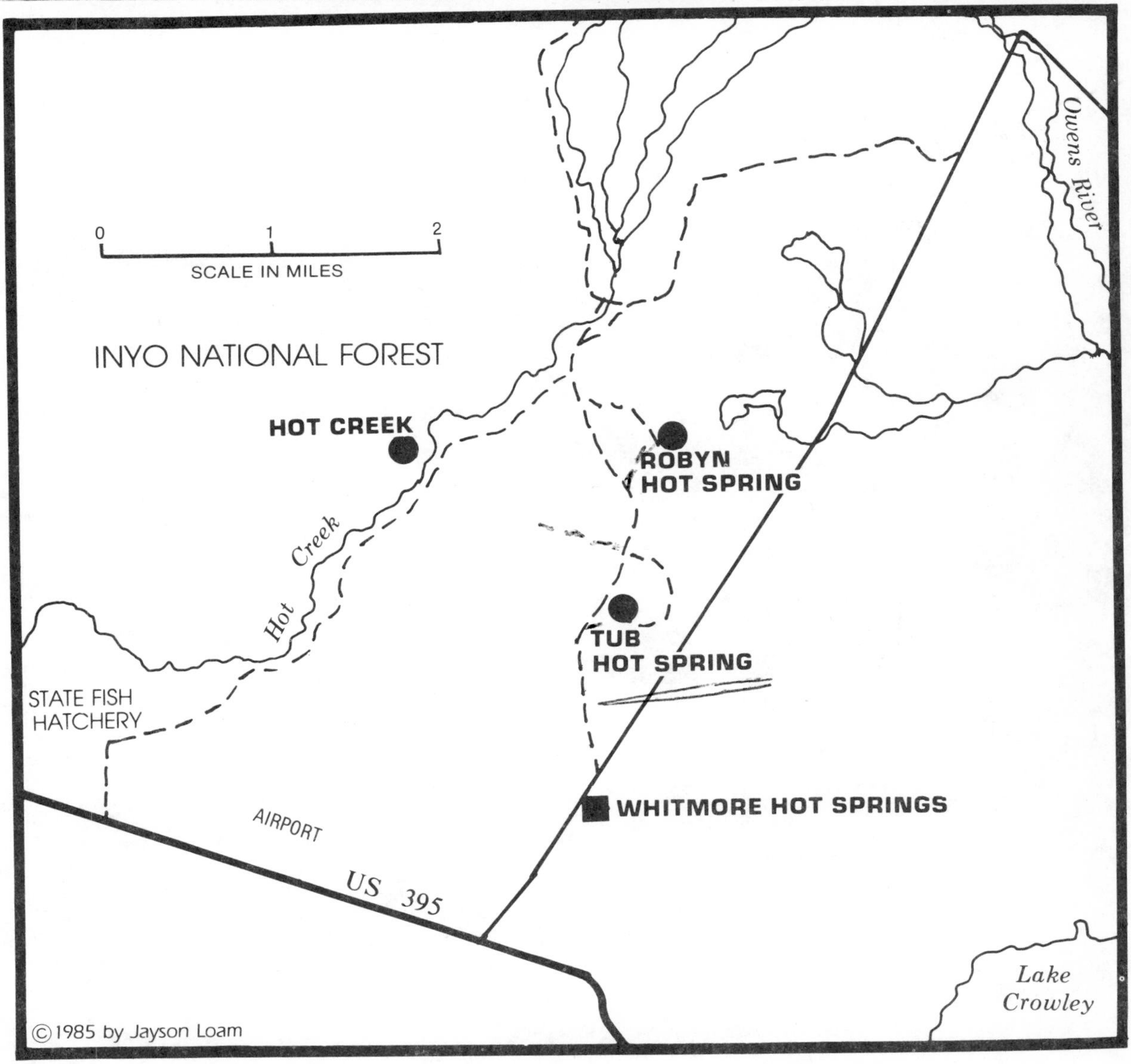

INYO NATIONAL FOREST

0 1 2
SCALE IN MILES

HOT CREEK

ROBYN
HOT SPRING

Hot Creek

TUB
HOT SPRING

STATE FISH
HATCHERY

WHITMORE HOT SPRINGS

AIRPORT

US 395

Owens River

Lake
Crowley

©1985 by Jayson Loam

The Tub Hot Spring: The barren wastelands surrounding this tiny pool help convey a convincing away-from-it-all feeling.

Robyn Hot Springs: Sheepherders built this cozy geothermal retreat many decades ago and volunteers have been trying to keep it together ever since.

#209 THE TUB HOT SPRING

See map page 55

● **Near the town of Mammoth Lakes**

non- commercial

Small remote soaking pool with fine view of the High Sierra. Elevation 7,200 ft. Open all year, not accessible by road in winter.

Natural mineral water flows out of the ground at 114° through a hose to a volunteer-built rock and cement tub, large enough for four. The water temperature in the pool is controlled by diverting the hot water flow while cooling takes place. The apparent local custom is clothing optional.

No services are available on the premises. There is a limited amount of unmarked level space on which overnight parking is not prohibited. It is five miles to the nearest restaurant, motel, service station, store, etc.

Source maps: *Inyo National Forest.* USGS *Mt. Morrison.*

#210 ROBYN HOT SPRING

See map page 55

● **Near the town of Mammoth Lakes**

non- commercial

Small remote soaking pool in treeless foothills. Elevation 7,000 ft. Open all year; not accessible by road in winter.

Natural mineral water flows out of the ground at 113° through a pipe to a shallow, crumbling cement block pool, large enough for one person. Water temperature in the pool is controlled by diverting the hot water flow while the cooling takes place. The apparent local custom is clothing optional.

No services are available on the premises. There is a limited amount of unmarked level space on which overnight parking is not prohibited. It is six miles to a restaurant, motel, service station, store, etc.

Source maps: *Inyo National Forest.* USGS *Mt. Morrison.*

See map — page 55

#211 WHITMORE HOT SPRINGS

■ **Route 3, Box 200** **(619) 935-4741**
Bishop, CA 93546 **PR**

Conventional public swimming pool in treeless Sierra foothills. Jointly operated by Mono County and Los Angeles City Parks and Recreation Department. Elevation 7,000 ft. Open daytime; mid-April to mid-October.

Natural mineral water is pumped to the pool from a well at 90°. Depending on air temperature and wind conditions, pool temperature averages 82°. Pool water is treated with chlorine. Bathing suits are required. No credit cards are accepted.

No services are available on the premises. Overnight parking is not prohibited on the large gravel parking lot. It is four miles to a store and service station, and 12 miles to a restaurant and hotel.

Directions: Drive one mile east off of US 395, northwest of Lake Crowley. Watch for sign on US 395.

▲ *Keough Hot Ditch:* These parents explored several pools along the ditch to find just the right temperature for the family.

#212 KEOUGH HOT DITCH

● **near Keough Hot Springs** **non-commercial**

Runoff from Keough Hot Springs cools as it flows through a series of volunteer-built rock pools in a treeless foothill gully. Elevation 4,100 ft. Open all year.

Natural mineral water flows out of the ground at 128° on Keough Hot Springs property, then wanders northeast over BLM land for about a mile before joining with a cold water surface stream. Volunteer-built rock dams create several primitive pools of various depths, each one cooler than the preceding one upstream. The apparent local custom is clothing optional

No services available on the premises. There is a limited amount of level unmarked space on which overnight parking is not prohibited. It is one mile to an RV park, and eight miles to a restaurant, store, service station, etc.

Directions: Seven miles south of Bishop on US 395, turn west on Keough Hot Springs Road approximately 500 yards. At the only intersection with paved road (old 395) turn north 200 yards to end of the road at a cold stream. Walk an additional 50 yards north to Keough Ditch. Either stream may be followed to where they join, forming a warm swimming pond.

Keough Hot Springs: The notice on the door allows the owner to comply with county health laws without building a new pool.

#213 KEOUGH HOT SPRINGS

Route 1, Box 9 **(619) 873-3167**
Bishop, CA 93514 **PR + RV**

Older hot springs resort in the Sierra foothills. The bath house is closed, and the swimming pool access is limited. It is advisable to phone for current information. Elevation 4,200 ft. Open all year.

Natural mineral water flows out of the ground at 128°. The enclosed swimming pool (87° to 95°) and the wading pool (100°) use flow-through mineral water—no chlorine added. Bathing suits are required.

Snack bar and partial RV hook-ups are available on the premises. No credit cards are accepted. It is eight miles to the nearest restaurant, motel, service station, and store.

Directions: go seven miles south of Bishop on US 395, then follow signs west from US 395.

The High Hot Ones

A special report by Tom Winnett, co-author of *Sierra North* and *Sierra South*.

There are several hot springs in California that you can't drive to and can't reach via a short walk. Most of them are in the backcountry of the High Sierra. Although almost no one would make the long hike to one of these springs just to soak, if one is hiking near the springs, one should certainly visit them.

For a free catalog of trail guide books and source maps for all of the western states, including Hawaii, send a request with your name and address to:

Wilderness Press
2440 Bancroft Way Berkeley, CA 94704

If you wish to order *Sierra North* or *Sierra South,* enclose $12.70 (each).

#214 FISH CREEK HOT SPRING

Elevation 7,200 ft.

Near Fish Creek, 12 miles south of Reds Meadow, in the Devil's Postpile area. Also called Iva Bell Hot Springs after a baby that legend says was born nearby, this spring is well used—relatively—considering its distance from roads.

Go south from Reds Meadow on the Fish Creek Trail to beyond Island Crossing in Fish Valley. Just past the Sharktooth Creek Trail, cross that creek to Iva Bell Camp. The hot spring is about 100 yards up a path that goes through the campground there. There were three useable pools when checked in 1981.

Source map: USGS *Devil's Postpile.*

#215 BLAYNEY HOT SPRINGS

Elevation 7,600 ft.

Beside the South Fork of the San Joaquin River 9½ miles in from the roadend at Florence Lake in Fresno County. You can cut the distance by 3½ miles by taking the boat-taxi up Florence Lake. Anyone walking the part of the John Muir Trail in this region has only to hike 1¼ miles off the Muir Trail down the Florence Lake Trail to reach the hot springs.

About 200 yards west of signs on the Florence Lake Trail that indicate the Muir Trail is 1½ miles away both to the east and the north, an unsigned trail goes south ¼ mile down to riverside campsites. From the campsite on the south side of the river a faint trail goes southwest to the springs.

The springs are a single mud-bottomed hole in a grassy meadow, with a temperature of about 102°. Nearby is a warmish, small swimming lake for washing off the muddy water. You must cross the South Fork of the San Joaquin River to reach the springs, and will probably have to wade. As always with mountain streams, take extreme care.

Very close by is the Muir Trail Ranch, where for money you can be a paying guest and use their private hot springs in the same meadow. For information write the owner, Adeline Smith, at Box 176, Lakeshore, CA 93634 from mid-June to October, or Box 269, Ahwahnee, CA 93601 in other months.

Source map: USGS *Blackcap Mountain.*

Blayney Hot Springs: A fine squishy bottom.

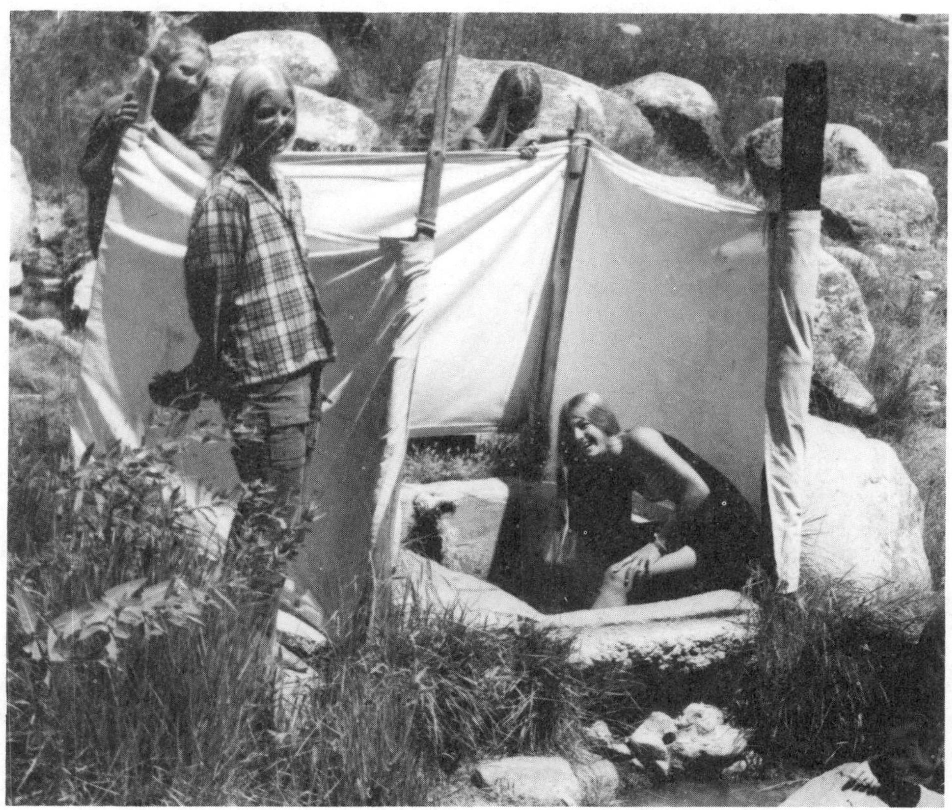

Kern Hot Spring: The longest hike of all.

#216 KERN HOT SPRING

Elevation 6,900 ft.

Beside the upper Kern River, 31½ miles west from Whitney Portal or 37 miles east from Crescent Meadow, near Giant Forest in Sequoia National Park. This hot spring is deeper into the wilderness than any other in California. By a great piece of luck it is right beside the Kern River, so you can dip into the river's cold waters to cool the spring's 115° if desired.

Situated in the mile-deep canyon of the upper Kern River, this spring has a magnificent view in all directions. And well it should, considering that it is at least three days' walk from the nearest roadend. However, if you are hiking across the superb wilderness of the upper Kern, you won't want to miss the ineffable thrill of soaking your aching bones in this superb hot spring.

Source map: USGS *Kern Peak.* Located near the top center of this quadrangle map.

#217 JORDAN HOT SPRINGS

Elevation 6,400 ft.

Near Ninemile Creek east of the Kern River in the southernmost part of Golden Trout Wilderness. Although this spring is in a federal wilderness area, the resort that was there before the wilderness was established is still operating (supplied by pack train) and you will have to pay a small sum to soak. You can also buy hot meals, cabin rentals and limited groceries.

The nearest roadend is at the end of paved Sequoia National Forest Road 21S03, reached via County Road J41 from south of Little Lake on US 395. From the roadend hike north to Casa Vieja Meadows and then northwest down Ninemile Creek to Jordan Hot Springs.

Source map: USGS *Hockett Peak.*

#218 SALINE VALLEY HOT SPRINGS

near the town of Olancha

non-commercial

A sometimes crowded spring-fed oasis located on a barren slope of BLM land in a remote desert valley northwest of Death Valley. Elevation 2,900 ft. Open all year but the last few miles of access road can be impassable when wet.

Natural mineral water flows out of two source springs at 107°. Volunteers have installed pipes to carry this water to a variety of man-made cement and rock pools for soaking, shampooing, dish washing, etc. By mutual agreement no one bathes in the source pools. The rate of flow through the soaking pools is sufficient to eliminate any need for chemical treatment of the water. The apparent local custom is clothing optional.

There are no services except crude volunteer-built latrines on the premises, but there is an abudannce of level space on which overnight parking is not prohibited. It is 90 miles, half gravel surface, to a store, cafe, service station, etc.

Temperatures regularly soar over the 100° mark in the summer, so this desert location with very little natural shade is preferred in the winter and spring. It takes many hours of driving to reach these springs from almost anywhere, so the location becomes very crowded, and should be avoided, on major holidays and three day weekends. During the week is the ideal time to enjoy the peace and quiet of the desert.

Source maps: So. Cal. Auto Club *Death Valley*. USGS *Waucoba Wash* and *New York Butte*.

Saline Valley Hot Springs: Cement and rock soaking pools have been built in a strip of shade below the source springs.

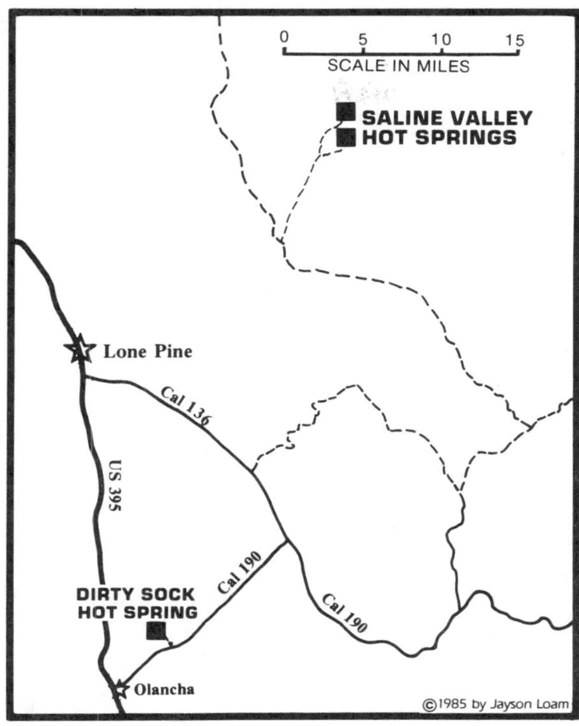

The *Saline Valley* source springs, on top of vast tufa mounds, are kept free of personal use so that uncontaminated water may be piped to the specialized pools which have been built in the willows.

#219 DIRTY SOCK HOT SPRING

Near the town of Olancha non-commercial

Large shallow pool, slimy green with algae, in an open desert area. Elevation 3,600 ft. Open all year.

Natural mineral water flows up from the bottom of a circular cement-edged pool at 90°, and flows out at various lower temperatures, depending on wind and air temperature. The murky water gives an uninviting appearance. The apparent local custom is clothing optional.

No services are available on the premises and there are no remaining buildings. There are many acres of unmarked level space on which overnight parking is not prohibited. It is five miles to the nearest restaurant, motel, service station and store.

Directions: From the intersection of US 395 and Cal 190, go five miles northeast on Cal 190. There are no signs on the highway so look for a narrow paved road on the northwest side, and follow it 300 yards to the spring.

California Hot Springs: Pools are expected to be ready for use in early 1985.

#220 CALIFORNIA HOT SPRINGS

P.O. Box 146 (805) 548-6242
California Hot Springs, CA 93207 PR

Historic resort in the process of major restoration and expansion. Located in rolling foothills at the edge of Sequoia National Forest. Elevation 3,100 ft. Open all year.

Natural mineral water flows out of several artesian wells at a temperature of 126°, and is piped to the pool area. There will be two concrete and tile hydropools, each large enough to hold 20 persons. Water temperature will be maintained at 100° with a flow-through process which eliminates the need for chlorination. There will also be one large swimming pool containing chlorinated and filtered mineral water at a temperature of approximately 85°. Bathing suits will be required.

The restored main building will contain a delicatessen, and shops selling gifts, art and local craft products. Massage will be available on the premises. An RV park is also part of the long range plan. MasterCard, Visa and American Express will be accepted. It is two miles to a motel, store and service station.

Directions: From the town of Earlimart, on Cal 99, take Tulare County Route J22 east for 38 miles to the resort.

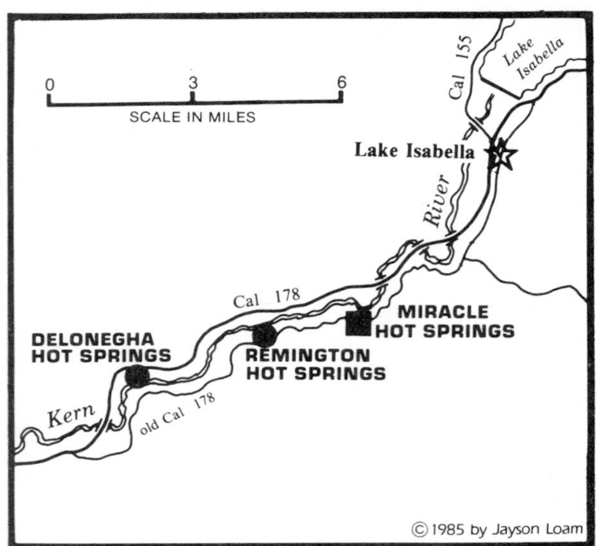

Miracle Hot Springs: The geothermal water for all six riverside soaking pools comes out of a single spring but careful valve control provides a variety of temperatures. The casual rock and cement construction retains the naturalness of the setting.

#221 MIRACLE HOT SPRINGS (see map)

■ **Star Route 1, Box 100 (619) 379-8350**
Miracle Hot Springs, CA 93301 PR + MH + CRV

Older resort, whose lodge building burned in 1976, carrying on with a store, bath house, RV park and six inviting outdoor soaking pools. Located on the tree-shaded south bank of the Kern River, a major all-year stream. Elevation 2,400 ft. Open all year.

Natural mineral water flows out of a spring at 123°, and is piped to pools and bath house. Each of the six rock and cement pools at the river's edge is maintained at a different temperature, ranging from 85° to 110°, using a flow-through process which eliminates the need for chemical treatment of the water. The bath house has men's and women's sections, each containing individual tubs in which the water temperature is controlled by each bather. The mineral content of the hot mineral water is so low that it is used in the showers. Bathing suits are required at the outdoor soaking pools, but are not required in the bath house.

Facilities include small trailers for rent by the night or week, camping and RV spaces along the river, and a seasonal store, gas pump and snack bar. No credit cards are accepted. It is four miles to a restaurant.

#222 REMINGTON HOT SPRINGS

(see map)

Near the town of Isabella non-commercial

A delightful two-person cement tub in an unspoiled primitive riverside setting of rocks and trees. Located in the Kern River Canyon, down a steep trail from old Hwy #178. Elevation 2,200 ft. Open all year except during high water in the river.

Natural mineral water emerges from the ground at 104°, and at more than 100 gallons per minute. This flow comes directly up through the bottom of a volunteer-built cement tub, providing a form of hydrojet action, and maintaining pool temperature at 104°. Twenty yards uphill is a drainable one-person rock and cement pool fed by a smaller flow of 96° water. Even though the site has obviously been used for many years, there is almost no unsightly trash. The apparent local custom is clothing optional.

There are no services available on the premises. It is six miles to a motel, restaurant and service station.

Directions: From the Miracle Hot Springs store, on old Hwy 178, go west 1½ miles to a large turn-off space with a telephone pole in the middle. Overnight parking is not prohibited. The steep unmaintained trail leads directly to the riverbank springs, 300 yards below. Keep it beautiful by packing out whatever you pack in.

Remington Hot Springs: This first-rate gem on the edge of the Kern River is worth every gasp of the 300-yard scramble down and up.

#223 DELONEGHA HOT SPRINGS

photos are on page 66 (see map)

Near the town of Isabella non-commercial

A primitive riverside hot spring where volunteers try to build creative soaking pools faster than vandals and flood waters can destroy them. Located in the dramatic Kern River canyon, only 30 yards from Cal 178, which accounts for scattered piles of broken bottles and empty cans. Elevation 2,100 ft. Open all year.

Natural mineral water emerges from both sides of a giant rock at 108°. On one side a rock and cement pool large enough for ten people has been built. On the other side, plastic hoses carry hot mineral water to cast iron bath tubs at river's edge. The rate of cooling in pools is dependent upon air temperature and wind conditions. The apparent local custom is clothing optional.

There are no services available on the premises. It is 11 miles to a restaurant, store, etc.

Directions: 30 miles east of Bakersfield, Cal 178 splits into the "old" route on the south side and the "new" route on the north side. From that split take the "new" route across a bridge and go approximately ½ mile, just past the first hill on the right edge of the road. Watch for an unusually large turn-out area and many paths leading down the embankment toward the river and the springs.

Delonegha Hot Springs: Over several decades commercial firms and unpaid volunteers have built improvements, only to have them destroyed by vandals or swept away by flood waters. Be prepared to see some changes.

#224A BAKERSFIELD HILTON INN
☐ 3535 Rosedale Hwy. (805) 327-0681
Bakersfield, CA 93308 Hydropool MH

#224B REGAL OAK INN
☐ 1011 Oak St. (805) 325-0772
Bakersfield, CA 93304 Hydropool MH

#224C RAMADA INN
☐ 2620 Pierce Rd. (805) 327-9651
Bakersfield, CA 93308 Hydropool MH

#224D RIO BRAVO RESORT
☐ 11200 Lake Ming Rd. (805) 325-0772
Bakersfield, CA 93306 Hydropool MH

#225 MUSTANG FAMILY FUN CENTER
☐ 110 N. Mooney Blvd. (209) 688-0561
Tulare, CA 93274 PR

Combination water slide and hot pool rental establishment, located on the edge of a major farming community.

Pools for rent to the public, using gas-heated tap water, treated with chlorine.

Ten private rooms, rented by the hour.

Water temp: 100-102°.

Special features: One pool is large enough for 16 persons. Showers are located in Men's and Women's changing rooms, rather than in private rooms. Bathing suits: required on water slide, not required in private rooms.

Services available: snack bar.

Credit cards accepted: none.

Phone for rates, reservations and directions.

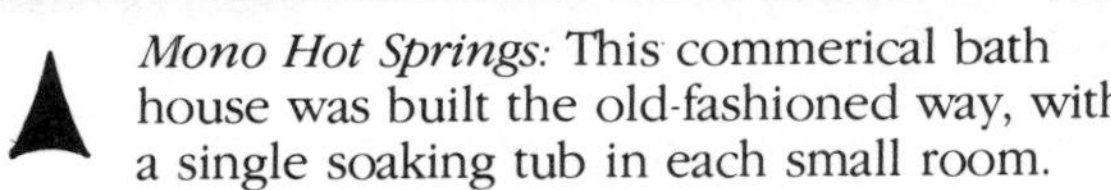
Mono Hot Springs: This commerical bath house was built the old-fashioned way, with a single soaking tub in each small room.

#226 MONO HOT SPRINGS

(Summer) Mono Hot Springs, CA 93642
(Winter) Lake Shore, CA 93634 PR + CRV + MH

A variety vacation resort, offering fishing, hiking and camping in addition to mineral baths. Located on the south fork of the San Juaquin River near Thomas Edison Lake in the Sierra National Forest. Elevation 6,500 ft. Open May to October.

Natural mineral water flows from a spring at 107°, then is piped to a bath house containing ten individual soaking tubs in small private rooms. Customers may add cold tap water as desired to control temperature.

A cafe, store, service station, campground and RV spaces are available on the premises. Visa and MasterCard are accepted.

On the south side of the river, directly across from the resort bath house, on National Forest land, is another hot spring supplying two old cement soaking pools which average a temperature of 101°. Bathing suits are advisable at this location in the daytime.

Directions: From the city of Fresno, on US 99, go 80 miles northeast on Cal 168. The last 15 miles are steep, winding and rough.

Across the river from *Mono Hot Springs Resort* are these non-commercial remains of an old bath house. The Forest Service plans to remove the dangerous jagged cement.

#227A SNUGGLE TUBS

5169 N. Blackstone (209) 222-7484
Fresno, CA 93710 PR

Recreation oriented rent-a-tub establishment, located on a main city street.

Pools for rent to the public, using gas-heated tap water, treated with chlorine.

11 private rooms, rented by the hour. Water temp. 100°, will adjust on request.

Services available: Beer & wine bar, with room service.

Credit cards accepted: Visa and MasterCard.

Phone for rates, reservations and directions.

#227B PICCADILLY INN—AIRPORT

5115 E. McKinley Ave. (209) 251-6000
Fresno, CA 93727 Hydropool MH

#227C BEST WESTERN TRADEWINDS MOTEL

(209) 237-1881
2141 N. Pkwy Dr. at Clinton Ave.
Fresno, CA 93705 Hydropool MH

#227D HACIENDA INN

2550 W. Clinton Ave. (209) 486-3000
Fresno, CA 93705 Hydropool MH

#227E PICADILLY INN—SHAW

2305 W. Shaw Ave. (209) 226-3850
Fresno, CA 93711 Hydropool MH

#227F SMUGGLER'S INN

3737 N. Blackstone Ave. (209) 226-2200
Fresno, CA 93726 Hydropool MH

#228 MERCEY HOT SPRINGS

Box 1363 (no phone)
Los Banos, CA 93635 PR + MH

An older hot springs resort, located in rolling desert hills on the west side of the San Joaquin Valley. Elevation 1,200 ft. Open September 1 to July 1.

Natural mineral water flows from the ground at 119° and cools to 105° as it is piped to the bath house. There are five individual tubs in small private rooms.

Endonphin Therapy and massage are available on the premises. Cabins (community kitchen) and RV spaces are also available. No credit cards are accepted. It is 36 miles to a restaurant, store, etc.

Directions: From the intersection of I-5 and Fresno County Route J1, follow signs 13 miles west on Little Panoche Road.

#229 BEST WESTERN
PEA SOUP ANDERSEN'S INN

12367 S. Hwy 33 (209) 826-5534
Santa Nella, CA 95322 Hydropool MH

#230 HOLIDAY INN

1612 Sisk Rd. (209) 521-1612
Modesto, CA 95350 Hydropool MH

#231 OAKWOOD LAKE RESORT

on Woodward Ave. (209) 239-9566
Manteca, CA 95336 Hydropool CRV

#232A SPAS FOR YOU

4919 Pacific Ave. (209) 477-8827
Stockton, CA 95207 PR

Combination rent-a-tub and retail spa sales establishment located on a main suburban street.

Pools for rent to the public, using gas-heated tap water, treated with chlorine.

12 private enclosures, rented by the hour. Water temp. 95-97°, will adjust on request.

Credit cards accepted: Visa and MasterCard.

Phone for rates, reservations and directions.

#232B HOLIDAY INN & HOLIDOME

221 N. Center St. (209) 466-3993
Stockton, CA 95202 Hydropool MH

#232C STOCKTON HILTON

2323 Grand Canal Dr. (209) 957-9090
Stockton, CA 95207 Hydropool MH

#234 FAR HORIZONS 49ER TRAILER VILLAGE

on Hwy 49 (209) 245-6981
Plymouth, CA 95669 Hydropool RV

#235 RANCHO MURIETA RESORT

14813 Jackson Rd. (916) 985-7200
Rancho Murieta, CA 95683 Hydropool MH

Floating World: Skylight, colorful tile and glistening shower stalls are typical of new rent-a-tub facilites.

#236A FLOATING WORLD

303 Harbor World (415) 331-2555
Sausalito, CA 94965 PR

A combination of Japanese beauty, Swedish deep relaxation and American high technology, with skylit suites and contoured cedar tubs. Located a few yards from the harbor.

Pools for rent to the public, using gas-heated tap water, treated with bromine and electronic filtering.

Ten private rooms, rented by the hour. Water temp. 102-105°. Sauna included.

One private room, rented by the hour, with a tub large enough for ten people. Water temp. 102-105°.

Services available: massage, juice bar.

Credit cards accepted: Visa and MasterCard.

Phone for rates, reservations and directions.

Shibui Gardens: The classic redwood tub experience, in an atmosphere of friendly informality, is a *Shibui* tradition.

All customers in the three *Shibui Gardens* hot tubs are welcome to take a refreshing plunge in the adjacent cold tub.

#236B F. JOSEPH SMITH'S MASSAGE THERAPY

☐

158 Almonte Blvd. (415) 383-8260
Mill Valley, CA 94941 PR

Informal therapy establishment, with redwood hot tubs, located in a Marin County suburb.

Pools for rent to the public, using gas-heated tap water, treated with bromine.

Two private enclosures, rented by the hour. Water temp. 104-108°.

Special features: One of the tubs is for communal use.

Bathing suits: optional everywhere except front office.

Other facilities: Private sauna available for rent.

Services available: massage.

Credit cards accepted: none.

Phone for rates, reservations and directions.

#236C TRAVELODGE—MILL VALLEY

☐

707 Redwood Hwy (415) 383-0340
Mill Valley, CA 94941 PR + MH

A conventional motel with one enclosed outdoor redwood hot tub.

One pool for rent to the public, using gas-heated tap water, treated with chlorine.

One private enclosure, rented by the hour. Water temp. 102°. Sauna included.

One communal swimming pool for registered guests.

Bathing suits: optional in private enclosure.

Other facilities: motel rooms.

Credit cards accepted: Visa and MasterCard.

Phone for rates, reservations and directions.

#236D SHIBUI GARDENS

☐

19 Tamalpais Ave. (415) 457-0283
San Anselmo, CA 94960 PR

An inviting blend of Marin County natural redwood hot tubs and Japanese landscaping. Located on a suburban side street.

Pools for rent to the public, using gas-heated tap water, treated with bromine.

Three private enclosures, rented by the hour. Water temp. 102-105°.

One communal cold pool, no charge to customers.

Bathing suits: optional inside pool and sauna spaces.

Other facilities: private indoor sauna.

Services available: massage.

Phone for information about rates, reservations, credit cards and directions.

Realax in Fairfax: If you are brave you may have a cold shower in this hot tub.

#236E REALAX IN FAIRFAX

☐ 10B School Street Plaza (415) 454-1922
Fairfax, CA 94930 PR

One of the first dozen informal soaking and stress reduction centers in the Bay Area. Located in a Marin County suburb.

Pools for rent to the public, using gas-heated tap water, treated with bromine.

Two private enclosures, rented by the hour. Water temp. 106°.

One communal hydropool large enough for 25 people, day rate charge. Water temp. 106°.

One communal cold plunge, day rate charge.

Special features: one communal sauna, day rate.

Bathing suits: optional everywhere.

Services available: massage.

Credit cards accepted: Visa and MasterCard.

Phone for rates, reservations and directions.

#236F BEST WESTERN CORTE MADERA INN
1815 Redwood Hwy (415) 924-1502
☐ Sausalito, CA 94965 Hydropool MH

#237A BEST WESTERN ROYAL BAY INN
44 Admiral Callaghan Lane (707) 643-1061
☐ Vallejo, CA 94590 Hydropool MH

#237B GATEWAY MOTOR HOTEL
2070 Solano Ave. (707) 552-1600
☐ Vallejo, CA 94590 Hydropool MH

#238A SHERATON HOTEL & CONFERENCE CENTER
45 John Glenn Dr. (415) 825-7700
☐ Concord, CA 94520 Hydropool MH

#238B CONCORD HILTON
1970 Diamond Blvd. (415) 827-2000
☐ Concord, CA 94520 Hydropool MH

#239A TO YOUR HEALTH

☐ 1948 Contra Costa Blvd. (415) 676-2014
Pleasant Hill, CA 94523 PR

Recreation oriented rent-a-tub establishment, located in the Pleasant Hill Plaza shopping center.

Pools for rent to the public, using gas-heated tap water, treated with bromine.

Seven private rooms, rented by the hour. Water temp: cool pools 80-90°, hot pools, 101-103°. Sauna included.

Services available: massage, juice bar

Credit cards accepted: Visa and MasterCard

Phone for rates, reservations and directions.

#239B AMERICAN FAMILY HOT TUB

☐ 88 Trelany Lane (415) 827-2299
Pleasant Hill, CA 94523 PR

Combination rent-a-tub and retail spa sales establishment located a few yards west of Contra Costa Blvd.

Pools for rent to the public, using gas-heated tap water, treated with chlorine.

12 private outdoor enclosures, rented by the hour. Water temp. 102-104°.

Services available: juice bar

Credit cards accepted: Visa and MasterCard

Phone for rates, reservations and directions.

#240 NEW AGE FINNISH TUB & SAUNA

☐ 242 25th St. (415) 234-1012
Richmond, CA 94804 PR

A state-certified massage school located on the premises of a pioneering rent-a-tub location.

Pools for rent to the public, using gas-heated tap water, treated with chlorine.

Two private outdoor enclosures, rented by the hour. Water temp: 98-99°.

Other facilities: two saunas available for private rental.

Services available: massage and massage training.

Phone for rates, reservations and directions.

#241A THE BERKELEY SAUNA

☐ 1947 Milvia St. (415) 845-2341
Berkeley, CA 94704 PR

A stress reduction establishment, located a few yards north of University Avenue.

Pools for rent to the public, using gas-heated tap water, treated with bromine.

Two private rooms, rented by the hour. Water temp. 104-106°.

Other facilities: Samadhi float tank and three private saunas for rent.

Services available: massage.

Credit cards accepted: Visa and MasterCard

Phone for rates, reservations and directions.

Springwater: Prospective spa buyers get a chance to try various types of tubs.

#241B GRAND CENTRAL SAUNA & HOT TUB CO.

☐ 1915 University Ave. (415) 843-4343
Berkeley, CA 94704 PR

One of a chain of urban locations, established by Grand Central, a pioneer in the private room rent-a-tub business.

Pools for rent to the public, using gas-heated tap water, treated with chlorine.

16 private rooms, rented by the hour. Water temp. 102-108°. Sauna included.

Services available: juice bar

Credit cards accepted: none

Phone for rates, reservations and directions.

#241C WATER WORKS

☐ 1799 University Ave. (415) 548-1510
Berkeley, CA 94703 PR

A combination rent-a-tub and retail spa sales establishment, located on a main urban street.

Pools for rent to the public, using gas-heated tap water, treated with chlorine.

Nine private rooms, rented by the hour. Water temp. 102-104°. Sauna included.

Credit cards accepted: Visa and MasterCard

Phone for rates, reservations and directions.

#241D ALBANY SAUNA AND HOT TUBS

☐ 1002 Solano Ave. (415) 525-6262
Albany, CA 94706 PR

One of the first dozen rent-a-tub establishments in the Bay Area. Located a few blocks west of San Pablo Ave.

Pools for rent to the public, using gas-heated tap water, treated with chlorine.

Three private outdoor enclosures, rented by the hour. Water temp. 105-106°.

Other facilities: four private saunas available for rent.

Services available: massage, juice bar

Credit cards accepted: Visa and MasterCard

Phone for rates, reservations and directions.

#241E PARADISE HOT TUBS

☐ 811 San Pablo Ave. (415) 527-8990
Albany, CA 94706 PR

Recreation oriented rent-a-tub establishment located on an urban main street.

Pools for rent to the public, using gas-heated tap water, treated with chlorine.

Six private rooms, rented by the hour. Water temp. 104°.

Other facilities: Two tanning units.

Services available: Adult movie (videotape) rental.

Credit cards accepted: Visa and MasterCard

Phone for rates, reservations and directions.

#241F BERKELEY MARINA MARRIOTT
☐ 200 Marina Blvd. (415) 548-7920
Berkeley, CA 94710 Hydropool MH

#242A IN HOT WATER

☐ 5496 College (415) 654-8484
Oakland, CA 94618

Urban rent-a-tub establishment with a strong emphasis on holistic health.

Pools for rent to the public, using gas-heated tap water, treated with chlorine.

Six private rooms, rented by the hour. Water temp. 105°.

Special features: Staffed with Holistic Heath Institute graduates.

Other facilities: Three private saunas available for rent.

Services available: massage, acupressure.

Credit cards accepted: Visa and MasterCard

Phone for rates, reservations and directions.

#242B SPRINGWATER

☐ 5854 College Ave. (415) 428-2557
Oakland. CA 94618 PR

A combination rent-a-tub and retail spa sales establishment, located on a suburban main street.

Pools for rent to the public, using gas-heated tap water, treated with bromine.

Eight private rooms, rented by the hour. Water temp. summer - 104°, winter - 106°.

Special features: Two redwood tubs, six fiberglass tubs.

Other facilities: Two private saunas.

Credit cards accepted: Visa and MasterCard

Phone for rates, reservations and directions.

#242C TRAVELODGE AT OAKLAND AIRPORT
☐ 150 Hegenberger Rd. (415) 635-5300
Oakland, CA 94621 Hydropool MH

#242D HYATT REGENCY HOTEL
☐ 1101 Broadway (415) 893-1234
Oakland, CA 94612 Hydropool MH

New Age Finnish Tub & Sauna: This is one of the first commercial fiberglass tubs.

#242E CLAREMONT RESORT HOTEL
☐ Ashby & Domingo Aves. (415) 843-3000
Oakland, CA 94623 Hydropool MH

#243A GRAND CENTRAL SAUNA & HOT TUB CO.

☐ 17389 Hesperian Blvd. (415) 278-8827
San Lorenzo, CA 94580 PR

One of a chain of urban locations, established by Grand Central, a pioneer in the private room rent-a-tub business.

Pools for rent to the public, using gas-heated tap water, treated with chlorine.

16 private rooms, rented by the hour. Water temp. 102-104°. Sauna included.

Services available: juice bar

Credit cards accepted: none

Phone for rates, reservations and directions.

#243B PLAZA INTERNATIONAL INN
☐ 410 W. A St. (415) 785-0260
Hayward, CA 94541 Hydropool MH

#244 HOWARD JOHNSON'S MOTOR LODGE
☐ 6680 Regional St. (415) 828-7750
Dublin, CA 94566 Hydropool MH

#245 BEST WESTERN THUNDERBIRD LODGE
☐ 5400 Mowry Ave. (415) 792-4300
Fremont, CA 94538 Hydropool MH

#246A THE HOT TUBS

☐ 2200 Van Ness Ave. (415) 441-TUBS
San Francisco, CA 94109 PR

One of the few stress reduction establishments offering tile tubs and decks in a chrome and glass urban environment. Located on a main street, just west of downtown.

Pools for rent to the public, using gas-heated tap water, treated with chlorine.

20 private rooms, rented by the hour. Water temp. 105-106°. Sauna included.

Services available: massage, juice bar.

Credit cards accepted: none.

Phone for rates, reservations and directions.

Grand Central Sauna & Hot Tub Co..
The first urban rent-a-tub facility, just off Market St. in San Francisco.

#246B GRAND CENTRAL SAUNA & HOT TUB CO.

☐ 15 Fell St. (415) 431-1370
San Francisco, CA 94102 PR

The first one of a chain of urban locations, established by Grand Central, a pioneer in the private room rent-a-tub business.

Pools for rent to the public, using gas-heated tap water, treated with chlorine.

26 private rooms, rented by the hour. Water temp. 102-104°. Sauna included.

Services available: juice bar.

Credit cards accepted: none.

Phone for rates, reservations and directions.

#246C FAMILY SAUNA SHOP

☐ 2308 Clement (415) 221-2208
San Francisco, CA 94121 PR

One of the pioneer stress reduction centers in San Francisco. Located in the Richmond District.

Pools for rent to the public, using gas-heated tap water, treated with chlorine.

Two private rooms, rented by the hour. Water temp. 108°.

Other facilities: four private saunas, available for rent.

Services available: massage.

Phone for rates, reservations and directions.

#246D OCEAN PARK MOTEL

☐ 2690 46th Ave. (415) 775-4600
San Francisco, CA 94116 Hydropool MH

#246E SAN FRANCISCO TRAVELODGE

☐ 1707 Market St. (415) 621-6775
San Francisco, CA 94103 Hydropool MH

#246F TROPICAL GARDENS

☐ 200 San Pedro Rd. (415) 755-8827
Colma, CA 94015 PR

Recreation oriented rent-a-tub establishment, sharing quarters with a racquetball facility and health club. Located a few blocks south of Daly City.

Pools for rent to the public, using gas-heated tap water, treated with chlorine.

16 private rooms, rented by the hour. Water temp. 102-104°. Sauna included in 8 of the rooms.

Other facilities: Racquetball and handball courts, Nautilus conditioning, swimming pool and locker room.

Credit cards accepted: none.

Phone for rates, reservations and directions.

Watercourse Way: Some of the suites in this new rent-a-tub establishment have adjoining hot and cold tubs.

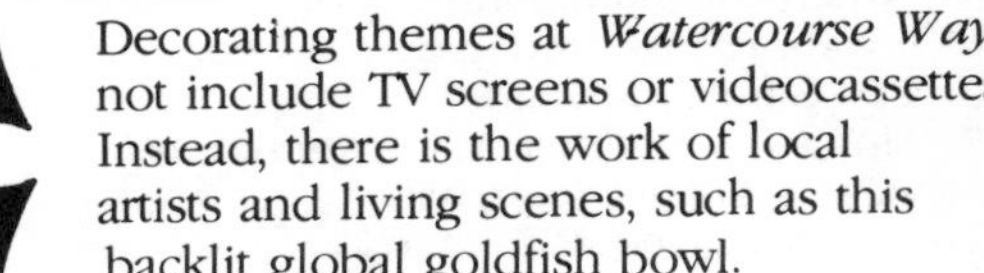

Decorating themes at *Watercourse Way* do not include TV screens or videocassettes. Instead, there is the work of local artists and living scenes, such as this backlit global goldfish bowl.

#247 WATERCOURSE WAY

☐ 165 Channing Way, Palo Alto, CA 94301 — (415) 329-8827 — PR

An innovative bathing center, with a sushi bar, offering a variety of enjoyable rooms and experiences. The beautiful oriental decor creates a comfortable and interesting environment.

Pools for rent to the public, using gas-heated tap water, treated with bromine.

Nine individually decorated private rooms, rented by the hour, each with a different combination of hot pool, cold pool, sauna and steam bath. Water temperature in the pools is approximately 103°.

Special features: for larger groups, two rooms can be joined.

Bathing suits: optional in private rooms.

Other facilities: flotation tank for private rental.

Services available: massage, sushi bar.

Credit cards accepted: Visa and MasterCard.

Phone for rates, reservations and directions.

#248 GRAND CENTRAL SAUNA & HOT TUB CO.

☐ 170 El Camino Real (415) 961-4000
Mountain View, CA 94040 PR

One of a chain of urban locations, established by Grand Central, a pioneer in the private room rent-a-tub business.

Pools for rent to the public, using gas-heated tap water, treated with chlorine.

22 private rooms, rented by the hour. Water temp. 103-105°. Sauna included.

Bathing suits: optional in private rooms.
Services available: juice bar.
Credit cards accepted: none.
Phone for rates, reservations and directions.

#249A AMBASSADOR INN

☐ 910 E. Fremont (408) 738-0500
Sunnyvale, CA 94087 Hydropool MH

#249B HILTON INN

☐ 91250 Lakeside Dr. (408) 738-4888
Sunnyvale, CA 94086 Hydropool MH

#250A GRAND CENTRAL SAUNA & HOT TUB CO.

☐ 376 Saratoga (408) 247-8827
San Jose, CA 95129 PR

One of a chain of urban locations, established by Grand Central, a pioneer in the private room rent-a-tub business.

Pools for rent to the public, using gas-heated tap water, treated with chlorine.

21 private rooms, rented by the hour. Water temp. 102-104°. Sauna included.

Bathing suits: optional in private rooms.
Services available: juice bar.
Credit cards accepted: none.
Phone for rates, reservations and directions.

#250B HYATT SAN JOSE AT SAN JOSE AIRPORT

☐ 1740 N. First St. (408) 298-0300
San Jose, CA 95112 Hydropool MH

#250C BEST WESTERN SANDMAN MOTEL

☐ 2585 Seaboard Ave. (408) 263-8800
San Jose, CA 95131 Hydropool MH

#250D SANTA CLARA MARRIOTT HOTEL

☐ 101 & Great America Pkwy (408) 988-1500
Santa Clara, CA 95054 Hydropool MH

#251 LUPIN NATURIST CLUB

☐ P.O. Box 1274 (408) 353-2250
Los Gatos, CA 95031 PR + MH + CRV

A clothing-optional resort where both sexes are equal and the differences are accepted as natural. Located on 120 acres of tree-shaded tranquility in the Santa Cruz mountains. Elevation 200 ft. Open all year.

Gas-heated well water, bromine treated, is used in two outdoor fiberglass tubs available without extra charge to all members and registered guests. Temperature: 102-104°. Bromine-treated well water is also used in two outdoor swimming pools, one of which is heated and covered with a plastic dome in the winter. Bathing suits are prohibited in all pools. Clothing is optional elsewhere on the grounds.

Lodge rooms, RV and camping spaces, and dining room meals are available on the premises. MasterCard and Visa are accepted. It is seven miles to a store and service station.

This is a private club, not open to the public for drop-in visits. Phone first for information about guest passes and directions.

Lupin Naturist Club: A canyon-side deck around this hot pool gives the impression of soaking in a giant tree house.

Kiva Retreat: The addition of a communal sunning patio is a popular expansion of stress-reducing rent-a-tub facilities.

A policy of clothing optional at *Kiva Retreat* means that parents and children have freedom of choice, even in the pools.

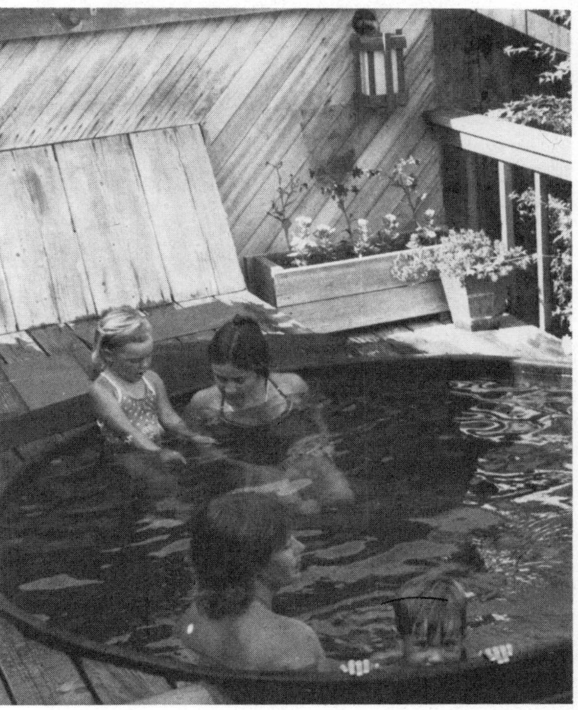

#252A KIVA RETREAT

☐ 702 Water St. (408) 429-1142
Santa Cruz, CA 95060 PR

Unusual hot pool rental establishment, featuring a communal patio area with the feel of a primitive hot spring (trees, grass, flowers, clothing optional) available near the city center.

Pools for rent to the public, using gas-heated tap water, treated with chlorine and bromine.

Two private enclosures, rented by the hour. Water temp. 104°.

One communal patio, day rate charge, including large hot tub, cold tub plunge, sauna, and adjoining indoor dressing and social rooms.

Bathing suits: optional everywhere except front desk.

Services available: massage.

Credit cards accepted: none.

Phone for rates, reservations and directions.

Heartwood Spa: Outdoor communal pools and positive body attitudes are part of many New-Age health-maintenance programs.

#252B HEARTWOOD SPA

☐ 3150A Mission Dr. (408) 462-2192
Santa Cruz, CA 95065 PR

Unusual hot pool rental establishment, featuring a communal patio area with the feel of a primitive hot spring (trees, grass, flowers, clothing optional), available on a suburban side street.

Pools for rent to the public, using gas-heated tap water, treated with chlorine.

One private enclosure, rented by the hour. Water temp. 105°.

One communal patio, day rate charge, including large hot tub, cold tub plunge and sauna.

Bathing suits: optional everywhere except front desk.

Services available: massage.

Credit cards accepted: none.

Phone for information about rates, reservations and directions.

#252C FAMILY SAUNA SHOP

☐ 320C Cedar St. (408) 427-2803
Santa Cruz, CA 95060 PR

Primarily a fitness-oriented sauna establishment, with one enclosed private hot tub space. Located near the city center.

One pool for rent to the public, using gas-heated tap water, treated with chlorine.

One private enclosure, rented by the hour. Water temp. 108-110°, will adjust on request.

Other facilities: Four private sauna rooms, each with two dressing spaces.

Services available: massage and exercise classes.

Credit cards accepted: Visa and MasterCard.

Phone for rates, reservations and directions.

#252D CARBONERO CREEK TRAVEL TRAILER PARK

☐ on Scotts Valley Rd. (408) 438-1288
Scotts Valley, CA 95066 Hydropool CRV

#253 TAN OAKS PARK

☐ P.O. Box 1356 (408) 842-7838
Gilroy, CA 95021 PR + MH + CRV

A member-oriented nudist club, located on a cool, green forested slope of the Santa Cruz Mountains. Elevation 2,000 ft. Open May to October.

Gas-heated well water, bromine-treated, is used in an outdoor redwood hot tub. Temperature is maintained at 102°. There is also a solar-heated outdoor swimming pool, with water temperature at approximately 80°. Bathing suits are not permitted in the pools; clothing is optional elsewhere on the grounds.

Cabins, clubhouse, sauna, and a volleyball court are available on the premises. No credit cards are accepted. It is 11 miles to a restaurant, store and service station.

This is a private club, not open to the public for drop-in use. However, guest passes are available on a limited basis. Phone for information and directions.

Different Soaks: The open-roof garden along one wall of this hot tub room gives a feeling of out-of-doors while retaining the comfort of an indoor installation.

#254 KOA—SANTA CRUZ
☐ on Spring Valley Rd. (408) 772-0551
Watsonville, CA 95076 Hydropool CRV

#255A DIFFERENT SOAKS
☐ 1157 Forest Ave. (408) 646-8293
Pacific Grove, CA 93950 PR

Unusually spacious hot-pool rental, and retail spa sales establishment, located in a suburb of Monterey.

Pools for rent to the public, using gas-heated tap water, treated with bromine.

Five private rooms, rented by the hour. One room has a tub large enough for ten persons, and rooms can be combined for larger groups. Water temp. 102-103°.

Special features: each room has a dressing space and has a landscaped open-roof garden along one wall.

Credit cards accepted: none.

Phone for information about rates, reservations and directions.

#255B 17 MILE DRIVE VILLAGE
☐ on 17 Mile Drive (408) 373-2721
Pacific Grove, CA 93950 Hydropool CRV

#255C HILTON INN RESORT
Rte. 1 at Monterey-Aguaito Exits
☐ (408) 373-6141
Monterey, CA 93940 Hydropool MH

#255D DOUBLETREE INN
☐ No. 2 Portola (408) 649-4511
Monterey, CA 93940 Health Spa MH

#255E BEST WESTERN VICTORIAN INN
☐ 487 Foam St. (408) 373-8000
Monterey, CA 93940 Hydropool MH

#255F BEST WESTERN RAMONA INN
☐ 2332 Fremont St. (408) 373-2445
Monterey, CA 93940 Hydropool MH

#256A HYATT DEL MONTE
☐ 1 Old Golf Course Rd. (408) 372-7171
Carmel, CA 93921 Hydropool MH

#256B BEST WESTERN CARMEL RESORT INN
☐ P.O. Box 2266 (408) 624-3113
Carmel, CA 93921 Hydropool MH

Blackthorne Spas: A superb combination of natural beauty and colorful tile patterns.

#257A BLACKTHORNE SPAS

4 Pilot Road (408) 659-3241
□ Carmel Valley, CA 93924 PR

A unique combination of retail spa sales, hydropool rentals, and landscaping, using themes from **Shogun** in the various enclosures. Located in rustic Carmel Valley.

Pools for rent to the public, using gas-heated tap water, treated with chlorine and hydrogen peroxide.

Five private outdoor enclosures, rented by the hour Water temp. 102-104°.

Special features: Two of the tubs are acrylic, two are tile, and one is redwood.

Credit cards accepted: Visa and MasterCard.

Phone for information about rates, reservations and directions.

#257B ROBLES DEL RIO LODGE

200 Punta Del Monte (408) 659-2264
□ Carmel Valley, CA 93924 Health Spa MH

#257C VALLEY LODGE

P.O. Box 93 (408) 659-2261
□ Carmel Valley, CA 93924 Hydropool MH

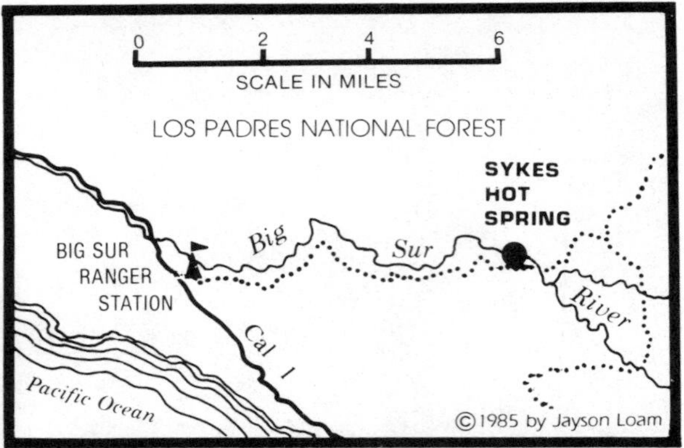

#258 PARAISO HOT SPRINGS

(408) 678-2882

■ **Soledad, CA 93960** **PR + MH + CRV**

A quiet resort for adults, with several acres of tree-shaded grassy areas, located on the west slopes of the Salinas Valley. Elevation 1,200 ft. Open all year.

Natural mineral water flows out of the ground at 108°, and is piped to pools. There are two outdoor swimming pools, averaging 70° and 85° respectively, and an indoor soaking pool with a temperature of 108°. All pools are treated with chlorine. Bathing suits required. No cut-offs permitted.

Cottages, RV spaces, overnight camping and a small store are available on the premises. No credit cards. It is eight miles to a restaurant and service station.

Directions: From US 101, exit on Arroyo Seco Road, one mile south of Soledad. Go one mile to stop sign, then turn on to Paraiso Springs Road uphill for six miles to resort at end of road.

#259 TASSAJARA BUDDHIST MEDITATION CENTER

■ **Tassajara Springs** **(408) 659-2229**
Carmel Valley, CA 93924 **MH**

Primarily a Buddhist Monastery, with limited accommodations available to the public from May 1 to Labor Day. Located in wooded mountains southeast of Monterey. Elevation 1,500 ft.

Please, no drop-in visitors. Prior reservation and confirmation required for all uses. Guests are expected to respect the spirit of a monastic community.

Natural mineral water flows out of the ground at 110°, into two large enclosed soaking pools, which average 108°. This water, which is not chemically treated, cools as it flows into nearby streambed soaking areas. The outdoor swimming pool is maintained at approximately 70°. There are also men's and women's steam baths. Bathings suits are required.

Rooms and meals are included as part of confirmed reservation arrangements. The use of meditation facilities is also included. No credit cards are accepted. It is 20 miles to a store, cafe, service station, etc.

#260 SYKES HOT SPRING (see map)

● **Near the village of Big Sur non-commercial**

Remote undeveloped hot spring on the Big Sur River in the Ventana Wilderness portion of Los Padres National Forest. Elevation 1,110 ft. May be submerged during high water in the river.

Natural mineral water flows out of the ground at 100° from under a fallen tree, into a volunteer-built shallow pool. This location is a 10-mile hike on the Pine Ridge Trail and a Wilderness Permit must be obtained from the Forest Service before entering the area. However, this spring is near one of the most popular hiking routes in the Wilderness, so the distance is no assurance of quiet or privacy during the summer months.

The access trail appears on USGS *Ventana Cones* and *Partington Ridge,* but the hot spring is not shown. The Forest Service issues a trail map to those holding Wilderness Permits, and, on request, will mark the hot spring location on that map.

There are no services available at the location. When you obtain your Wilderness Permit, check your preparations, including water supply, with the ranger.

#261 VENTANA INN

□ Big Sur, CA 93920 (408) 667-2331 Hydropool MH

#262 ESALEN INSTITUTE

■ **Big Sur, CA 93920** **(408) 667-2335** **PR + MH**

Primarily an educational/experiential center rather than a hot spring resort. Located on Cal 45 miles south of Monterey and 50 miles north of San Simeon. Elevation 100 ft. Open all year.

Esalen is a pioneer in the growth center movement, specializing in residential programs which focus on education, philosophy and the physical and behavioral sciences. Access to the grounds is permitted only to workshop participants and people registered for room and board, which is occasionally available on short notice. Phone or write for a catalog of programs being offered; attendance is by prior registration and confirmation only.

Natural mineral water flows out of the ground at 120°, into a bath house built on a cliff face fifty feet above a rocky ocean beach. Within the bath house, which is open toward the ocean, are four concrete soaking pools and eight individual bath tubs. There are also two adjoining outdoor soaking pools. Water temperature is determined within each tub by admitting controlled amounts of hot mineral water and cold well water. This flow-through process, plus frequent cleaning of pools, makes chemical treatment of the water unnecessary. Clothing is optional in and around the bath house.

During late night hours on weekdays the baths are available to the public for a nominal charge. Phone first for information about the current schedule and parking instructions.

Facilities include housing and a dining room for registered guests. Massage is available on the premises. Visa, MasterCard and American Express are accepted. It is 11 miles to a restaurant, store and service station.

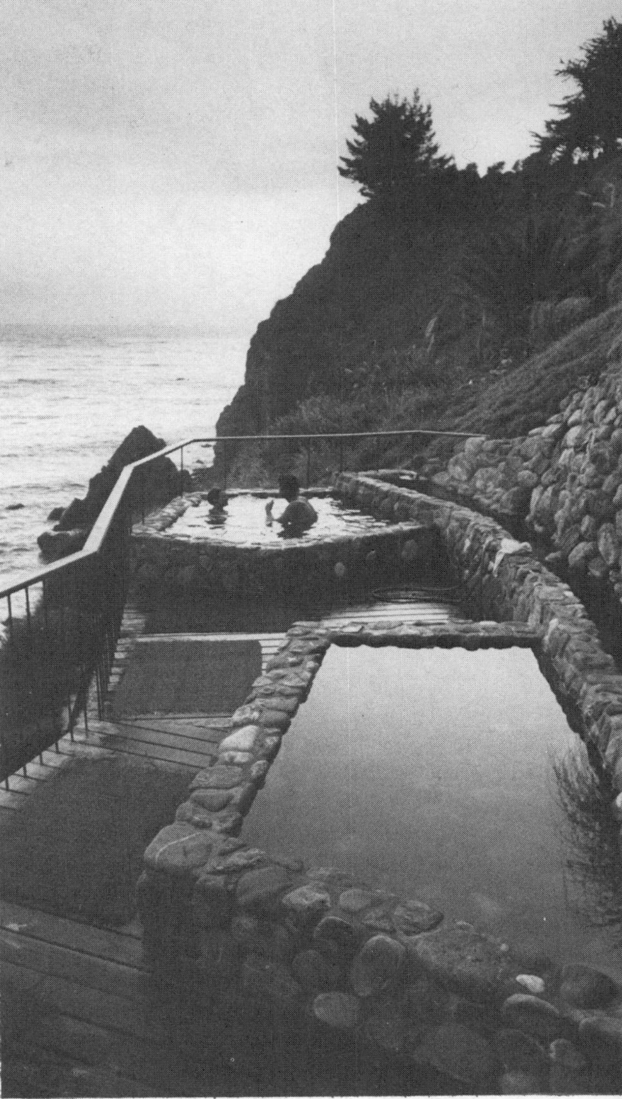

▲ *Esalen Institute:* One of the few places where the crashing of ocean waves below may be heard while soaking in a hot tub.

Sycamore Mineral Springs: Hot mineral water in a redwood tub can feel almost as good as a real hot springs out in the woods.

Most of the *Sycamore* tubs are screened by tree branches so that skinnydipping is practical, even during daylight hours.

#263A DISCOVERY MOTOR INN

☐ 1800 Monterey St. (805) 544-8600
San Luis Obispo, CA 93401 Hydropool MH

#263B BEST WESTERN
ROYAL OAK MOTOR HOTEL

☐ 214 Madonna Rd. (805) 544-4410
San Luis Obispo, CA 93401 Hydropool MH

#264A SYCAMORE MINERAL SPRINGS

■ **1215 Avila Beach Dr. (805) 595-7302**
San Luis Obispo, CA 93401 PR + MH/P

The first rent-a-tub establishment to combine natural mineral water and redwood hot tubs in tree-shaded outdoor spaces for rent by the hour. Located on a rural hill, two miles from the ocean. Elevation 40 ft. Open all year.

Natural mineral water is pumped from a well at 90° and gas heated to 110° before being piped to 25 tubs scattered over the hillside. Each tub has a faucet-controlled source of cold tap water, so the water temperature in each tub is under the control of the customer. Each tub also has its own jet pump, filter and automatic chlorinator. One tub is eighteen feet in diameter, capable of holding more than 50 persons at a time. The apparent local custom is clothing optional in those tubs screened by the natural shrubbery and/or lattice panels.

Motel rooms (some with hot tubs on the balcony) are available on the premises. There is also a seasonal cafe, serving beer and wine. On request, directions to a nearby clothing-optional state beach will be given. MasterCard and Visa credit card are accepted . Phone for rates and reservations.

Directions: From US 101, four miles south of San Luis Obispo, take the Avila Beach exit, then go one mile west on Avila Beach Dr. and watch for resort sign on south side of road.

Mustang Water Slide at Lopez Lake: Parents soak while children slide.

#264B AVILA HOT SPRINGS SPA & RV PARK

■ **250 Avila Rd.** **(805) 595-2359**
San Luis Obispo, CA 93401 **PR + CRV**

Combination hot spring resort and RV park located in a foothill hollow at a freeway exit. Elevation 40 ft. Open all year.

Natural mineral water is pumped out of a well at 130° and piped to various pools. There are six indoor tiled Roman tubs, in which the water temperature is determined by the amount of hot mineral water and cold tap water admitted. These tubs are drained and refilled after each use, so no chemical treatment is needed. There is an outdoor swimming pool (88°), and an outdoor soaking pool (107°), which use natural mineral water treated with chlorine. Bathing suits are required except in private tub rooms.

Massage, snack bar, RV and camping spaces and a small store are available on the premises. It is three miles to a motel, restaurant, and service station.

Visa, MasterCard and American Express accepted.

Directions: From US 101, four miles south of San Luis Obispo, take the Avila Beach exit, and go north one block to resort entrance.

#265A SEA CREST MOTEL
□ 2241 Price St. (805) 773-4608
Pismo Beach, CA 93449 Hydropool MH

#265B PISMO BEACH TRAVELODGE
□ 230 Five Cities Dr. (805) 773-1841
Pismo Beach, CA 93449 Hydropool MH

#265C BEST WESTERN SHORE CLIFF LODGE
□ 2555 Price St. (805) 773-4671
Pismo Beach, CA 93449 Hydropool MH

#266 MUSTANG WATER SLIDE AT LOPEZ LAKE
□ Near the town of Arroyo Grande PR

Recreation concession, including hot pools, on the grounds of a county park in hills north of Lopez Lake. Elevation 700 ft. Open seven days per week, June 1 to September 15; weekends starting approximately April 1 and closing approximately November 1.

Gas-heated well water, chlorine-treated, is used in soaking pools which are available without extra charge to those who have paid by the hour to use the two adjoining 600 ft. water slides. Water temperature in the four cement and tile hot pools varies from 90° to 102°. Bathing suits are required at all times.

A snack bar is available on the premises.

RV and camping spaces are available in the county park. It is ten miles to a motel, restaurant, store and service station.

Directions: From the city of Arroyo Grande, on US #101, follow Lopez Lake signs northeast and around the lake to County Recreation Area main gate. Pay use fee and follow signs to water slide.

#267 KOA—SANTA MARIA
□ on Preisker Lane (805) 992-7214
Santa Maria, CA 93454 Hydropool RV

#268 BEST WESTERN FLAGWAVER MOTOR INN
□ 937 N. H St. (805) 736-5605
Lompoc, CA 93436 Hydropool MH

#269 BEST WESTERN
PEA SOUP ANDERSEN'S INN
□ 51 E. Hwy 246 (805) 688-3216
Buellton, CA 93427 Hydropool MH

#270A BEST WESTERN KING FREDERIK
□ 1617 Copenhagen Dr. (805) 688-5515
Solvang, CA 93463 Hydropool MH

#270B SVENGAARD'S DANISH LODGE
□ 1711 Mission Dr. (805) 688-3277
Solvang, CA 93463 Hydropool MH

 *Las Cruces Hot Spring:* An ideal primitive setting with water that is less than hot.

#271 LAS CRUCES HOT SPRINGS

(see map)

Near Gaviota State Park **non-commercial**

Two primitive mud-bottom pools on a tree-shaded slope, a few miles from the ocean. Elevation 500 ft. Open all year.

Natural mineral water emerges from the ground at 96°, directly into a small soaking pool, and then flows into a larger pool which averages 90°. Both of these volunteer-built pools have dirt sides and cloudy water. The apparent local custom is clothing optional.

There are no services available on the premises, and overnight parking is prohibited in the parking area at the bottom of the trail. It is three miles to a campground with RV hook-ups; six miles to a restaurant, store, etc.

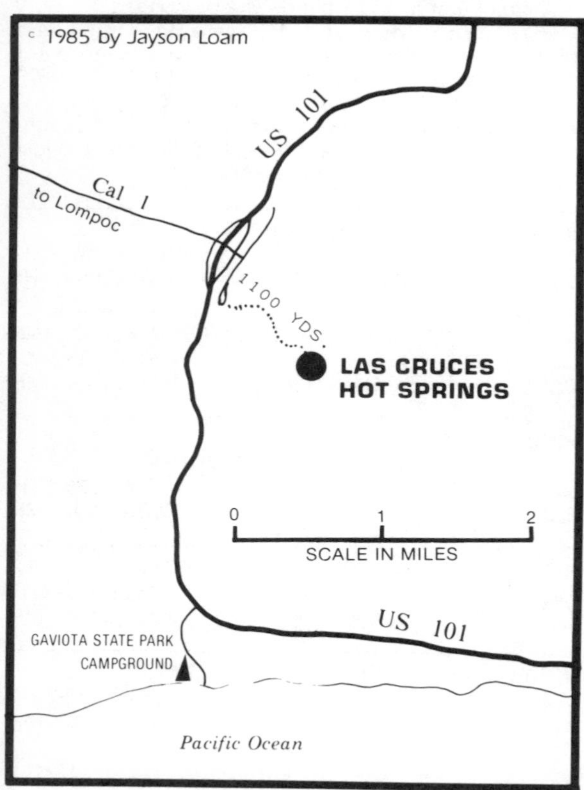

#272 SHIBUKI GARDENS

6576 Trigo Rd. (805) 685-4617
Isla Vista, CA 93117 PR

Clean, inviting rent-a-tub establishment, located in a residential neighborhood adjoining the UC Santa Barbara campus.

Pools for rent to the public, using gas-heated tap water, treated with chlorine.

One private room, rented by the hour. Water temp. 102-104°, will adjust on request.

Eight private outdoor enclosures, rented by the hour. Water temp. 102-104°, will adjust on request.

Special features: Roofless enclosures are tree-shaded.

Other facilities: Separate private sauna room for rent.

Services available: juice bar

Credit cards accepted: none

Phone for rates, reservations and directions.

 *Big Caliente Hot Springs:* Legend says it was the rugged 30 miles drive to this springs which prompted Santa Barbara soakers to invent the redwood hot tub. It is still popular with those who do not own a tub.

#273 BIG CALIENTE HOT SPRINGS

(see map)

Near the city of Santa Barbara

non-commercial

An improved non-commerical hot spring located in a sparsely wooded canyon reached over ten miles of gravel road. Elevation 1,500 ft. Open all year, subject to fire closure.

Natural mineral water flows out of a bluff at 115° then through a faucet-controlled pipe to a 6′ by 10′ concrete pool. Water temperature in the pool is determined by the inflow of hot water. There is general compliance with an official "NO NUDE BATHING" sign, except when everyone present agrees to ignore the sign.

There are government-built restrooms and changing rooms nearby, and a year-round running stream twenty yards away. There are no other services available on the premises. It is 25 miles to a restaurant, store, service station, etc.

Little Caliente Spring is a small rock and mud volunteer-built pool another five miles beyond Big Caliente. Public access is infrequent, due to fire closures in the summer and flood closures in the winter.

Source map: *Los Padres National Forest.*

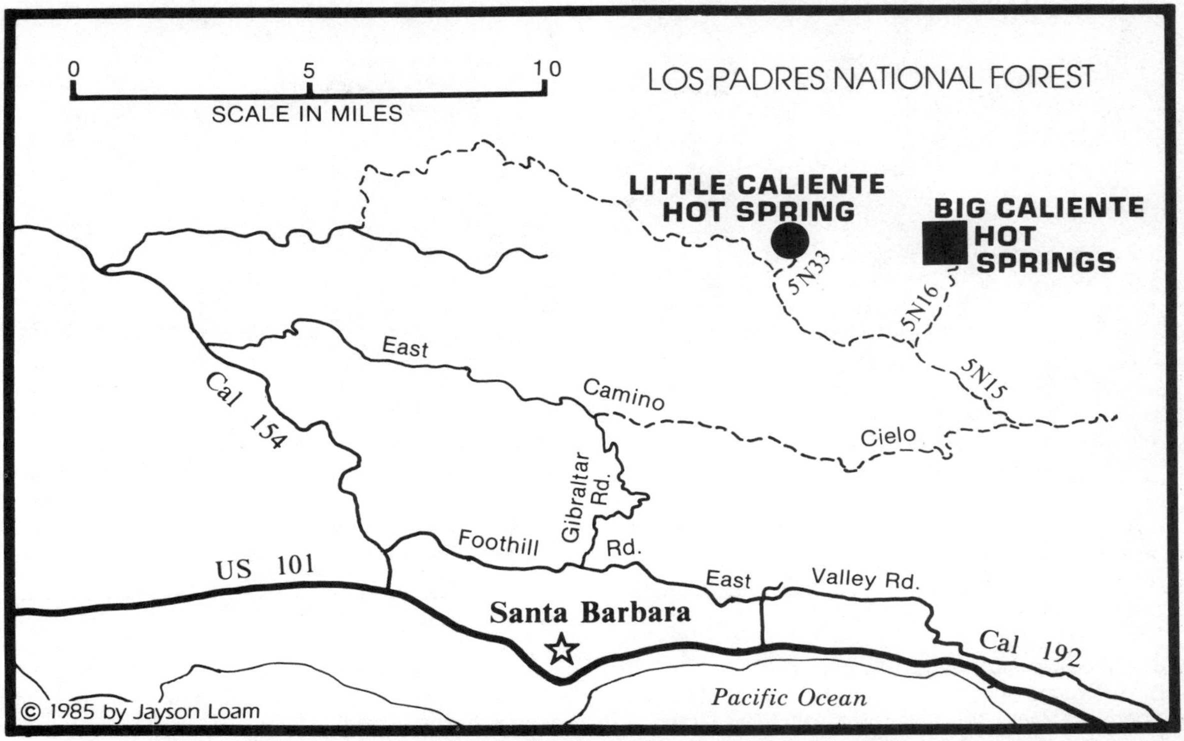

LOS PADRES NATIONAL FOREST

0 5 10
SCALE IN MILES

LITTLE CALIENTE
HOT SPRING

BIG CALIENTE
HOT
SPRINGS

5N33
5N16
5N15
East Camino Cielo
Cal 154
Gibraltar Rd.
Foothill Rd.
US 101
East Valley Rd.
Santa Barbara
Cal 192
Pacific Ocean

 *The Hourglass:* One of the larger outdoor enclosures gets its daily cleaning.

 *Magic Waters:* Water purity and hot pool equipment are tested every day.

#274A THE HOURGLASS

☐ 213 W. Cota (805) 963-1436
Santa Barbara, CA 93101 PR

Basic private space rent-a-tub facility located on a residential street near downtown Santa Barbara.

Pools for rent to the public, using gas-heated tap water, treated with chlorine.

Three private rooms, rented by the hour. Water temp. 104°.

Eight private enclosures, rented by the hour. Water temp. 104°.

Services available: juice bar

Credit cards accepted: none

Phone for rates, reservations and directions.

#274B MAGIC WATERS

☐ 4285 State St. (805) 964-6924
Santa Barbara, CA 93105 PR

Basic private space rent-a-tub facility located on a main suburban street.

Pools for rent to the public, using gas-heated tap water, treated with chlorine.

Ten private enclosures, rented by the hour. Water temp. 104°.

Credit cards accepted: none

Phone for rates, reservations and directions.

 *Montecito Hot Springs:* People soaking is no longer in the plans for this location.

#274C	BEST WESTERN ENCINA LODGE		
☐	2220 Bath St. Santa Barbara, CA 93105	(805) 682-7277 Hydropool	MH
#274D	BEST WESTERN PEPPER TREE MOTOR INN		
☐	3850 State St. Santa Barbara, CA 93105	(805) 682-2418 Hydropool	MH
#274E	TURNPIKE LODGE		
☐	4770 Calle Real Santa Barbara, CA 93110	(805) 964-3511 Hydropool	MH
#274F	SHERATON SANTA BARBARA		
☐	1111 E. Cabrillo Blvd. Santa Barbara, CA 93103	(805) 963-0744 Health Spa	MH
#274G	SANTA BARBARA MIRAMAR HOTEL		
☐	P.O. Box M Santa Barbara, CA 93102	(805) 969-2203 Health Spa	MH
#274H	QUALITY INN—SANDMAN		
☐	3714 State St. Santa Barbara, CA 93105	(805) 687-2468 Hydropool	MH
#274I	OCEAN PALMS HOTEL		
☐	232 W. Cabrillo Blvd. Santa Barbara, CA 93101	(805) 966-9133 Hydropool	MH

#275 MONTECITO HOT SPRINGS

(see map)

● **near the city of Santa Barbara** **non-commercial**

Small unimproved source springs near the ruins of a burned-down resort. Located in a rugged mountain canyon north of Santa Barbara. Elevation 1,500 ft. Open all year.

Natural mineral water flows from several springs at temperatures up to 115°. Much of the water is carried away in pipes installed by the Montecito Water District. The remaining surface run off cools as it flows through very shallow volunteer-built rock & mud pools, suitable for foot bathing.

There are no services available on the premises. It is five miles to a restaurant, store, service station, etc.

Directions: Follow Hot Springs Road uphill to end, which has parking space for only three vehicles, in between driveways serving private residences. Prepare for a climb of 800 ft. during a 1½ mile hike. The Hot Springs Trail starts upcanyon alongside a paved driveway for 300 yards, then continues under the trees until it veers right across the canyon bottom to join a fire-break road. This road leads to the masonry ruins of the old resort; follow pipes to the springs in the canyon beyond.

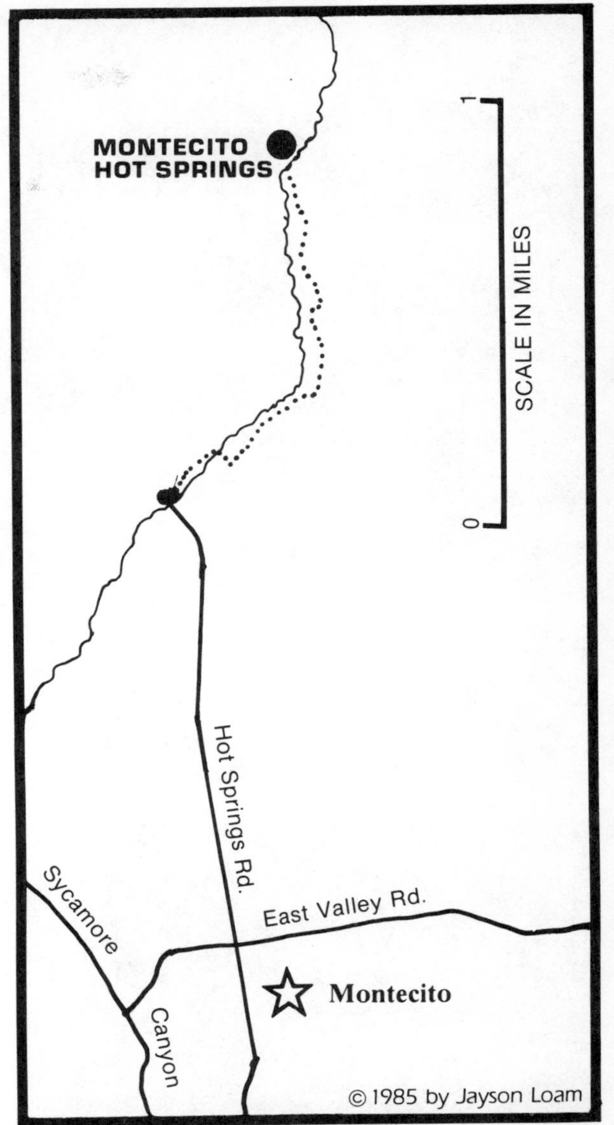

Matilija Hot Springs: By popular demand, this outdoor group soaking pool was added to the smaller indoor soaking tubs.

Big-rig drivers make a stop at *Matilija* for a hot mineral bath and a massage.

#276 THE MONTECITO INN

□ 1295 Coast Village Rd. (805) 969-7854
Montecito, CA 93108 Hydropool MH

#277 MATILIJA HOT SPRINGS

■ **788 West Hot Springs Rd. (805) 646-7667**
Ojai, CA 93023 PR

Older physical health center, located on the grounds of a county park in a tree-shaded foothill canyon. Elevation 800 ft. Open all year.

Natural mineral water is pumped from a well at 125° and cools as it is piped to a bath house. There are three fiberglass indoor hydropools and one enclosed outdoor hydropool. Water temperature in these pools is maintained at a temperature of 101-105° on a flow-through basis, with no chlorination. There are men's and women's sections in the bath house, each containing three individual bathtubs, which are drained and refilled with untreated mineral water after each use. Bathing suits are optional in private rooms and spaces.

Unheated tap water, chlorine-treated, is used in a large swimming pool which is open Memorial Day to Labor Day. Bathing suits are required in the swimming pool and adjoining park.

Physical therapy, including massage and reflexology, is available on the premises. No credit cards are accepted. It is five miles to a motel, store, service station, etc.

Directions: From the junction of Hwy 33 and 150 in Ojai, go five miles north on 33 (Maricopa Hwy) to Hot Springs Road. Follow signs west to resort.

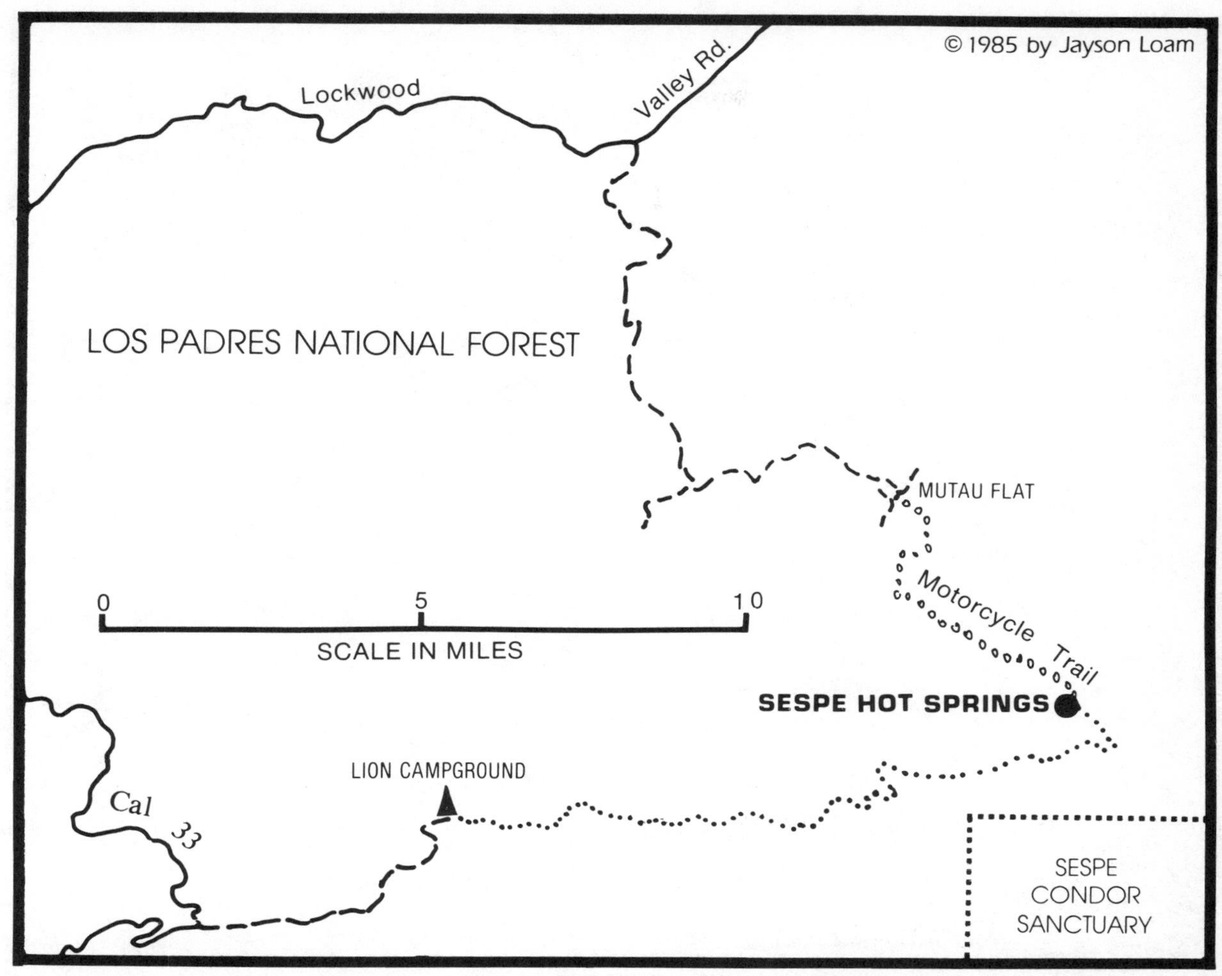

#279 SESPE HOT SPRINGS (see map)

Near the Sespe Condor Sanctuary
non-commercial

A remote undeveloped hot spring located in rugged desert mountains subject to some flash flooding. Elevation 2,800 ft. Open all year, subject to Forest Service closures.

Natural mineral water flows out of the side of a mountain at 185°, cooling as it flows through a series of shallow volunteer-built soaking pools. A sauna-shack steam bath has also been built over the spring mouth. The apparent local custom is clothing optional.

There are no services available on the premises. Access is via a nine-mile motorcycle trail from Mutau Flat, or via a 17-mile hiking trail from Lion Campground. A Forest Service permit is required to enter the area at any time. Be sure to inquire about fire season closures, flood warnings, and the adequacy of your preparations for packing in and packing out.

Source maps: *Los Padres National Forest*; USGS *Devil's Heart Peak*, plus adjoining quads as required by route chosen.

#278 ☐ LOS PADRES INN
1208 E. Ojai Ave. (805) 646-4365
Ojai, CA 93023 Hydropool MH

#280 ☐ BEST WESTERN INN OF VENTURA
708 E. Thompson Blvd. (805) 648-3101
Ventura, CA 93001 Hydropool MH

#281A ☐ OXNARD HILTON
600 Esplanade Dr. (805) 485-9666
Oxnard, CA 93030 Hydropool MH

#281B ☐ CASA SIRENA MARINA HOTEL
3606 Peninsula Rd. (805) 985-6311
Oxnard, CA 93030 Hydropool MH

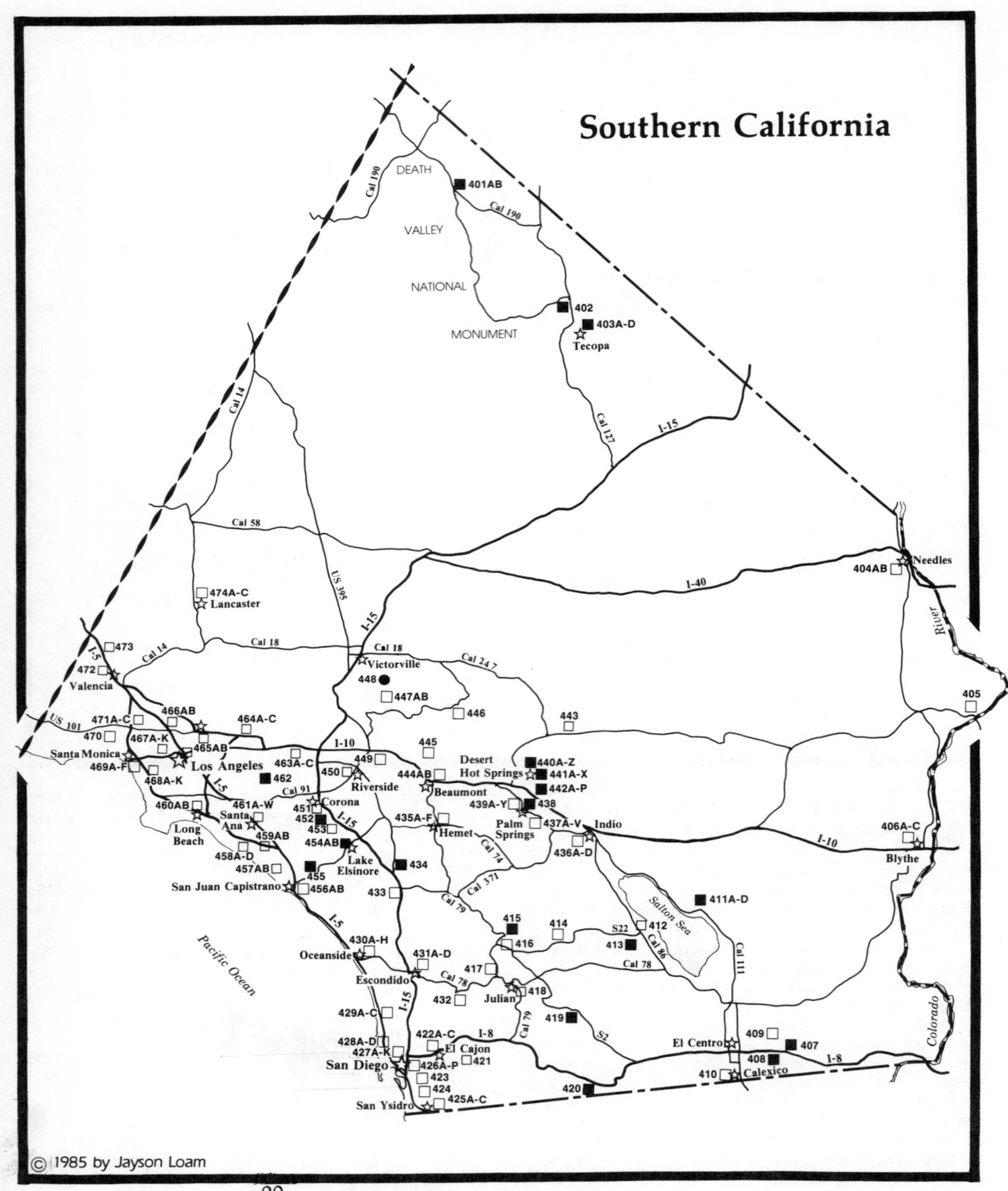
Southern California
DEATH
VALLEY
NATIONAL
MONUMENT
401AB
Cal 190
Cal 190
402
403A-D
Tecopa
Cal 14
Cal 127
I-15
Cal 58
US 395
I-40
Needles
404AB
474A-C
Lancaster
River
I-15
473
I-5
Cal 14
Cal 18
Cal 18
Victorville
Cal 24 7
472
Valencia
448
447AB
446
405
466AB
471A-C
US 101
470
464A-C
443
467A-K
465AB
I-10
445
Santa Monica
469A-F
Los Angeles
463A-C
449
Desert
Hot Springs
440A-Z
441A-X
468A-K
462
450
Riverside
444AB
Beaumont
442A-P
I-5
Cal 91
460AB
461A-W
451
Corona
439A-Y
438
Long
Beach
Santa
Ana
452
453
I-15
435A-F
Hemet
Palm
Springs
437A-V
Indio
406A-C
459AB
454AB
Cal 74
436A-D
I-10
Blythe
458A-D
457AB
455
Lake
Elsinore
434
San Juan Capistrano
456AB
433
Cal 371
411A-D
Cal 79
Salton Sea
I-5
415
414
S22
412
Pacific Ocean
430A-H
416
413
Cal 86
Cal 111
Oceanside
431A-D
Cal 78
417
Escondido
Cal 78
I-15
432
Julian
418
429A-C
Cal 79
419
S2
Colorado
I-8
422A-C
428A-D
427A-K
El Cajon
El Centro
409
407
San Diego
426A-P
421
408
I-8
423
410
Calexico
424
420
425A-C
San Ysidro
©1985 by Jayson Loam

MAP AND DIRECTORY SYMBOLS

● **Unimproved natural mineral water pool**
■ **Improved natural mineral water pool**
□ Gas-heated tap or well water pool

——— Paved highway
– – – Unpaved road
• • • Hiking route

PR = Tubs or pools for rent by hour, day or treatment

MH = Rooms, cabins or dormitory spaces for rent by day, week or month

CRV = Camping or vehicle parking spaces, some with hookups, for rent by day, week, month or year

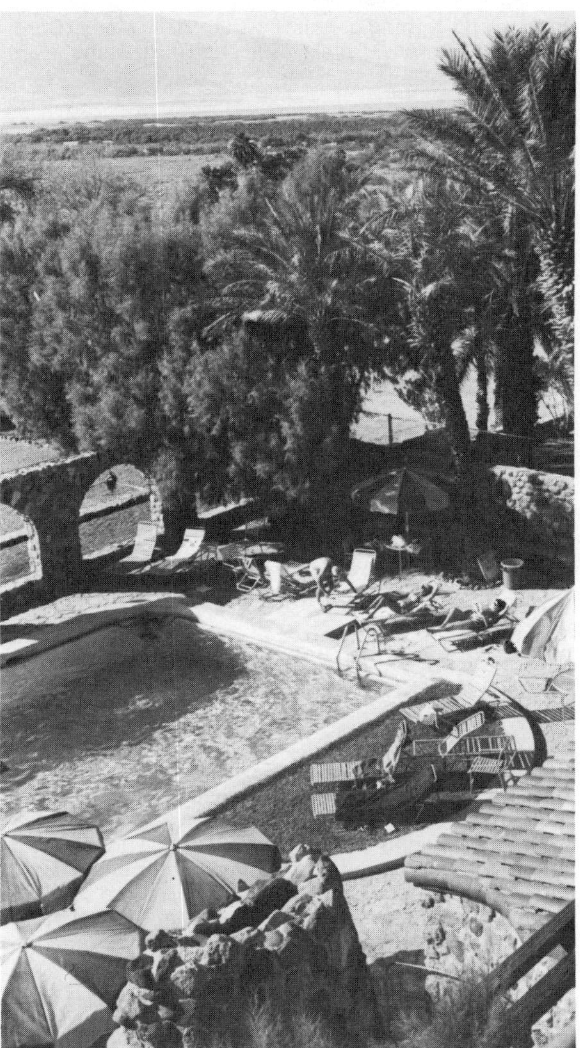

#401A FURNACE CREEK INN

■ **Box 1** **(619) 786-2345**
Death Valley, CA 92328 **MH**

An historic resort built around a lush oasis on a barren hillside overlooking Death Valley. Elevation sea level. Open all year.

Natural mineral water flows out of a spring at 89° to two outdoor pools and through a large, palm-shaded arroyo. The swimming pool maintains a temperature of approximately 85° as the flow-through rate is so great that no chemical treatment of the water is necessary. Bromine treated gas heated mineral water is used in the outdoor hydropool where the temperature is regulated by poolside controls in the 100 to 105° range. Bathing suits are required. Pools are for the use of registered guests only.

Facilities include two saunas, lighted tennis courts, rooms, restaurant and bar. Visa, MasterCard, American Express, Diners Club and Carte Blanche are accepted.

Note: Runover water from the spring and pools cools as it flows through a ditch down the slope below this resort. Volunteers have dug out shallow soaking pools along the ditch, which is on BLM land. Bathing suits are advisable in the daytime at this location.

◀ *Furnace Creek Inn:* Most of Death Valley is indeed a barren wasteland, but this palm-shaded poolside sun deck is a very nice vantage point from which to contemplate the desert. Some of the palms date back to when 20-mule teams served the borax mine.

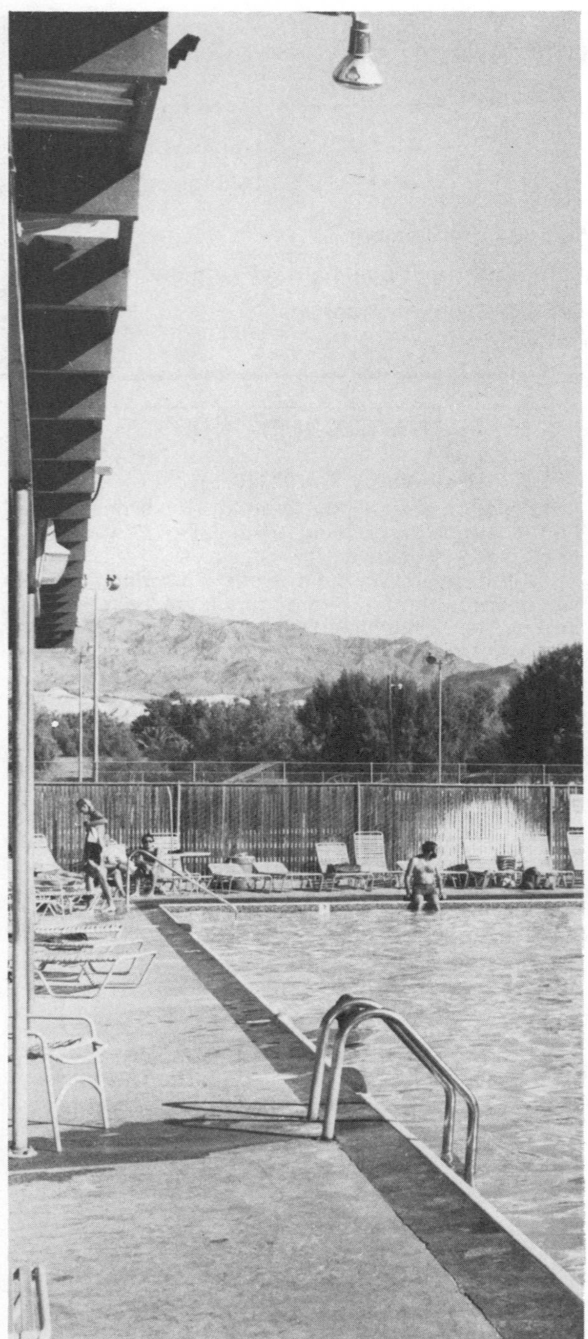

▲ *Furnace Creek Ranch:* Another oasis made possible by the same large mineral spring serving *Furnace Creek Inn.*

#401B FURNACE CREEK RANCH

■ **Box 1** **(619) 786-2345**
Death Valley, CA 92328 **PR + MH**

A large ranch style resort in a green oasis setting. Located on the edge of Death Valley, one mile west of Furnace Creek Inn. Elevation 178 ft. below sea level. Open all year.

Natural mineral water is piped from the 89° spring serving the Inn to a swimming pool at the Ranch. The rate of flow-through is so great that a temperature of approximately 85° is maintained and no chemical water treatment is necessary. Pool use is open to the public as well as to registered guests. Bathing suits are required.

Facilities include rooms, restaurant, bar, store, service station, overnight spaces, RV hookups, golf course and lighted tennis courts. Visa, MasterCard, American Express, Diners Club and Carte Blanche are accepted.

▲ *Shoshone Motel and Trailer Park:* This pool has a sparkling waterfall rather than jets.

#402 SHOSHONE MOTEL AND TRAILER PARK

■ **Box 143** **(619) 852-4367**
Shoshone, CA 92384 **PR + MH + CRV**

Older resort located on Cal 127 in desert foothills near the southern entrance to Death Valley. Elevation 1,600 ft. Open all year.

Natural mineral water flows out of a spring at 93°, and is piped to an outdoor swimming pool. The rate of flow-through is so great that a temperature of 92° is maintained, and no chemical treatment of the water is necessary. Pool use is available to the public as well as to registered guests. Bathing suits are required.

Facilities include rooms, restaurant, bar, store, service station, RV hookups and overnight spaces. Visa and MasterCard are accepted at the motel; no credit cards accepted at the trailer park.

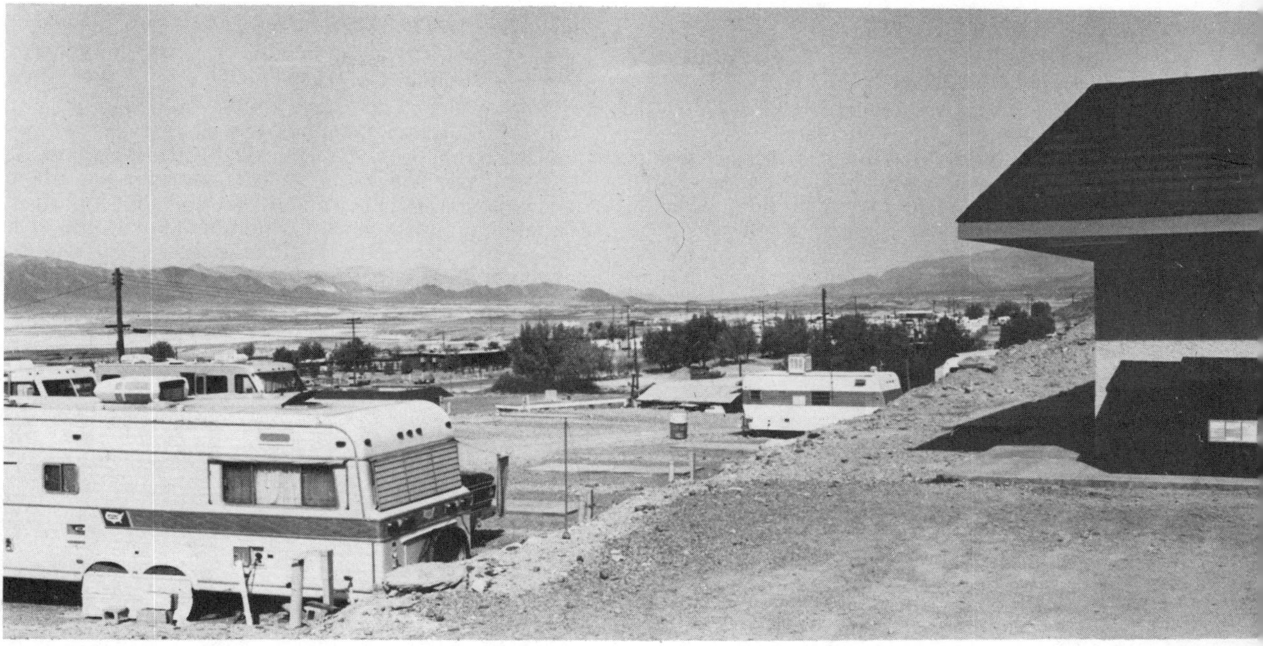

The new hydropool building (right) at *Tecopa Hot Springs Resort* overlooks new RV spaces and the surrounding desert.

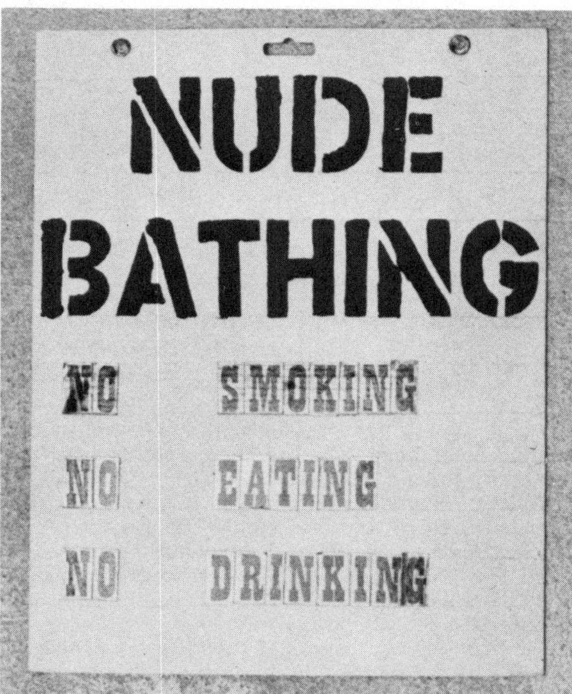

NUDE
BATHING
NO SMOKING
NO EATING
NO DRINKING

Tecopa Hot Springs Resort: Registered guests have free use of fiberglass tubs in private rooms, but also face a few rules.

#403A TECOPA HOT SPRINGS RESORT

Box 420 **(619) 852-4373**
Tecopa, CA 92389 **MH +CRV**

Newer motel, restaurant and RV park, located on the Tecopa loop of Cal 127 in desert foothills near the Dumont sand dunes. Elevation 1,400 ft. Open all year.

Natural mineral water flows from an artesian well at 108° and then is piped to seven hydropools in private rooms. Continuous flow-through maintains a temperature of approximately 107° and no chemical treatment of the water is necessary. Posted signs require nude bathing in these pools, which are for the use of registered guest only.

Facilities include rooms, restaurant, store, RV hookups and overnight spaces. It is one mile to a service station. Visa and MasterCard are accepted.

#403B ALI BABA'S MOTEL

■ **Box 336** **(619) 852-4422**
Tecopa, CA 92389

Small motel located on the Tecopa loop off of Cal 127. Elevation 1,400 ft. Open all year.

Natural mineral water flows out of an artesian well at 118° and is piped to two indoor pools. Some chlorination is added in the swimming pool, which is equipped with hydrojects and is maintained at 90°. The hydropool, in a separate private room, is maintained at 104° and the rate of flow through is so great that no chemical treatment of the water is necessary. Use of the pool is reserved for registered guests only. Bathing suits are required in the swimming pool and are optional in the private room.

Visa and MasterCard are accepted. It is one mile to a restaurant, store, etc.

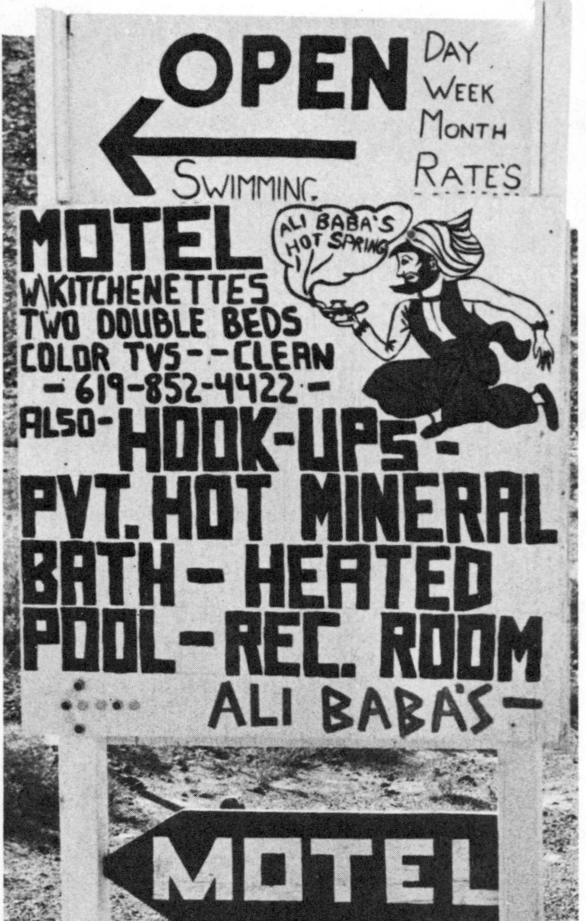

#403C ELIAS' HIDE-A-WAY

■ **Box 101** **(619) 852-4438**
Tecopa, CA 92389 **PR + CRV**

Small trailer park located on the Tecopa loop off of Cal 127. Elevation 1,400 ft. Open all year.

Natural mineral water flows out of an artesian well at 118° and is piped to two indoor soaking pools where the temperature is controlled between 100° and 108°, depending on the season. The rate of flow-through is so great that no chemical treatment of the water is necessary. The pools are available to the public as well as to registered guests.

Facilities include RV hookups and overnight spaces. No credit cards accepted. It is one mile to a motel, restaurant, store and service station.

▲ *Inyo County Tecopa Hot Springs:* Admittance to the separate men's and women's bath is free, and nude bathing is required, but mixed bathing is clearly prohibited.

#403D TECOPA HOT SPRINGS (OPERATED BY INYO COUNTY)

■ **Tecopa, CA 92389** **PR (free) + CRV**

A county-operated trailer park, bath house and campground, located on the Tecopa loop off Cal 127. Elevation 1,400 ft. Open all year.

Natural mineral water flows out of a spring at 108° and is piped to separate men's and women's bath houses. Each one has two soaking pools maintained at 105° and 100°, plus an enclosed outdoor sunbathing area. Posted signs require nude bathing and also prohibit mixed bathing.

RV hookups and overnight spaces are available on the premises. No credit cards accepted. It is two miles to a store and service station.

#404A NEEDLES MARINA PARK
on Marina Dr. (619) 326-2197
Needles, CA 92363 Hydropool CRV

#404B RAINBOW BEACH MARINA
on River Rd. (619) 326-3101
Needles, CA 92363 Hydropool CRV

#405 BERMUDA PALMS
on Parker Dam Rd. (619) 665-2784
Earp, CA 92242 Hydropool CRV

#406A BEST WESTERN TROPICS MOTEL
9274 E. Hobsonway (619) 922-5101
Blythe, CA 92225 Hydropool MH

#406B BEST WESTERN SAHARA MOTEL
825 W. Hobsonway (619) 922-7105
Blythe, CA 92225 Hydropool MH

#406C KOA — BLYTHE MARINA
on Riviera Dr. (619) 922-5350
Blythe, CA 92225 Hydropool CRV

#407 HIGHLINE SOUTH HOT WELL

near the town of Holtville

non- commercial

A cement soaking pool by an artesian well, located just off the I-8 right-of-way, on the east edge of Holtville. Elevation sea level. Open all year.

Natural mineral water flows out of an artesian well at 125° and splashes on the edge of a six-foot-by-six-foot cement pool. Pool temperature is controlled by diverting the hot flow after the water in the pool is as hot as desired. Because it takes so little hot water to maintain a pool temperature of more than 100° there is very little self-cleaning action and algae growth is rapid.

There are no services available and overnight parking is prohibited. However, a primitive BLM campground, with a 14-day limit, is located 20 yards north of the well.

Directions: At the east end of Holtville, take the Van Der Linden exit from I-8. Go north, taking the first right turn onto frontage road (Evans Hughes Hwy). Within the next few hundred yards you will cross over the Highline Canal and go past the Holdridge Road intersection. Watch for a large parking area on your right, directly opposite the BLM *Hot Springs Campground* sign on the north side of the road. The hot well and pool are visible on the west side of the parking area.

Highline South Hot Well: The flowing mineral water is sparkling clear for drinking, but thick with algae in the pool.

#408 HIGHLAND SERVICE

1675 Van Der Linden Rd. (619) 356-1742
Holtville, CA 92250

Normally a combination RV park, store and service station with natural mineral-water pools. However, the pools and RV park are closed and the property is for sale. Telephone or write for current information.

#409 BARBARA WORTH COUNTRY CLUB
2050 Country Club Dr. (619) 356-2806
Holtville, CA 92250 Hydropool MH

#410 CALEXICO TRAVEL TRAILER PARK
on Imperial Dr. (619) 357-5220
Calexico, CA 92231 Hydropool CRV

#411A FOUNTAIN OF YOUTH SPA

(see map)

■

Rte. 1, Box 12 (619) 348-1340
Niland, CA 92257 CRV

The largest and newest of the RV parks in this area, located on a desert slope overlooking the Salton Sea. Elevation 50 ft. below sea level. Open all year.

Natural mineral water flows out of an artesian well at 137° into several cooling tanks, from which it is piped to two pool areas, one of which is reserved for adults. The two outdoor swimming pools range in temperature from 85° to 90°. The five outdoor hydropools have a variety of temperatures, from 100° to 107°. The water in all pools is treated with chlorine. Bathing suits are required.

The facilities include a laundromat, store, RV hookups, overnight spaces and a recreation room. Services include massage, physical therapy, beauty and barber shop and a medical doctor in residence. No credit cards accepted.

It is four miles to a motel, restaurant and service station.

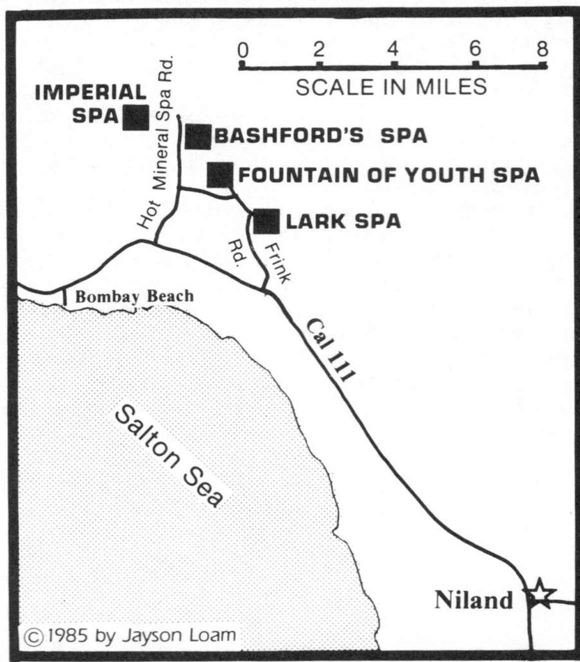

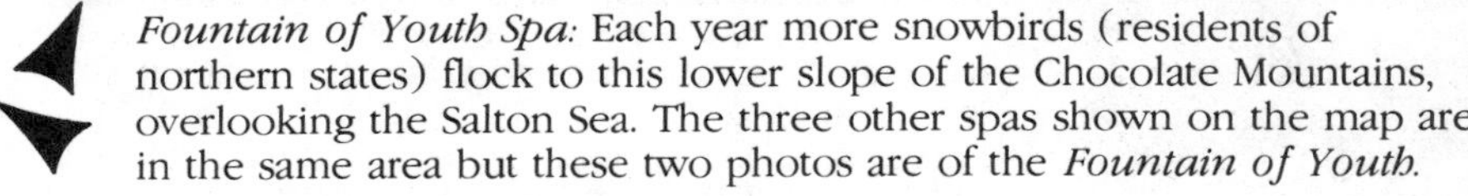

Fountain of Youth Spa: Each year more snowbirds (residents of northern states) flock to this lower slope of the Chocolate Mountains, overlooking the Salton Sea. The three other spas shown on the map are in the same area but these two photos are of the *Fountain of Youth.*

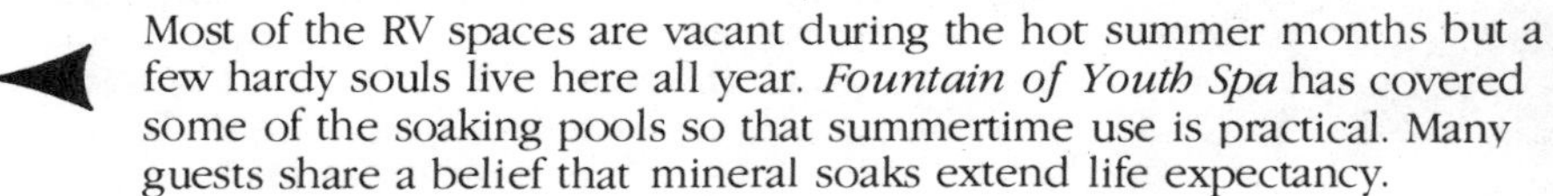

Most of the RV spaces are vacant during the hot summer months but a few hardy souls live here all year. *Fountain of Youth Spa* has covered some of the soaking pools so that summertime use is practical. Many guests share a belief that mineral soaks extend life expectancy.

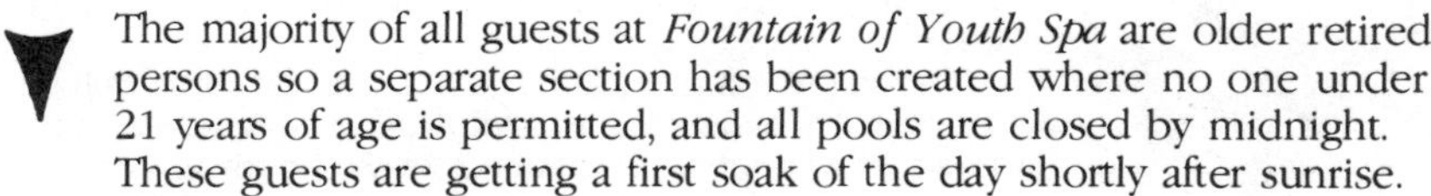

The majority of all guests at *Fountain of Youth Spa* are older retired persons so a separate section has been created where no one under 21 years of age is permitted, and all pools are closed by midnight. These guests are getting a first soak of the day shortly after sunrise.

Bashford's Hot Mineral Spa: These oversize bathtubs not only soothe aching muscles but also serve as a comfortable and attractive social center.

Imperial Sea View Hot Springs Spa: Hundreds of gallons per minute of scalding mineral water flow out of the black standpipe visible in the background.

#411B BASHFORD'S HOT MINERAL SPA

See map — page 96

Star Rte. Box 26 **(619) 348-1315**
Niland, CA 92257 **CRV**

Primarily an RV winter resort for adults, located on a desert slope overlooking the Salton Sea. Elevation 50 ft. below sea level. Open all year.

Natural mineral water flows out of an artesian well at 145° into two cooling tanks, from which it is piped to an outdoor swimming pool which is maintained at 84°, and to an outdoor hydropool which is maintained at 102°. The water in both pools is chlorine-treated. Mineral water is also piped to six outdoor soaking tubs with temperatures from 101° to 105°. These tubs are drained and refilled after each use so no chemical water treatment is needed. Bathing suits are required.

RV hookups, overnight spaces, a store and a laundry room are available on the premises. No credit cards accepted. It is four miles to a motel, restaurant and service station.

#411C IMPERIAL SEA VIEW HOT SPRINGS SPA

See map — page 96

HCO 1, Box 20 **(619) 348-1204**
Niland, CA 92257 **CRV + MH**

The original "Old Spa" location, with the first hot well drilled in this area, and recently expanded hot-water facilities. Located on a desert slope overlooking the Salton Sea. Elevation 50 ft. below sea level. Open all year.

Natural mineral water flows out of an artesian well at 165°, into a large holding and cooling tank, from which it is piped to seven outdoor pools. Five hydropools are maintained at a variety of temperatures from 96 to 104°. One mineral-water soaking pool is maintained at 96° and an adjoining fresh-water pool is maintained at 80°. All pools are treated with chlorine. Bathing suits are required.

RV hookups, overnight spaces, a store, and mobile-home rentals are available on the premises. No credit cards accepted. It is four miles to a motel, restaurant and service station.

Oh My God Hot Well: A carpet-and-cement-block dam is used to keep the hot water from the old standpipe in the smaller pool where this volunteer is working.

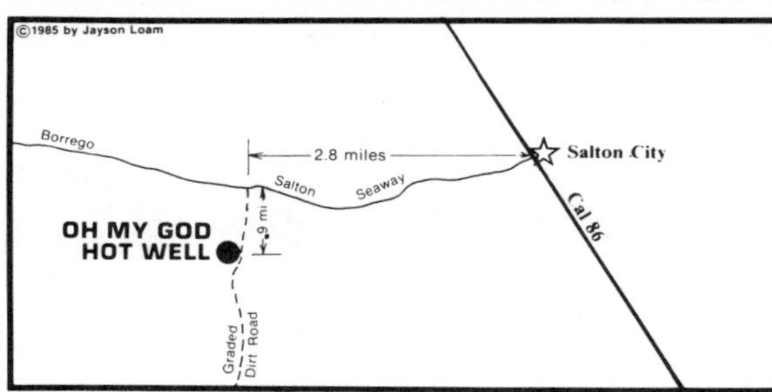

#411D LARK SPA **See map — page 96**

■ **Star Rte. 1, Box 10** **(619) 348-1340**
Niland, CA 92257 **CRV**

Primarily an RV winter resort for adults, located on a desert slope overlooking the Salton Sea. Elevation 50 ft. below sea level. Open all year.

Well water and mineral water, gas heated and chlorine treated is used in an outdoor hydropool maintained at 102°. Bathing suits are required. Overnight spaces and RV spaces are available on the premises. No credit cards accepted. It is one mile to a store and four miles to a motel, restaurant and service station.

#412 SALTON CITY SPA AND RV PARK

□ on Sea View Dr. (619) 394-4333
Salton City, CA 92274 Hydropool CRV

#413 OH MY GOD HOT WELL (see map)

● **near the town of Salton City**

non- commercial

A few very popular sand and rock pools built around a free flowing hot well on an unposted piece of private desert land west of the Salton Sea. Elevation sea level. Open all year.

Natural mineral water flows from the rusted pipe of an abandoned hot well at 108°. Volunteers have built a series of shallow connecting pools, making the first one small enough to maintain a temperature of approximately 104°, and the others considerably cooler, depending on the air temperature and wind conditions. The graded gravel road passes within a few yards of the pools, so there is often a wide variety of visitors. The regulars who built the pools are determined to keep a clothing optional policy, no matter how many clothed persons might be present.

There are no services, but there is an abundance of level space on which overnight parking is not prohibited. If you want a fire, be sure to bring your own wood, and some windbreak materials might also come in handy. It is four miles to a store, restaurant, service station, etc.

#414 DESERT SANDS

□ on Palm Canyon Dr. (619) 767-5554
Borrego Springs, CA 92004 Hydropool CRV

#415 WARNER SPRINGS RANCH

■ **P.O. Box 10** **(619) 782-3555**
Warner Springs, CA 92086 **MH (limited)**

A major 2,500 acre resort development in the process of being sold to 2,000 buyers of undivided proprietary interest. Located 75 miles northeast of San Diego, on CAI 79, in the mountains east of Palomar Observatory. Elevation 3,000 ft. Open all year.

Natural mineral water flows out from several springs at 137° and is then piped to and flows through an outdoor, Olympic-size swimming pool, maintaining a temperature of 101° and requiring no chemical treatment. A second Olympic size swimming pool uses chlorinated well water maintained at a temperature of 80°. Bathing suits are required.

Facilities include rooms, restaurant, bar, store, service station, golf course, airstrip and glider port, tennis courts, riding stables, crafts workshop and fitness gym. Massage is available on the premises.

During the transition from single ownership to multiple ownership this resort is not open to the public. However, prospective buyers may arrange for an orientation visit and a guest pass. Once the sale is complete, use of the facilities will be limited to the multiple owners and their personal guests. Telephone for current information on the status of this location.

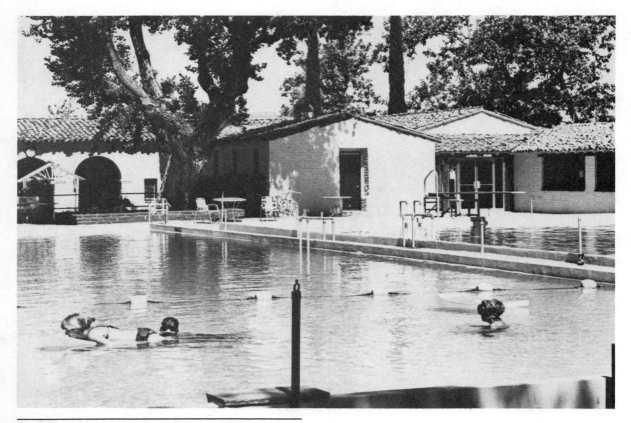

Warner Springs Ranch: The designers of this resort provide two Olympic-size swimming pools, but not one hydropool or smaller soaking pool. According to legend the location was cursed when a paleface landowner first denied traditional hot spring access to a local tribe. Maybe it is only a coincidence that all previous commerical ventures at *Warner* have failed.

#416 TIDO'S RV PARK
□ on Hwy. 79 (714) 782-3571
Warner Springs, CA 92086 Hydropool CRV

#417 LAKE HENSHAW RESORT
□ on Hwy 76 (619) 782-3487
Santa Ysabel, CA 92070 Hydropool CRV

#418 ACI
□ on CR 52 (714) 765-1463
Julian, CA 92036 Hydropool CRV

#419 AGUA CALIENTE COUNTY PARK

For reservations call (619) 565-3600
PR + CRV

A county operated desert campground located in a wildlife refuge area near the Anza Borrego Desert. No pets are permitted at any time! Elevation 1,000 ft. Open all year.

Natural mineral water flows out of several springs at 90° and is then piped to a variety of pools. Continuous flow through an outdoor swimming pool maintains a temperature of approximately 80° and eliminates the need for chemical treatment. A large indoor hydropool uses chlorine-treated mineral water, gas-heated to 102°. There are two indoor drain and refill roman tubs which are reserved for handicapped persons or others who require chlorine-free water. Bathing suits are required except in private-space roman tubs. Pool facilities are available to the public for day use as well as for those occupying campground spaces.

Facilities include RV hookups and overnight spaces. No credit cards accepted. It is ½ mile to a store and service station, ten miles to a restaurant and 30 miles to a motel. There is a nearby airstrip—Agua Caliente.

Agua Caliente County Park: This outdoor chlorine-free pool is popular with the youngsters, but a bit cool for parents.

This unique installation at *Agua Caliente County Park* is truly a whirlpool. Pumps create a current around a central island at a speed which provides good exercise.

▲ *Swallows/Sun Island Nudist Resort:* The hydropool is available to full-time residents as well as non-resident members.

#420 JACUMBA HOT SPRINGS HEALTH SPA

■ **Box 466** **(619) 766-4333**
Jacumba, CA 92034

An older motel spa, located just off of I-8, 80 miles east of San Diego. Elevation 3,600 ft. Open all year.

Natural mineral water flows out of a spring at 97° and is then piped to an indoor hydropool. Continuous flow-through maintains a temperature of 95° and eliminates the need for any chemical water treatment. Bathing suits are required.

Facilities include rooms, restaurant, bar and sauna. Massage is available on the premises. No credit cards accepted. It is one block to a store and service station and eight miles to RV hookups.

#421 SWALLOWS/SUN ISLAND NUDIST RESORT

□ 1631 Harbison Canyon Rd. (619) 445-3754
El Cajon, CA 92021 PR + MH + CRV

A large, well-equipped, traditional nudist park, located in a tree-shaded canyon 15 miles east of San Diego. Elevation 500 ft. Open all year.

Gas-heated well water, chlorine-treated, is used in an outdoor swimming pool with a temperature range of 75° to 80°, and in an outdoor hydropool with water temperature maintained at 104°. Bathing suits are not permitted in pool and clothing is prohibited everywhere, weather permitting.

Facilities include rooms, restaurant, tennis and volleyball courts, RV hookups and overnight camping. Visa and MasterCard are accepted. It is one mile to a store and eight miles to a service station.

This is a membership organization, not open to the public for drop-in visits, but prospective members may be issued a guest pass by prior arrangement. Resort rules prohibit guns, cameras, drugs and erotic behavior. Phone for more information and directions.

#422A	PLAZA INTERNATIONAL INN		
☐	683 N. Mollison Ave.	(619) 442-0973	
	El Cajon, CA 92021	Hydropool	MH
#422B	ROYAL INN		
☐	1274 Oakdale Ave.	(619) 442-0651	
	El Cajon, CA 92021	Hydropool	MH
#422C	CIRCLE RV RANCH		
☐	on Main St.	(619) 440-0040	
	El Cajon, CA 92020	Hydropool	RV
#423	NITE LITE INN		
☐	521 Roosevelt Ave.	(619) 474-6518	
	National City, CA 92050	Hydropool	MH
#424	RAMADA INN		
☐	91 Bonita Rd.	(619) 428-5521	
	Chula Vista, CA 92010	Hydropool	MH
#425A	INTERNATIONAL BORDER TRAVELODGE		
☐	815 San Ysidro Blvd.	(619) 428-5521	
	San Ysidro, CA 92073	Hydropool	MH
#425B	BORDER GATE RV PARK		
☐	on San Ysidro Blvd.	(619) 428-4411	
	San Ysidro, CA 92073	Hydropool	CRV
#425C	MOTEL 8 RV PARK		
☐	on Calle Primero	(619) 428-4486	
	San Ysidro, CA 92073	Hydropool	CRV
#426A	BAHIA HOTEL		
☐	998 W. Mission Bay Dr.	(619) 488-0551	
	San Diego, CA 92109	Hydropool	MH
#426B	BEST WESTERN BLUE SEA LODGE		
☐	707 Pacific Beach Dr.	(619) 483-4700	
	San Diego, CA 92109	Health Spa	MH
#426C	CATAMARAN MOTOR HOTEL		
☐	3999 Mission Blvd.	(619) 488-1081	
	San Diego, CA 92109	Hydropool	MH
#426D	EXECUTIVE HOTEL		
☐	1055 First Ave.	(619) 232-6141	
	San Diego, CA 92101	Hydropool	MH
#426E	HALF MOON INN		
☐	2303 Shelter Island Dr.	(619) 224-3411	
	San Diego, CA 92106	Hydropool	MH
#426F	THE SAN DIEGO HILTON BEACH AND TENNIS RESORT		
☐	1775 E. Mission Bay Dr.	(619) 276-4010	
	San Diego, CA 92109	Hydropool	MH
#426G	SAN DIEGO TRAVELODGE SPORTS ARENA		
☐	1101 Hollister St.	(619) 226-3711	
	San Diego, CA 92154	Hydropool	MH
#426H	BEST WESTERN POSADA INN		
☐	5005 N. Harbor Dr.	(619) 224-3254	
	San Diego, CA 92106	Hydropool	MH
#426I	THE GROSVENOR INN		
☐	3145 Sports Arena Blvd.	(619) 225-9999	
	San Diego, CA 92110	Hydropool	MH
#426J	TRAVELODGE HARBOR ISLAND		
☐	1960 Harbor Island Dr.	(619) 291-6700	
	San Diego, CA 92101	Hydropool	MH
#426K	BEST WESTERN RANCHO BERNARDO		
☐	17065 W. Bernardo Dr.	(619) 485-6530	
	San Diego, CA 92127	Hydropool	MH
#426L	DEL CORONADO HOTEL		
☐	1500 Orange Ave.	(619) 435-6611	
	Coronado, CA 92118	Health Spa	MH
#426M	SEAPOINT HOTEL		
☐	4875 N. Harbor Dr.	(619) 224-3621	
	Pt. Loma, CA 92106	Hydropool	MH
#426N	SANTA FE TRAVEL TRAILER PARK		
☐	on Santa Fe St.	(619) 272-4051	
	San Diego, CA 92109	Hydropool	CRV
#426O	NITE LITE INN		
☐	on Sports Arena Blvd.	(619) 225-9999	
	San Diego, CA 92110	Hydropool	CRV
#426P	CAMPLAND ON THE BAY		
☐	on Olney St.	(619) 274-6260	
	San Diego, CA 92109	Hydropool	CRV

#427A THE TUBS
7220 El Cajon Blvd. (619) 698-7727
☐ San Diego, CA 92115 PR

San Diego's original rent-a-tub establishment, located on a main suburban street near San Diego State University.

Pool for rent to the public, using gas-heated tap water, treated with chlorine.

Eleven private rooms, rented by the hour. Water temperature 102°. Sauna included in most rooms.

Special features: The VIP Suite, large enough for 12 persons, has a bathroom and steam bath in addition to a sauna.

Services available: juice bar.

Credit cards accepted: Visa and MasterCard.

Phone for rates, reservations and directions.

#427B TOWN AND COUNTRY HOTEL
500 Hotel Circle North (619) 291-7131
☐ San Diego, CA 92138 Hydropool MH

#427C RAMADA INN
2151 S. Hotel Circle (619) 291-6500
☐ San Diego, CA 92108 Hydropool MH

#427D PLAZA INTERNATIONAL HOTEL
1515 Hotel Circle West (619) 291-8790
☐ San Diego, CA 92108 Hydropool MH

#427E MISSION VALLEY INN
875 Hotel Circle South (619) 298-8281
☐ San Diego, CA 92108 Hydropool MH

#427F KINGS INN
1333 Hotel Circle South (619) 297-2231
☐ San Diego, CA 92138 Hydropool MH

#427G HANALEI HOTEL
2270 Hotel Circle Dr. (619) 297-1101
☐ San Diego, CA 92138 Hydropool MH

#427H FABULOUS INN — MISSION VALLEY
2485 Motel Circle Place (619) 291-7700
☐ San Diego, CA 92108 Hydropool MH

#427I CIRCLE 7/11 MOTEL
2201 W. Hotel Circle (619) 291-2711
☐ San Diego, CA 92108 Hydropool MH

#427J BEST WESTERN SEVEN SEAS LODGE
411 Hotel Circle South (619) 291-1300
☐ San Diego, CA 92108 Hydropool MH

#427K AMBASSADOR INN
5415 Clairemont Mesa Blvd. (619) 560-0545
☐ San Diego, CA 92117 Hydropool MH

#428A LA VALENCIA HOTEL
1132 Prospect St. (619) 540-0771
☐ La Jolla, CA 92037 Health Spa MH

#428B BEST WESTERN HOTEL AT LA JOLLA
7766 Fay Ave. (619) 454-3001
☐ La Jolla, CA 92037 Hydropool MH

#428C ROYAL INN
7830 Fay Ave. (619) 459-4461
☐ La Jolla, CA 92037 Hydropool MH

#428D SUMMER HOUSE INN
7955 La Jolla Shores Dr. (619) 459-0261
☐ La Jolla, CA 92038 Hydropool MH

#429A DEL MAR INN
720 Camino Del Mar (619) 755-9765
☐ Del Mar, CA 92014 Hydropool MH

#429B WINNERS CIRCLE LODGE
550 Via de la Valle (619) 755-6666
☐ Del Mar, CA 92014 Hydropool MH

#429C SURF & TURF RV PARK
on Turf Rd. (619) 755-5400
☐ Del Mar, CA 92014 Hydropool CRV

#430A LA COSTA RESORT MOTEL AND SPA
Costa Del Mar Rd. (619) 438-9111
☐ Carlsbad, CA 92008 Hydropool MH

#430B BEST WESTERN BEACH VIEW LODGE
3180 Carlsbad Blvd. (619) 729-1151
☐ Carlsbad, CA 92008 Hydropool MH

#430C BEST WESTERN BEACH TERRACE INN
2775 Ocean St. (619) 729-5951
☐ Carlsbad, CA 92008 Hydropool MH

#430D VILLA MARINA BOATEL — MOTEL
2008 Harbor Dr. N. (619) 722-1561
☐ Oceanside, CA 92054 Hydropool MH

#430E MARINA DEL MAR CONDOMINIUM RESORT
1202 N. Pacific St. (619) 722-4330
☐ Oceanside, CA 92054 Hydropool MH

#430F BEST WESTERN ROYAL SCOT
1680 Oceanside Blvd. (619) 722-1821
☐ Oceanside, CA 92054 Hydropool MH

#430G CASITAS POQUITOS RV PARK
on Hill St. (619) 722-4404
Oceanside, CA 92054 Hydropool RV

#430H PARADISE BY THE SEA
on Hill St. (619) 439-1376
Oceanside, CA 92054 Hydropool RV

#431A ESCONDIDO MOTOR HOTEL
2500 S. Escondido Blvd. (619) 747-5000
Escondido, CA 92025 Hydropool MH

#431B THE GOLDEN DOOR
P.O. Box 1567 (619) 744-5777
Escondido, CA 92025 Health Spa MH

#431C LAWRENCE WELK VILLAGE INN
8860 Lawrence Welk Dr. (619) 749-3000
Escondido, CA 92026 Hydropool MH

#431D TRAVELODGE WEST
1290 West Valley Pkwy. (619) 489-1010
Escondido, CA 92025 Hydropool MH

#432 SAN DIEGO COUNTRY ESTATES
2457 Van Vicente Rd. (619) 789-8290
Ramona, CA 92065 Hydropool MH

#433 RAINBOW CANYON GOLF RESORT
P.O. Box 129 (619) 676-5631
Temecula, CA 92390 Hydropool MH

Alive Polarity at Murietta Hot Springs: Mud baths are part of an elaborate health program available to the public.

Family participation is encouraged at *Murietta,* but only if everyone wears clothing in the indoor soaking tubs.

#434 ALIVE POLARITY AT MURIETTA HOT SPRINGS
28779 Via Las Flores (714) 677-7451
Murietta, CA 92362 PR + MH

A self-styled vegetarian family oasis for body, mind and spirit, located just off of I-15 and I-215, 30 miles north of Escondido and 50 miles south of San Bernardino. Elevation 800 ft. Open all year.

Natural mineral water flows out of a spring at 120° and is then piped to a variety of indoor pools and tubs. The outdoor Olympic-size swimming pool uses a combination of mineral water and cold well water to maintain a temperature of 85°. A similar combination of water is used to maintain a temperature of 102° in an outdoor hydropool and a temperature of 90° in an outdoor exercise pool. All pool water is chlorinated. Natural mineral water is also piped to 36 indoor soaking tubs, which are drained and refilled after each use, so no chemical water treatment is necessary. There are separate men's and womens mud-bath sections, each containing nine tubs. Bathing suits are required everywhere except in the mud baths, where they are not permitted. Only legally married couples or adults of the same sex may share a resort room. Spa facilities are available to the public as well as to registered guests.

Facilities include rooms, a vegetarian restaurant, tennis courts, a store and overnight parking. Massage, facials, skin glow rubs, energizing body wraps and a beauty shop are available on the premises. There are also numerous Alive Polarity programs for healing yourself and your family. Visa, MasterCard and American Express are accepted. It is five miles to RV hookups and a service station.

Phone for reservations and additional information.

#435A BEST WESTERN HEMET HOTEL
2625 W. Florida Ave. (714) 925-6605
☐ Hemet, CA 92343 Hydropool MH

#435B MOUNTAIN VALLEY RV PARK
on Lyon (714) 925-5812
☐ Hemet, CA 92343 Hydropool CRV

#435C GOLDEN VILLAGE ADULT TRAVEL TRAILER PARK
on Hwy 74/79 (714) 925-2518
☐ Hemet, CA 92343 Hydropool CRV

#435D AMERICANA MOBILE HOME AND RV PARK
on N. Palm Ave. (714) 652-1220
☐ Hemet, CA 92343 Hydropool CRV

#435E ROADRUNNER RV PARK
on Kirby (714) 925-2515
☐ Hemet, CA 92343 Hydropool CRV

#435F GOODWIN'S RV PARK
on State St. (714) 654-0670
☐ San Jacinto, CA 92383 Hydropool CRV

#436A ROYAL INDIO MOTEL
82-347 Hwy. 111 (619) 347-0911
☐ Indio, CA 92201 Hydropool MH

#436B BEST WESTERN DATE TREE MOTOR INN
81-909 Indio Blvd. (619) 347-3421
☐ Indio, CA 92201 Hydropool MH

#436C INDIAN WELLS RV ROUNDUP
on Jefferson St. (619) 347-0895
☐ Indio, CA 92201 Hydropool CRV

#436D CARRIAGE PLACE TRAVEL TRAILER PARK
on I-10 frontage road (619) 345-2236
☐ Indio, CA 92201 Hydropool CRV

#437A DE ANZA PALM SPRINGS OASIS
on Ave. 36 (619) 328-4813
☐ Cathedral City, CA 92234 Hydropool CRV

#437B DESERT HILLS MOBILE PARK
on Hwy 111 (619) 328-2758
☐ Cathedral City, CA 92234 Hydropool CRV

#437C ADOBE GARDEN HOTEL
45-406 Hwy 74 (619) 346-6185
☐ Palm Desert, CA 92260 Hydropool MH

#437D MARRIOTT'S RANCHO LAS PALMAS RESORT
41000 Bob Hope Dr. (619) 568-2727
☐ Rancho Mirage, CA 92270 Hydropool MH

#437E INDIAN WELLS RESORT HOTEL
764-661 Hwy 111 (619) 345-2581
☐ Indian Wells, CA 92260 Hydropool MH

#437F PALM DESERT LODGE
74-527 Hwy 111 (619) 346-3875
☐ Palm Desert, CA 92261 Hydropool MH

#437G THE PALM DESERT RESORT
40-999 Resorter Rd. (619) 345-2781
☐ Palm Desert, CA 92260 Hydropool MH

#437H SANDRA MOTOR LODGE
74-470 Abronia Trail (619) 346-8061
☐ Palm Desert, CA 92260 Hydropool MH

#437I SHADOW MT. RESORT & RACQUET CLUB
45-750 San Luis Rey (619) 346-6123
☐ Palm Desert, CA 92260 Hydropool MH

#437J INDIAN WELLS RACQUET CLUB RESORT
46-765 Bay Club Dr. (619) 345-2811
☐ Palm Desert, CA 92260 Hydropool MH

#437K ERAWAN GARDEN HOTEL
76-477 Hwy 111 (619) 346-8021
☐ Palm Desert, CA 92260 Hydropool MH

#437L CAROUSEL RESORT HOTEL
45-640 Hwy 74 (619) 346-6197
☐ Palm Desert, CA 92260 Hydropool MH

#437M GENE AUTRY HOTEL
4200 E. Palm Canyon Dr. (619) 328-1171
☐ Palm Springs, CA 92264 Hydropool MH

#437N SHERATON PLAZA — PALM SPRINGS
400 E. Tahquitz McCullum Way
☐ Palm Springs, CA 92262 (619) 320-6868
Health Spa MH

#437O SEVEN SPRINGS HOTEL
1269 E. Palm Canyon Dr. (619) 323-2775
☐ Palm Springs, CA 92262 Hydropool MH

#437P PALM SPRINGS TRAVELODGE
333 E. Palm Canyon Dr. (619) 327-1211
☐ Palm Springs, CA 92262 Hydropool MH

Palm Springs Spa Hotel: Two outdoor soaking pools have their own patio area. Although this spa is famous for its many beauty services for women, the grooming needs of men have not been ignored.

#438 PALM SPRINGS SPA HOTEL

■ **100 N. Indian Ave. (619) 325-1461**
Palm Springs, CA 92262

A major destination resort with an elaborate mineral-water spa, located in downtown Palm Springs. Elevation 500 ft. Open all year except spa closed June 21 to Labor Day.

Natural mineral water flows out of historic Indian wells on the property at a temperature of 106°, and is chlorine-treated for use in four outdoor pools; swimming pool at 84°, hydropool at 106°, soaking pool at 106° and another soaking pool at 96°. The spa has separate men's and women's sections, each containing 14 tile tubs, with mineral water temperature separately controllable up to 104°. These tubs are drained and refilled after each use, so no chemical treatment of the water is necessary. Each spa also has vapor-inhalation rooms, a steam bath and a dry sauna. Bathing suits are required in the outdoor pool area, optional in the bath house.

Services and facilities on the premises include massage, barber and beauty shop, rooms, restaurant, bar, stores, travel agent, airport pickup and group conference rooms. Visa, MasterCard, American Express and Diners Club accepted. Pool and spa facilities are available to the public as well as to registered guests.

Directions: Take the Indian Ave. exit from I-10 and drive south five miles to the resort.

#437Q PALM SPRINGS BILTMORE HOTEL
□ 1000 E. Palm Canyon Dr. (619) 323-1811
Palm Springs, CA 92262 Hydropool MH

#437R OCOTILLO LODGE
□ 1111 E. Palm Canyon Dr. (619) 327-1141
Palm Springs, CA 92262 Hydropool MH

#437S INTERNATIONAL HOTEL RESORT
□ 1800 E. Palm Canyon Dr. (619) 323-1711
Palm Springs, CA 92262 Hydropool MH

#437T BEST WESTERN TROPICAL HOTEL
□ 411 E. Palm Canyon Dr. (619) 327-1391
Palm Springs, CA 92262 Hydropool MH

#437U HAPPY TRAVELER RV PARK
□ on Mesquite Ave. (619) 325-8518
Palm Springs, CA 92262 Hydropool CRV

#437V GOLDEN SANDS RV PARK
□ on San Rafael Rd. (619) 327-4737
Palm Springs, CA 92262 Hydropool CRV

#439A RACQUET CLUB OF PALM SPRINGS
☐ 2743 N. Indian Ave. (619) 325-1251
Palm Springs, CA 92263 Hydropool MH

#439B QUALITY INN AT PALM SPRINGS
☐ 2743 N. Indian Ave. (619) 325-2371
Palm Springs, CA 92263 Hydropool MH

#439C WESTERN HOST MOTOR HOTEL
☐ 1633 S. Palm Canyon Dr. (619) 325-9177
Palm Springs, CA 92262 Hydropool MH

#439D VILLA HERMOSA APARTMENT HOTEL
☐ 155 W. Hermosa Pl. (619) 325-5757
Palm Springs, CA 92262 Hydropool MH

#439E VAGABOND MOTOR HOTEL
☐ 1699 S. Canyon Dr. (619) 325-7211
Palm Springs, CA 92262 Hydropool MH

#439F TIKI SPA HOTEL & APARTMENTS
☐ 1910 S. Camino Real (619) 327-1349
Palm Springs, CA 92262 Hydropool MH

#439G SHERATON OASIS HOTEL
☐ 155 S. Bolardo Rd. (619) 323-2775
Palm Springs, CA 92262 Hydropool MH

#439H PALM SPRINGS TENNIS CLUB
☐ 701 W. Barista Rd. (619) 340-0460
Palm Springs, CA 92262 Hydropool MH

#439I LA SIESTA VILLAS
☐ 247 W. Stevens Rd. (619) 325-2269
Palm Springs, CA 92262 Hydropool MH

#439J INGLESIDE INN
☐ 200 W. Ramon Rd. (619) 325-0046
Palm Springs, CA 92262 Hydropool MH

#439K HYATT LODGE
☐ 1177 S. Palm Canyon Dr. (619) 325-1356
Palm Springs, CA 92262 Hydropool MH

#439L DUNES HOTEL
☐ 390 S. Indian Ave. (619) 325-1172
Palm Springs, CA 92262 Hydropool MH

#439M AMERICANA CANYON HOTEL,
RACQUET AND GOLF RESORT
☐ 2850 S. Palm Canyon Dr. (619) 323-5656
Palm Springs, CA 92262 Health Spa MH

#439N BEST WESTERN CAMBRIDGE INN
☐ 1277 S. Palm Canyon Dr. (619) 325-5026
Palm Springs, CA 92262 Hydropool MH

#439O RAMADA INN — NORTH
☐ 1177 N. Palm Canyon Dr. (619) 325-5591
Palm Springs, CA 92262 Hydropool MH

#439P THE PALMS AT PALM SPRINGS
☐ 572 N. Indian Ave. (619) 325-1111
Palm Springs, CA 92262 Hydropool MH

#439Q PALM SPRINGS HILTON RIVIERA
☐ 1600 N. Indian Ave. (619) 327-8311
Palm Springs, CA 92262 Hydropool MH

#439R GRAND VIEW HOTEL
☐ 950 N. Indian Ave. (619) 325-2707
Palm Springs, CA 92262 Hydropool MH

#439S ALAN LADD'S SPANISH INN
☐ 640 N. Indian Ave. (619) 325-2285
Palm Springs, CA 92262 Hydropool MH

#439T CANYON VILLAS HOTEL
☐ 520 Murray Canyon Dr. (619) 320-6841
Palm Springs, CA 92262 Hydropool MH

#439U ESTRELLA INN
☐ 415 S. Belardo Dr. (619) 325-2236
Palm Springs, CA 92262 Hydropool MH

#439V LA MANCHA PRIVATE CLUB & VILLAS
☐ 444 Caballeros Ave. (619) 323-1773
Palm Springs, CA 92262 Hydropool MH

#439W MONACO VILLA REDUCING
& HEALTH RESORT
☐ 371 Camino Monte Vista (619) 327-1261
Palm Springs, CA 92262 Hydropool MH

#439X SUNDANCE VILLAS
☐ 378 Cabrillo Rd. (619) 325-3888
Palm Springs, CA 92262 Hydropool MH

#439Y OLYMPIC GOLD AND RACQUET CLUB
☐ 69375 Ramon Rd. (619) 324-4521
Palm Springs, CA 92264 Hydropool MH

DESERT HOT SPRINGS MOTELS AND SPAS

All of the establishments listed below are in or near the city of Desert Hot Springs, at an elevation of 1,200 ft. and are open all year.

Unless otherwise noted, all of them offer at least one swimming pool and one hydropool, where bathing suits are required. Locations which offer daytime spa use, or in-room pools, or natural mineral water from their own wells, are noted. It is one mile or less to a store, restaurant and service station.

Take the Desert Hot Springs exit from I-10, north of Palm Springs, and phone for further directions if necessary. For additional information about accommodations and the general area, phone, write or visit:

VISITOR INFORMATION CENTER
Chamber of Commerce
13560 Palm Drive   Desert Hot Springs, CA 92240   (619) 329-6403

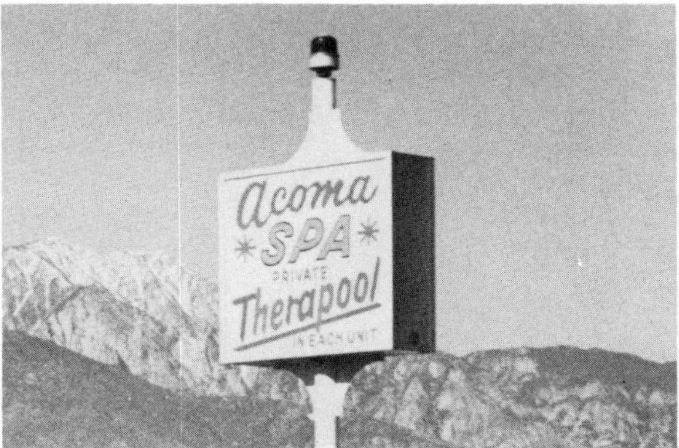

#440A ACOMA SPA MOTEL

■ **66313 Acoma Ave. (619) 329-6343**
Desert Hot Springs, CA 92240 MH
(in-room pools)

Visa and MasterCard accepted.

#440B A'DONNA SPA MOTEL

□ 66197 Cahuilla Ave. (619) 329-5118
Desert Hot Springs, CA 92240 MH

Visa and MasterCard accepted.

#440C AMBASSADOR ARMS SPA MOTEL

■ **12921 Tamar Dr. (619) 329-5446**
Desert Hot Springs, CA 92240 MH

Visa and MasterCard accepted.

#440D ATLAS-HI LODGE

□ 13336 Avenida Hermosa (619) 329-5446
Desert Hot Springs, CA 92240 MH

No credit cards accepted.

Best Western Ponce DeLeon:
One of the newer and larger hotels which feature recreation rather the therapy.

#440E BEST WESTERN PONCE DE LEON HOTEL

■ **11000 Palm Dr. (619) 329-0484**
Desert Hot Springs, CA 92240 PR +
(in-room pools) MH

Open to public for day-rate spa use. Restaurant and bar on the premises. Visa, MasterCard, American Express, Carte Blanche and Diners Club accepted.

#440F BLUE WATER MANOR

■ **66729 Eighth St.** **(619) 329-6912**
Desert Hot Springs, CA 92240 **MH**

Visa and MasterCard accepted.

#440G CACTUS LODGE

■ **68061 Calle Azteca** **(619) 329-0584**
Desert Hot Springs, CA 92240 **MH**

Visa and MasterCard accepted.

#440H CACTUS SPRINGS LODGE

■ **68075 Club Circle Dr.** **(619) 329-5776**
Desert Hot Springs, CA 92240 **MH**

Visa and MasterCard accepted.

Desert Hot Springs Spa: This central patio pool area is so large it even has it own mini-shopping center along one side.

#440I CARAVAN MOTEL

■ **66810 Fourth St.** **(619) 329-7124**
Desert Hot Springs, CA 92240 **PR + MH**

Open to public for day-rate spa use.
Visa and MasterCard accepted.

#440J DAVID'S SPA MOTEL

□ 11220 Palm Dr. (619) 329-6202
Desert Hot Springs, CA 92240 MH

Visa and MasterCard accepted.

#440K DESERT HOT SPRINGS SPA

■ **10805 Palm Dr.** **(619) 329-6495**
Desert Hot Springs, CA 92240 **PR** + MH

Open to public for day-rate spa use.
Restaurant and bar on the premises.
Visa, MasterCard, American Express, Carte Blanche and Diners Club accepted.

#440L EL MYRA LODGE
■ **66705 E. Sixth St.** **(619) 329-6015**
Desert Hot Springs, CA 92240 **MH**
Open to public for day-rate spa use.
Visa and MasterCard accepted.

#440M EL REPOSO SPA
□ 66334 W. Fifth St. (619) 329-6632
Desert Hot Springs, CA 92240 PR + MH
Open to public for day-rate spa use.
Visa, MasterCard, American Express, Carte Blanche and Diners Club accepted.

#440N FRIENDSHIP DESERT HOLIDAY
□ 67221 Pierson Blvd. (619) 329-1464
Desert Hot Springs, CA 92240 MH
No credit cards accepted.

#440O GREEN BRIAR INN
□ 66445 Second St. (619) 329-5109
Desert Hot Springs, CA 92240 MH
No hydropool. No credit cards accepted.

#440P HACIENDA RIVIERA SPA
□ 67375 Hacienda Ave. (619) 329-7010
Desert Hot Springs, CA 92240 PR
Spa only—no rooms. No credit cards accepted.

#440Q HIGHLANDER LODGE
□ 68187 Club Circle Dr. (619) 329-7123
Desert Hot Springs, CA 92240 MH
Visa and MasterCard accepted.

#440R HILLVIEW MOTEL
□ 11740 Mesquite Ave. (619) 329-5317
Desert Hot Springs, CA 92240 MH
No credit cards accepted.

#440S KISMET LODGE
■ **13340 Mountain View** **(619) 329-6451**
Desert Hot Springs, CA 92240 **MH**
No credit cards accepted.

#440T LAS PRIMAVERAS MOTEL & SPA
■ **66659 Sixth St.** **(619) 251-1677**
Desert Hot Springs, CA 92240 **MH**
Visa and MasterCard accepted.

#440U LIDO PALMS SPA MOTEL
■ **12801 Tamar Dr.** **(619) 329-6033**
Desert Hot Springs, CA 92240 **MH**
No credit cards accepted.

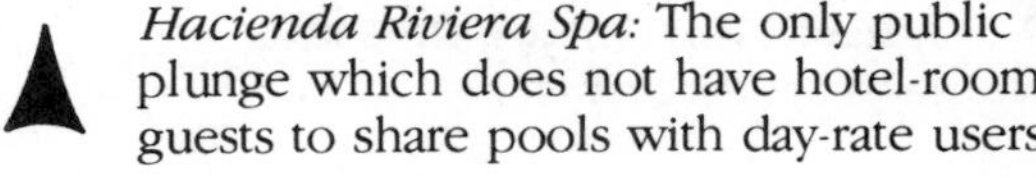

Hacienda Riviera Spa: The only public plunge which does not have hotel-room guests to share pools with day-rate users.

Linda Vista Lodge: Typical medium-size resort, offering wind-protected pools and a balcony view of Mt. San Jacincto.

#440V LINDA VISA LODGE
■ **67200 Hacienda Ave. (619) 329-6401**
Desert Hot Springs, CA 92240 MH
Visa and MasterCard accepted.

#440W LORANE MANOR SPA
■ **67751 Hacienda Ave. (619) 329-9090**
Desert Hot Springs, CA 92240 MH
No credit cards accepted.

#440X MA-HA-YAH LODGE
■ **68111 Calle Las Tiendas (619) 329-5420**
Desert Hot Springs, CA 92240 MH
No credit cards accepted.

#440Y MARY ANN MANOR
■ **12890 Quinta Way (619) 329-6051**
Desert Hot Springs, CA 92240 MH
No credit cards accepted.

#440Z MECCA
■ **12885 Eliseo Rd. (619) 329-6932**
Desert Hot Springs, CA 92240 MH
No swimming pool. No credit cards accepted.

#441A MIRACLE MANOR
■ **12589 Reposo Way (619) 329-6641**
Desert Hot Springs, CA 92240 MH
Visa and MasterCard accepted.

#441B MISSION LAKES COUNTRY CLUB INN
□ 8484 Clubhouse Blvd. (619) 329-6481
Desert Hot Springs, CA 92240 MH
Visa and MasterCard accepted.

#441C MOHLER'S DESERT PALMS SPA
□ 11330 Palm Dr. (619) 329-6271
Desert Hot Springs, CA 92240 MH
Visa and MasterCard accepted.

#441D MONTE VISTA SPA
■ **12697 Eliseo Rd. (619) 251-1668**
Desert Hot Springs, CA 92240 MH
No credit cards accepted.

#441E THE MOORS SPA MOTEL
■ **12673 Reposo Way (619) 329-7121**
Desert Hot Springs, CA 92240 MH
No credit cards accepted.

#441F PALMER LODGE SPA
■ **11171 Ocotillo Rd. (619) 329-6030**
Desert Hot Springs, CA 92240 MH
No credit cards accepted.

#441G PYRAMID SPA MOTEL
□ 66563 E. Fifth St. (619) 329-5652
Desert Hot Springs, CA 92240 MH
Visa and MasterCard accepted.

 *Tropical Motel and Spa:* Older single-story motel which offers day-rate use of pools.

#441H ROYAL FOX INN
■ **14500 Palm Dr.** **(619) 329-4481**
Desert Hot Springs, CA 92240 **MH**
(in-room pools)
Restaurant and bar on the premises.
Visa, MasterCard and American Express accepted.

#441I SAHARA MOTEL
■ **66666 E. Sixth St.** **(619) 329-6666**
Desert Hot Springs, CA 92240 **MH**
No credit cards accepted.

#441J SANDPIPER INN & SPA
■ **12800 Foxdale Dr.** **(619) 329-6455**
Desert Hot Springs, CA 92240 **MH**
No credit cards accepted.

#441K SAN JACINTO MOTEL
□ 12561 Palm Dr. (619) 329-5258
Desert Hot Springs, CA 92240 MH
No credit cards accepted.

#441L SAN MARCUS MOTEL
□ 66540 San Marcus Rd. (619) 329-5304
Desert Hot Springs, CA 92240 MH
No credit cards accepted.

#441M SKYLINER SPA
■ **12840 Inaja St.** **(619) 329-3031**
Desert Hot Springs, CA 92240 **MH**
No credit cards accepted.

#441N SONESTA INN
■ **13355 Palm Dr.** **(619) 329-5539**
Desert Hot Springs, CA 92240 **MH**
Visa, MasterCard and Carte Blanche accepted.

#441O SPA TOWN HOUSE MOTEL
□ 66540 E. Sixth St. (619) 329-6014
Desert Hot Springs, CA 92240 MH
No credit cards accepted.

#441P STARDUST MOTEL
■ **66634 Fifth St.** **(619) 329-5443**
Desert Hot Springs, CA 92240 **MH**
No credit cards accepted.

#441Q STRAW HAT LODGE
□ 66365 Seventh St. (619) 329-6269
Desert Hot Springs, CA 92240 MH
No credit cards accepted.

#441R SUNSET INN
■ **67585 Hacienda Ave.** **(619) 329-4488**
Desert Hot Springs, CA 92240 **PR + MH**
Open to public for day rate spa use. Restaurant and bar on the premises.
Visa, MasterCard and American Express accepted.

#441S TAMARIX SPA MOTEL
□ 66185 Acoma (619) 329-6615
Desert Hot Springs, CA 92240 MH
Visa and MasterCard accepted.

#441T TRADE WINDS
■ **11021 Sunset Ave.** **(619) 329-9102**
Desert Hot Springs, CA 92240 **MH**
Visa and MasterCard accepted.

#441U TRAMVIEW LODGE
■ **11149 Sunset Ave.** **(619) 329-6751**
Desert Hot Springs, CA 92240 **MH**
No credit cards accepted.

#441V TROPICAL MOTEL & SPA
■ **12962 Palm Dr.** **(619) 329-6610**
Desert Hot Springs, CA 92240 **MH**
Visa and MasterCard accepted.

#441W WALDORF HEALTH RESORT
■ **11190 Mesquite Ave.** **(619) 329-6491**
Desert Hot Springs, CA 92240 **MH**
Visa and MasterCard accepted.

#441X WHITE HOUSE SPA-TEL
■ **11285 Mesquite Ave.** **(619) 329-7125**
Desert Hot Springs, CA 92240 **MH**
Visa and MasterCard accepted.

RV AND MOBILE HOME RESORTS NEAR DESERT HOT SPRINGS

All of the establishments listed below are in or near the city of Desert Hot Springs at an elevation of 1,200 ft. and are open all year.

Unless otherwise noted, all of them pump natural hot mineral water from their own wells and provide at least one chlorine-treated hydropool, where bathing suits are required. A store, restaurant and service station are within five miles of all locations.

Take the Desert Hot Springs exit from I-10, north of Palm Springs, and phone for further directions if necessary.

#442A AMERICAN ADVENTURE

■ **70405 Dillon Rd.** **(619) 329-5371**
Desert Hot Springs, CA 92240 **CRV**

A family-oriented membership recreation resort, not open to the public for drop-in visits, but willing to issue guest passes to prospective members. Facilities include one swimming pool, three hydropools and a sauna. No credit cards accepted.

American Adventure: This mini-golf course is part of an amusement park atmosphere, with modern music coming out of the pool loudspeakers at all times.

#442B CORKHILL RV AND MOBILE HOME PARK

■ **17989 Corkhill Rd.** **(619) 329-5976**
Desert Hot Springs, CA 92240 **CRV**

Older RV park with all pools enclosed and covered. There is one swimming pool, one hydropool, one soaking pool and one cold pool. No credit cards accepted.

#442C DESERT HOT SPRINGS TRAILER PARK

■ **66434 W. 5th** **(619) 329-6041**
Desert Hot Springs, CA 92240 **CRV**

Older trailer park within the city limits. No credit cards accepted.

Palm Drive Trailer Court: These residents devote an hour each weekday morning to an extensive program of vigorous exercises. The entire fitness routine is conducted in a soaking pool, led by the resident manager.

#442D MIRACLE MANOR

■ **17325 Johnson Rd.** **(619) 329-1384**
Desert Hot Springs, CA 92240

Older mobile and RV park, with overnighters welcome. Outdoor swimming pool. No credit cards accepted.

#442E DESERT VIEW ADULT MOBILE PARK

■ **18555 Roberts Rd.** **(619) 329-7079**
Desert Hot Springs, CA 92240 **CRV**

Strictly a mobile park, with no RV's and no overnighters. Outdoor swimming pool and two indoor hydropools. No credit cards accepted.

#442F GOLDEN LANTERN MOBILE VILLAGE

■ **17300 Corkhill Rd.** **(619) 329-6633**
Desert Hot Springs, CA 92240 **CRV**

Recently expanded park, with one outdoor swimming pool and three enclosed soaking pools. Mobile spaces, RV hookups and overnight spaces available. There is a restaurant, store and service station next door. No credit cards accepted.

#442G HOLMES HOT SPRINGS MOBILE PARK

■ **69530 Dillon Rd.** **(619) 329-7934**
Desert Hot Springs, CA 92240 **CRV**

Older RV park, with one outdoor swimming pool and one outdoor soaking pool. RV hookups and overnight spaces available. No credit cards accepted.

#442H MAGIC WATERS MOBILE HOME PARK

□ 17551 Mt. View Rd. (619) 329-2600
Desert Hot Springs, CA 92240 CRV

Older mobile home park. Gas-heated well water is used in an outdoor swimming pool and an indoor hydropool. Mobile spaces, RV hookups and overnight spaces available. No credit cards accepted.

#442I MOUNTAIN VIEW MOBILE HOME PARK

■ **125525 Mt. View Rd.** **(619) 329-5870**
Desert Hot Springs, CA 92240 **CRV**

Modern mobile park with one outdoor swimming pool and one enclosed hydropool. Also men's and women's saunas. Mobile spaces, RV hookups and overnight spaces available. No credit cards accepted.

#442J PALM DRIVE TRAILER COURT

■ **14881 Palm Dr.** **(619) 329-8341**
Desert Hot Springs, CA 92240 **CRV**

Older trailer court with two soaking pools and one hydropool, open 24 hours. Mobile spaces, RV hookups and overnight spaces available. No credit cards accepted.

#442K ROYAL FOX RV PARK

14500 Palm Dr. **(619) 329-4481**
Desert Hot Springs, CA 92240 **CRV**

Large new RV facility, operated as part of the Royal Fox Inn complex. A swimming pool, two hydropools, steam baths and two saunas are available to registered guests in the RV park as well as to motel guests. RV hookups are equipped with instant telephone connections through the motel switchboard.

Visa, MasterCard and American Express are accepted.

Sam's Family Spa: This is one of the first multi- purpose spas, offering motel rooms in addition to RV spaces.

#442L SAM'S FAMILY SPA

70875 Dillon Rd. **(619) 329-6457**
Desert Hot Springs, CA 92240 **PR + *MH* + CRV**

One of the largest multi-service resorts in the area with all facilities open to the public for day use as well as to registered guests. The outdoor swimming pool uses chlorinated mineral water, but the children's wading pool and four covered hydropools use flow-through mineral water which requires no chemical treatment.

Facilities include a co-ed sauna, motel rooms, restaurant, RV hookups, overnight spaces, store, laundromat, children's playground and gymnasium. No credit cards accepted.

The central pool complex at *Sam's Family Spa* includes these four unchlorinated mineral pools, which offer various temperatures ranging from 95° to 106°.

Sands RV Country Club: When you live on the grounds of an upscale resort, why not have the benefit of an upscale golf cart?

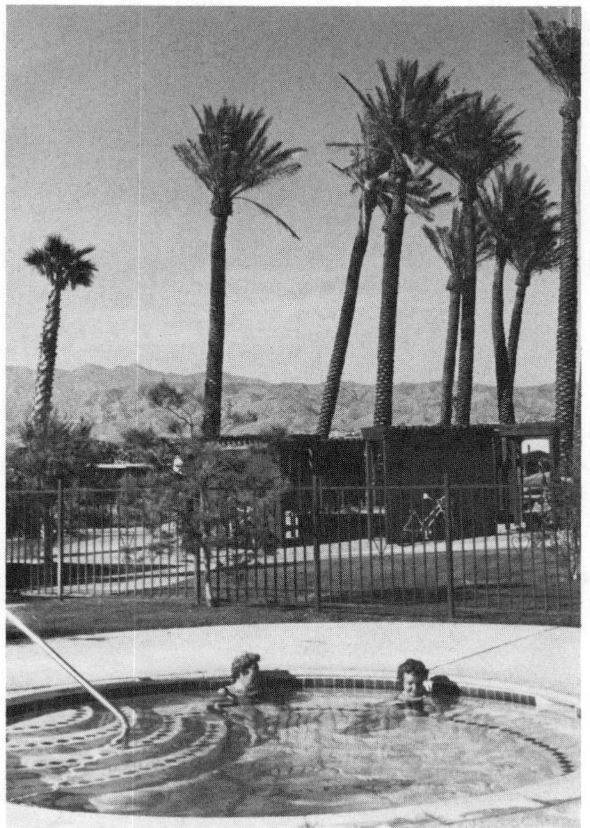

Unfortunately, the *Sands RV Country Club* did not hit a hot well, so all pools have chlorinated tap water. Most patrons don't notice the difference, or don't care.

#442 M SANDS RV COUNTRY CLUB

☐ 16400 Bubbling Wells Rd. (619) 251-1030
Desert Hot Springs, CA 92240

Large new RV resort, open to the public for day use as well as to registered guests. Gas-heated tap water, chlorine treated, is used in the outdoor swimming pool and the outdoor hydropool. Facilities include a co-ed sauna, golf course, RV hookups and overnight spaces. Visa and MasterCard are accepted.

Sky Valley Park: This easternmost resort on Dillon road has built a reputation for beautiful landscaping and customer comfort.

#442N SKY VALLEY PARK

74565 Dillon Rd. (619) 329-7415
Desert Hot Springs, CA 92240

Large, modern, landscaped mobile home and RV park. There are two outdoor swimming pools, one outdoor hydropool, two enclosed hydropools and one indoor hydropool. Facilities include men's and women's saunas, mobile spaces, RV hookups and overnight spaces. No credit cards accepted.

Sky Valley East: This extensive new addition has an even more spacious pool, patio and recreation building complex.

Separate rules are posted for each of the two separate pool areas; an arrangement appreciated by both children and seniors.

#442O SKY VALLEY EAST

74711 Dillon Rd. (619) 329-2909
Desert Hot Springs, CA 92240

Large new addition to Sky Valley Park. One swimming pool, an outdoor hydropool and an enclosed hydropool are on a separate patio reserved for adults. An adjoining patio contains an outdoor swimming pool and outdoor hydropool designed for family use. Facilities include men's and women's saunas, mobile spaces, RV hookups and overnight spaces. No credit cards accepted.

The creative use of old telephone poles at both *Sky Valley* parks relieves the starkness of desert sand and patio cement.

ADULT POOL RULES
SHOWER BEFORE SWIMMING.
PERSONS OVER 17 YEARS ONLY IN ADULT POOLS
NO SMOKING IN POOLS
NO FOOD OR ALCOHOLIC BEVERAGES IN POOL AREA
WEAR SWIM SUITS ONLY
NO GLASS CONTAINERS
POOL HOURS
8 AM-10 PM DAILY 8 AM-11 PM WEEK-ENDS
VIOLATORS OF THESE RULES WILL BE ASKED TO LEAVE
SKY VALLEY EAST

FAMILY POOL RULES
SHOWER BEFORE SWIMMING.
NO FOOD OR ALCOHOLIC BEVERAGES IN POOL AREA.
NO SMOKING IN POOLS.
NO CHILDREN UNDER AGE 2 IN ANY POOL.
NO SPLASHING *in* THERAPY POOLS.
POOL HOURS
8 AM-10 PM DAILY 8 AM-11 PM WEEK-ENDS
VIOLATORS OF THESE RULES WILL BE ASKED TO LEAVE
SKY VALLEY EAST

#442P WAGNER MOBILE HOME VILLAGE

18801 Roberts (619) 329-6043
Desert Hot Springs, CA 92240

Older mobile park, with one outdoor swimming pool, one indoor hydropool and two indoor cold pools. Mobile spaces and RV hookups are available. No overnighters. No credit cards accepted.

#443 ☐ **JOSHUA'S TRAILER VILLAGE**
on Hwy 62 — (619) 366-2210
Joshua Tree, CA 92252 — Hydropool CRV

#444A ☐ **BREEZE LAKES RV PARK**
on Manzanita Rd. — (714) 845-5919
Beaumont, CA 92223 — Hydropool CRV

#444B ☐ **EL RANCHO BROOKSIDE**
on Brookside Ave. — (714) 795-2524
Cherry Valley, CA 92223 — Hydropool CRV

#445 ☐ **HOLIDAY MOBILE RANCH**
on County Line Rd. — (714) 795-3616
Yucaipa, CA 92399 — Hydropool CRV

#446 ☐ **THUNDER CLOUD LODGE**
P.O. Box 1773 — (714) 866-4543
Big Bear Lake, CA 92315 — Hydropool MH

#447A ☐ **LAKE ARROWHEAD HILTON LODGE**
P.O. Box 1669 — (619) 337-8577
Lake Arrowhead, CA 92352 — Health Spa MH

#447B ☐ **ARROWHEAD HEALTH AND FITNESS RETREAT**
P.O. Box 417 — (619) 337-8577
Lake Arrowhead, CA 92352 — Hydropool MH

Deep Creek Hot Springs: One of the ten most beautiful hot springs in the West—worth every step of the gentle six-mile trail or the steep two-mile trail.

#448 DEEP CREEK HOT SPRINGS

● **near the town of Hesperia** **(see map)**
non-commercial

Beautiful remote springs on the south bank of Deep Creek, at the bottom of a spectacular canyon in the San Bernardino National Forest. Elevation 3,000 ft. Open all year.

Natural mineral water flows out of several rock fissures at 108°, directly into volunteer-built rock and sandbag soaking pools at the edge of Deep Creek, which flows all year. Water temperature in any one pool will depend on the amount of creek water admitted. The apparent local custom is clothing optional.

There are no services and overnight camping is not permitted in the canyon near the springs. It is six miles by an all-year trail to a forest service campground. There is also a steep 2½-mile trail down the north side of the canyon from Bowen Ranch, where a fee is charged for admission to the ranch, and for overnight parking. Note: the trail from Bowen Ranch ends on the north bank of Deep Creek, which runs so high during spring run-off that it is not safe to try to ford. From either campground it is ten miles to a store, restaurant, service station, etc.

Source maps: *San Bernardino National Forest.* USGS *Lake Arrowhead.*

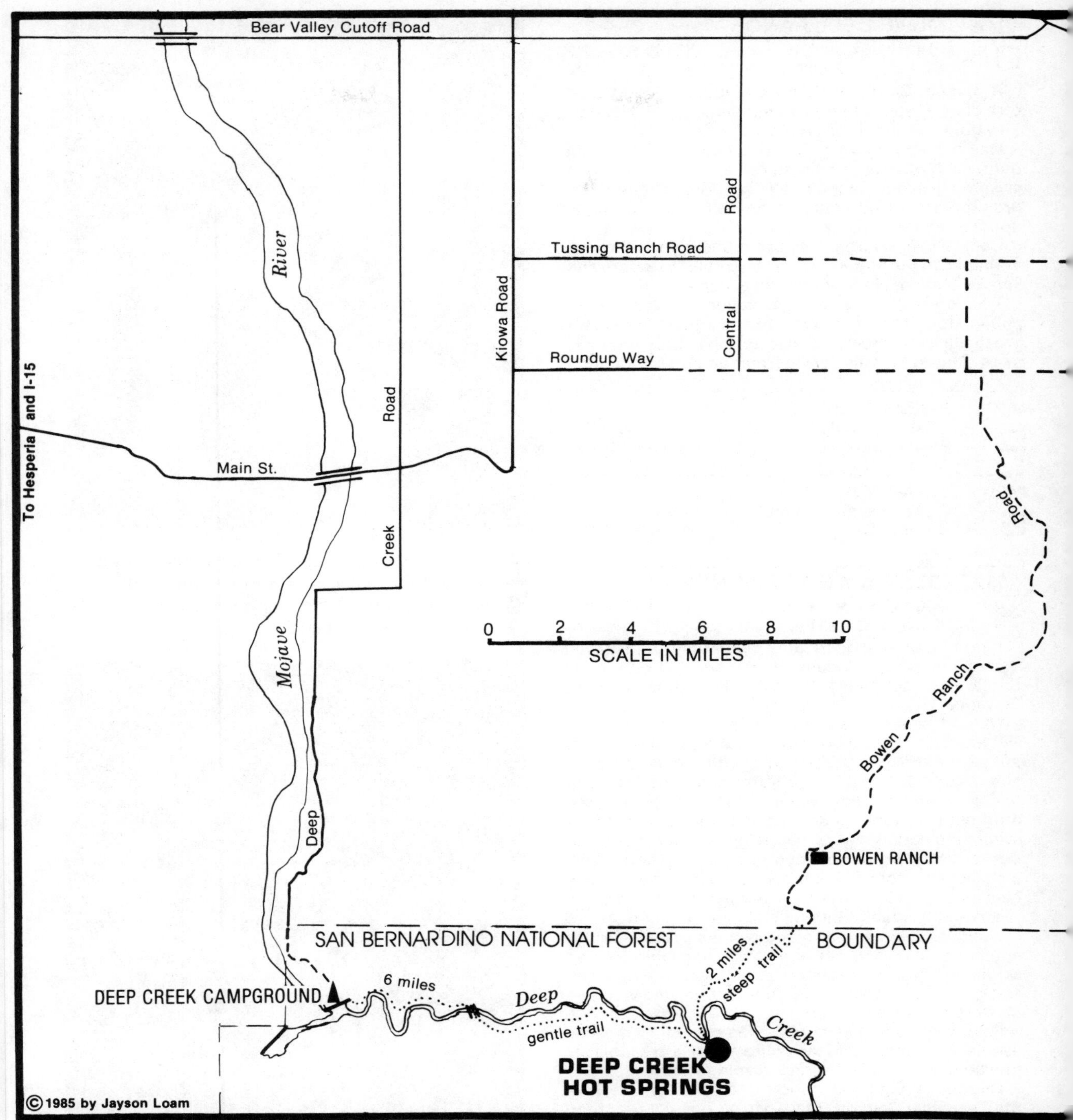
Bear Valley Cutoff Road
River
Mojave
Deep
Creek
Road
Kiowa Road
Tussing Ranch Road
Roundup Way
Central
Road
To Hesperia and I-15
Main St.
0 2 4 6 8 10
SCALE IN MILES
Road
Ranch
Bowen
BOWEN RANCH
SAN BERNARDINO NATIONAL FOREST BOUNDARY
DEEP CREEK CAMPGROUND
6 miles
Deep
gentle trail
2 miles
steep trail
Creek
DEEP CREEK HOT SPRINGS
© 1985 by Jayson Loam

#449 OLIVE DELL RANCH

☐ Rte. 1, Box 393 (714) 825-6619
Colton, CA 92324 PR + MH + CRV

A pioneer Southern California nudist park, located on a dry and sunny hilltop 60 miles east of Los Angeles. Elevation 1,000 ft. Open all year.

Gas-heated well water, chlorine treated, is used in an outdoor hydropool maintained at 105°, and in a swimming pool maintained at 75°. Clothing is prohibited in the pools and in the main recreation area, optional elsewhere.

Cabins, cafe, overnight camping and RV hookups are available on the premises. It is three miles to a store and service station. No credit cards accepted.

This is a membership organization not open to the public for drop-in visits, but a guest pass for prospective members is available by prior arrangement. Phone or write for information and directions.

#450 RIVERSIDE INN

☐ 1150 University Ave. (714) 682-2771
Riverside, CA 92507 Hydropool MH

#451 GLEN IVY RV RESORT

☐ on Temescal Canyon Rd. (714) 737-4261
Corona, CA 91720 Hydropool RV

#452 GLEN IVY HOT SPRINGS

■ **2500 Glen Ivy Road (714) 737-4712**
Corona, CA 91719 PR

Large, well equipped and beautifully landscaped day-use resort spa, located on the dry east side of the Santa Ana mountains, 70 miles from Los Angeles, Elevation 700 ft. Open all year.

Natural mineral water is pumped from two wells at 90° and 110°, and piped to a wide variety of pools. There are seven sunken hydrojet tubs with temperatures of 104° to 106°, using continuous flow-through unchlorinated mineral water. The other pools have automatic filters and chlorinators. An outdoor swimming pool is maintained at 85°, a covered soaking pool at 103°, two outdoor hydropools at 101° and 106°, a shallow outdoor floating pool at 100° and a red clay bath pool at 100°. The hydrojet pools are in a patio reserved for adults. Bathing suits are required.

Facilities include men's and women's locker rooms equipped with hair blowers, a suntanning table, a co-ed sauna and a cafe. Massage, herbal blanket wraps and salt glow rub are available on the premises. Visa and MasterCard are accepted.

During the summer months some evening musical events are planned and the entire resort is available for private group charter during evening hours.

Directions: Eight miles south of Corona, on I-15, take the Temescal Canyon Road exit, go one mile south to Glen Ivy Road, turn west and go one mile to resort at end of road.

Glen Ivy Hot Springs: The snack bar can be seen at the other end of the all-weather soaking pool (above). The sunken roman tubs (below) have jets and unchlorinated water.

The whisper of a sparkling fountain sets the tone for this new addition to *Glen Ivy's* multi-purpose pools.

Glen Ivy's famous red clay is to be smeared on with vigor, then allowed to dry, so it will crack, tickle and clean out the pores.

PLEASE
SHOWER
NO

Glen Eden Sun Club: The showers, restaurant and recreation room are to the left of the pools, with game courts uphill to the right.

453 GLEN EDEN SUN CLUB

□ P.O. Box 641 (714) 734-4650
Corona, CA 91720

Large, well-equipped traditional nudist park, located on the dry side of the Santa Ana mountains, 70 miles from Los Angeles. Elevation 700 ft. Open all year.

Gas-heated well water is used in an outdoor hydropool maintained at 105° and indoor soaking pool maintained at 85°. The solar-heated swimming pool averages 75° from May to November. All pools have automatic filters and chlorinators. Bathing suits are prohibited in the pools. There is no requirement of full nudity regardless of weather conditions, but posted signs state that individual dress is expected to conform to that of the majority at any given time.

Facilities include tennis and volleyball courts, sauna, restaurant, RV hookups, overnight spaces and recreation rooms. Visa and MasterCard are accepted. It is eight miles to a motel, store and service station.

This is a membership organization not open to the public for drop-in visits, but prospective members may be issued a guest pass by prior arrangement. Telephone or write for information and directions.

#454A JO-RAY MOTEL

■ **316 N. Main (714) 674-9997**
Lake Elsinore, CA 92330 PR MH

Older motel and spa located several blocks north of downtown Lake Elsinore. Elevation 1,300 ft. Open all year.

Natural mineral water flows out of an artesian well at 100° and is the piped to three pools and to the bathtubs in all rooms. The outdoor swimming pool is maintained at 104°. All pools are chlorine treated, and are available to the public as well as to registered guests. Bathing suits are required.

Facilities include sauna and recreation room. Massage is available on the premises. Visa and MasterCard are accepted. It is five blocks to a restaurant, store and service station.

#454B HAN'S MOTEL AND MINERAL SPA

■ **215 W. Graham (714) 674-3511**
Lake Elsinore, CA 92330 MH

An older motel in downtown Lake Elsinore. Elevation 1,300 ft. Open all year.

Natural mineral water flows out of an artesian well at 120° and is piped to two pools and to the bathtubs in every room. The outdoor swimming pool is maintained at 86° and the indoor hydropool is maintained at 105°. The water in both pools is chlorine treated and bathing suits are required.

Visa and MasterCard are accepted. It is two blocks to a restaurant, store and service station.

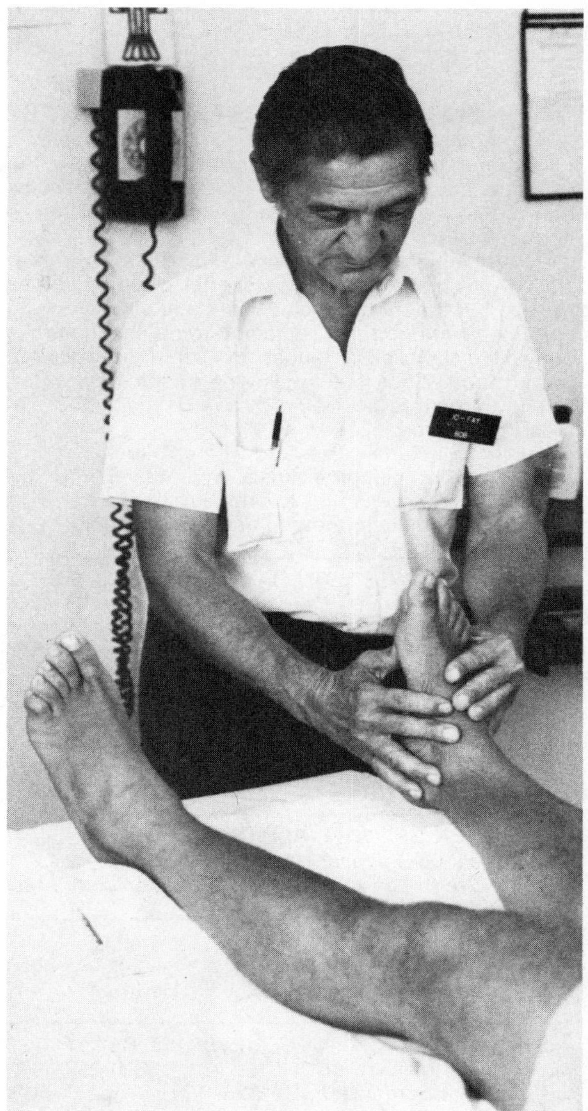

Jo-Ray Motel: When a body needs more than just a hot bath, it's time for a massage.

#455 SAN JUAN CAPISTRANO HOT SPRINGS

■ **P.O. Box 58** **(714) 728-0400**
San Juan Capistrano, CA,92693 **PR CRV**

A unique combination of outdoor redwood hot tubs, natural mineral water and pastoral setting under the trees. Located on the Ortega Highway (Cal 74) 13 miles east of San Juan Capistrano. Elevation 800 ft. Open 24 hours all year.

Natural mineral water flows out of several springs at 125° and is piped to 16 widely scattered redwood tubs rented by the hour each with its own automatic chlorinator and jets. Water temperature in each tub is controlled by using faucet to admit the desired proportions of hot mineral water and cold well water. Bathing suits are advisable during daylight hours in most of the tubs.

Facilities include men's and women's locker rooms and overnight camping. Visa and MasterCard are accepted. It is seven miles to a restaurant, store and RV hookups; 12 miles to a motel and service station.

#456A BEST WESTERN DAVIS MOTOR LODGE
□ 34862 Pacific Coast Hwy (714) 756-2200
San Juan Capistrano, CA 92616
Hydropool MH

#456B BEST WESTERN CAPISTRANO INN
□ 27171 Ortega Hwy (714) 438-5661
San Juan Capistrano, CA 92675
Hydropool MH

#457A BEN BROWN'S ALISO CREEK INN
□ 31106 S. Coast Hwy. (714) 499-2271
South Laguna, CA 92677 Hydropool MH

#457B VACATION VILLAGE
□ 647 S. Coast Hwy. (714) 494-8566
Laguna Beach, CA 92652 Hydropool MH

#458A SHERATON INN — NEWPORT BEACH
□ 434 MacArthur Blvd. (714) 833-0570
Newport Beach, CA 92660 Hydropool MH

#458B NEWPORTER INN
□ 1107 Jamboree Rd. (714) 644-1700
Newport Beach, CA 92660 Hydropool RV

#458C COMFORT INN
□ 2430 Newport Blvd. (714) 631-7840
Costa Mesa, CA 92626 Hydropool MH

#458D AMBASSADOR INN
□ 2277 Harbor Blvd. (714) 645-4840
Costa Mesa, CA 92626 Hydropool MH

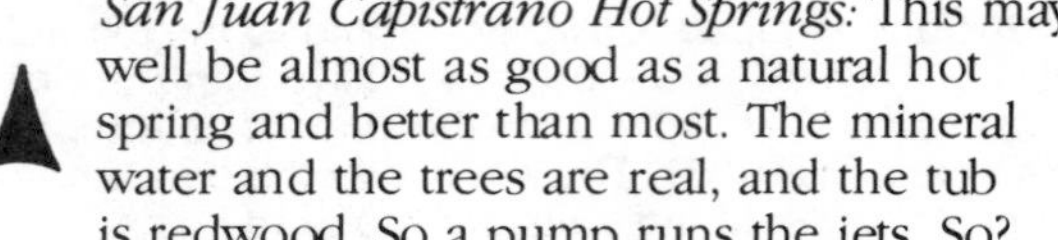

San Juan Capistrano Hot Springs: This may well be almost as good as a natural hot spring and better than most. The mineral water and the trees are real, and the tub is redwood. So a pump runs the jets. So?

#459A THE REGISTRY HOTEL
18800 MacArthur Blvd. (714) 752-8777
Irvine, CA 92715 Hydropool MH

#459B BEST WESTERN IRVINE HOST MOTOR HOTEL
1717 E. Dyer Rd. (714) 540-1515
Irvine, CA 92705 Hydropool MH

#460A BEACHTOWN MOTEL
4201 E. Pacific Coast Hwy. (213) 597-7701
Long Beach, CA 90804 Hydropool MH

#460B HYATT LONG BEACH
6400 E. Pacific Coast Hwy. (213) 434-8451
Long Beach, CA 90803 Hydropool MH

#461A AMBASSADOR INN—SANTA ANA
939 E. 17th St. (714) 558-9231
Santa Ana, CA 92701 Hydropool MH

#461B AMBASSADOR INN—SOUTH COAST PLAZA
2900 S. Brison St. (714) 540-2300
Santa Ana, CA 92704 Hydropool MH

#461C RAMADA INN
1600 E. First St. (714) 835-3051
Santa Ana, CA 92701 Hydropool MH

#461D BEST WESTERN EL CAMINO INN
3191 N. Tustin (714) 998-0360
Orange, CA 92665 Hydropool MH

#461E ORANGELAND RECREATION VEHICLE PARK
on Struck Ave. (714) 633-0414
Orange, CA 92667 Hydropool CRV

#461G CONCORD INN
1111 S. Harbor Blvd. (714) 533-8830
Anaheim, CA 92805 Hydropool MH

#461H HOWARD JOHNSON'S MOTOR LODGE
1380 S. Harbor Blvd. (714) 776-6120
Anaheim, CA 92805 Hydropool MH

#461I JOLLY ROGER INN
640 W. Katella Ave. (714) 772-7621
Anaheim, CA 92802 Hydropool MH

#461J RAMADA INN - ANAHEIM/DISNEYLAND
1331 E. Katella Ave. (714) 978-8088
Anaheim, CA 92805 Hydropool MH

#461K SAGE MOTOR INN
1650 S. Harbor Blvd. (714) 772-0440
Anaheim, CA 92802 Hydropool MH

#461L SANDMAN INN - HARBOR
921 S. Harbor Blvd. (714) 956-5730
Anaheim, CA 92805 Hydropool MH

#461M SANDMAN INN - KATELLA
1800 E. Katella Ave. (714) 634-9121
Anaheim, CA 92805 Hydropool MH

#461N ANAHEIM HARBOR INN TRAVELODGE
2171 S. Harbor Blvd. (714) 750-3100
Anaheim, CA 92802 Hydropool MH

#461O ANAHEIM PARK MOTOR LODGE
915 S. West St. (714) 778-0350
Anaheim, CA 92802 Hydropool MH

#461P THE ANAHEIM MARRIOTT
700 W. Convention Way (714) 750-8000
Anaheim, CA 92802 Hydropool MH

#461Q ANAHEIM STADIUM TRAVELODGE
1700 E. Katella Ave. (714) 774-7817
Anaheim, CA 92805 Hydropool MH

#461R BEST WESTERN GALAXY MOTEL
1735 S. Harbor Blvd. (714) 772-1520
Anaheim, CA 92802 Hydropool MH

#461S BEST WESTERN INN OF TOMORROW
1110 W. Katella Ave. (714) 778-1880
Anaheim, CA 92805 Hydropool MH

#461T COMFORT INN
2200 S. Harbor Blvd. (714) 750-5211
Anaheim, CA 92802 Hydropool MH

#461U MIDWAY TRAILER CITY
on Midway Dr. (714) 774-3860
Anaheim, CA 92805 Hydropool CRV

#461V CAVALIER MOTOR LODGE
11811 Harbor Blvd. (714) 750-1000
Buena Park, CA 92640 Hydropool MH

#461W QUALITY INN - BUENA PARK
7555 Beach Blvd. (714) 522-7360
Buena Park, CA 90620 Hydropool MH

#462 LA VIDA MINERAL SPRINGS

■ **6155 Carbon Canyon Road (714) 528-7861**
Brea, CA 92621 PR + MH

Primarily a motel spa with some outdoor pools open to the public for day use during the summer months. Located in the rural foothills of northern Orange County. Elevation 700 ft. Open all year.

Natural mineral water flows out of a spring at 120° and is piped to the bath house and pools. The outdoor swimming pool uses chlorine-treated mineral water and averages 80°. The outdoor hydropool also used chlorine-treated mineral water and averages 103°. In the bath house there are separate men's and women's sections, each containing eight sunken tile tubs and a sauna. These tubs are drained and cleaned after each use so no chemical water treatment is needed. Bathing suits are required except in the bath house.

Massage, rooms, a cafe and a bar are available on the premises. No credit cards accepted. It is one mile to a store, three miles to a service station and ten miles to RV hookups.

Directions: From the town of Brea, go seven miles northwest on CAI 142 and watch for signs at the location on the west side of the road.

#463A BEST WESTERN UPLANDER MOTOR HOTEL
☐ 81 W. Foothill Blvd. (714) 982-8821
Upland, CA 91786 Hydropool MH

#463B BEST WESTERN ONTARIO AIRPORT MOTEL
☐ 209 N. Vineyard Ave. (714) 983-9600
Ontario, CA 91764 Hydropool MH

#463C SAMOA MOBILE HOME VILLAGE NO. 2
☐ on Sultana Ave. (714) 983-8318
Ontario, CA 91751 Hydropool RV

#464A GRANADA ROYALE HOMOTEL
☐ 1211 E. Garvey (213) 915-3441
Covina, CA 91724 Hydropool MH

#464B EL DORADO MOTOR INN
☐ 140 N. Azusa Ave. (213) 331-6371
West Covina, CA 91791 Hydropool MH

#464C INDUSTRY HILLS SHERATON RESORT
☐ One Industry Pkwy. (714) 965-0861
Industry, CA 91744 Hydropool MH

#465A VAGABOND MOTOR HOTEL
☐ 3633 N. Rosemead Blvd. (213) 288-6661
Rosemead, CA 91770 Hydropool MH

#465B BEST WESTERN PASADENA INN
☐ 3570 E. Colorado Blvd. (213) 796-9100
Pasadena, CA 91107 Hydropool MH

#466A BEST WESTERN GOLDEN KEY HOTEL
☐ 136 S. Orange St. (213) 247-6111
Glendale, CA 91204 Hydropool MH

#466B SAFARI INN
☐ 1911 W. Olive Ave. (213) 845-8586
Burbank, CA 91506 Hydropool MH

Splash - The Relaxation Spa: Funky old wood tubs are definitely out and vivid decorator designs are in, in the city.

#467A SPLASH - THE RELAXATION SPA

☐ 8054 W. 3rd St. (213) 653-4410
Los Angeles, CA 90048 PR

The most elaborate rent-a tub facility in the Los Angeles area, located two miles south of Hollywood.

Pools for rent to the public, using gas-heated tap water, treated with bromine.

18 private rooms, rented by the hour. Water temperature 96° to 104° with poolside control by the customer plus a cold-spray mist.

Special features: special suites offering fill and drain tubs in which soap and shampoo may be used, or eucalyptus steam, or private bathroom, or sauna. Fantasy suites have a party-size hot tub with sauna, steam room, wet bar, fireplace, video unit and waterfall.

Services available: juice bar, limousine pick-up.

Credit cards accepted: Visa, MasterCard and American Express.

Phone for rates, reservations and directions.

#467B RAMADA INN HOLLYWOOD
☐ 1160 N. Vermont Ave. (213) 660-1788
Los Angeles, CA 90029
Hydropool on each floor MH

#467C FRANKLIN PLAZA MOTEL
☐ 7230 Franklin Ave. (213) 874-7450
Los Angeles, CA 90046 Hydropool MH

#467D THE WESTIN BONAVENTURE
☐ 350 S. Figueroa St. (213) 624-1000
Los Angeles, CA 90071 Health Clubl MH

#467E THE UNIVERSITY HILTON
☐ 3540 S. Figueroa St. (213) 748-4141
Los Angeles, CA 90007 Hydropool MH

#467F BEST WESTERN EXECUTIVE MOTOR INN MID WILSHIRE
☐ 603 S. New Hampshire Ave. (213) 385-4444
Los Angeles, CA 90005 Hydropool MH

#467G AMBASSADOR HOTEL, TENNIS & HEALTH CLUB
☐ 3400 Wilshire Blvd. (213) 387-7011
Los Angeles, CA 90010 Health Spa MH

#467H SUNSET MARQUIS HOTEL & VILLAS
☐ 1200 N. Alta Loma Rd. (213) 657-1333
Los Angeles, CA 90046 Health Spa MH

#467I L'ERMITAGE HOTEL
☐ 9291 Burton Way (213) 278-3344
Beverly Hills, CA 90210 Hydropool MH

Splash—The Relaxation Spa: Early rental tubs were small and in small rooms. Now they are large, in large rooms, with many luxurious, recreation-oriented options.

#467J CLARK PLAZA HOTEL
☐ 141 S. Clark Dr. (213) 278-9310
Beverly Hills, CA 90048 Hydropool MH

#467K CENTURY PLAZA
☐ Avenue of the Stars (213) 277-2000
Los Angeles, CA 90067 Health Club MH

#468A SPLASH - THE RELAXATION SPA
☐ 10932 Santa Monica Blvd. (213) 479-4657
West Los Angeles, CA 90025 PR

The rent-a-tub establishment that pioneered poolside controls and other luxury options in the Los Angeles area. Located one mile south of the UCLA campus.

Pools for rent to the public, using gas-heated tap water, treated with bromine.

Five private rooms, rented by the hour. Water temperture 90° to 104° with poolside control by customer. Sauna, steam bath and cold-water mist included in each room.

Special features: Environmental habitat unit also available.

Services available: massage, limousine pick-up.

Credit cards accepted: Visa, MasterCard, American Express.

Phone for rates, reservations and directions.

#468B	WESTWOOD MARQUIS HOTEL 930 Hilgard Ave. Los Angeles, CA 90024	(213) 208-8765 Health Spa MH	☐
#468C	HOLIDAY INN WESTWOOD PLAZA HOTEL 10740 Wilshire Blvd. Los Angeles, CA 90024	(213) 475-8711 Hydropool MH	☐
#468D	BRENTWOOD MOTOR INN 199 North Church Lane Los Angeles, CA 90049	(213) 476-6255 Hydropool MH	☐
#468E	LOS ANGELES AIRPORT HILTON 5711 W. Century Blvd. Los Angeles, CA 90045	(213) 410-4000 Health Club MH	☐
#468F	HYATT LOS ANGELES AIRPORT 6225 W. Century Blvd. Los Angeles, CA 90045	(213) 670-9000 Health Club MH	☐
#468G	BEST WESTERN AIRPORT PARK HOTEL 600 Ave. of Champions Inglewood, CA 90301	(213) 623-5151 Hydropool MH	☐
#468H	HACIENDA HOTEL 525 N. Sepulveda Blvd. El Segundo, CA 90245	(213) 615-0015 Hydropool MH	☐
#468I	BEST WESTERN BARNABY'S 3501 Sepulveda Blvd. Manhattan Beach, CA 90266	(213) 545-8466 Hydropool MH	☐

Hot Tub Fever: Urban rent-a-tub facilities no longer try to provide a "natural" hot-spring atmosphere. Instead, the emphasis is on manufactured options, such as this hammock, which contribute to the comfort, convenience and pleasure of the customers.

Promotional material from *Hot Tub Fever* makes a point of encouraging older couples to enjoy a soak with romantic extras, such as real fireplaces. Special daytime rates are also available to senior groups.

#468J PACIFICA HOTEL
☐ 6161 Centinela Ave. (213) 649-1776
Culver City, CA 90231 Hydropool MH

#468K AMFAC HOTEL - LOS ANGELES
☐ 8601 Lincoln Blvd. (213) 670-8111
Los Angeles, CA 90045 Health Club MH

#469A HOT TUB FEVER
☐ 3131 Olympic Blvd. (213) 829-1737
Santa Monica, CA 90404 PR

The first rent-a-tub facility in the Los Angeles area, located near the boundary between the cities of Santa Monica and Los Angeles.

Pools for rent to the public, using gas-heated tap water, treated with chlorine.

13 private rooms rented by the hour. Water temperatures 98° - 102°, will adjust on request. Sauna included in all rooms.

Special features: Each of the two largest rooms also has a bathroom, fireplace, videocassette unit and steam bath.

Services available: massage, by appointment.

Credit cards accepted: Visa and MasterCard.

Phone for rates, reservations and directions.

#469B CLUB CARIBBEAN
☐ 2335 Lincoln Blvd. (213) 821-3113
Marina del Rey, CA 90291 PR

Basic rent-a-tub facilty, converted from motel buildings, located on a main street near Marina del Rey Harbor.

Pools for rent to the public, using gas-heated tap water, treated with chlorine.

14 private rooms rented by the hour. Water temperature 98°, will adjust on request.

Special features: Unique decorating themes and video movies available in some of the rooms.

Credit cards accepted: Visa, MasterCard and American Express.

Phone for rates, reservations and directions.

#469C BEST WESTERN JAMAICA INN
☐ 4175 Admiralty Way. (213) 823-5333
Marina Del Rey, CA 90266 Hydropool MH

#469D MARINA CITY CLUB RESORT HOTEL
☐ 4333 Admiralty Way (213) 822-0611
Marina Del Rey, CA 90291 Health Club MH

#469E MARINA DEL REY MARRIOTT INN
☐ Lincoln Blvd. (213) 822-8555
Marina Del Rey, CA 90291 Hydropool MH

#469F PACIFIC SHORE HOTEL
☐ 1819 Ocean Ave. (213) 451-8711
Santa Monica, CA 90401 Hydropool MH

#471A L.A. WATERWORKS

11739 Ventura Blvd. (818) 508-6001
Studio City, CA 91604 PR

New private-room rent-a-tub facility, located on a main street in the San Fernando Valley.

Pools for rent to the public, using gas-heated tap water treated with bromine.

Nine private rooms rented by the hour. Water temperatures 75 - 104°, will adjust on request. All rooms have a sauna, skylight, bathroom and cold-water mist. The two largest rooms also have a fireplace, bidet and closet. Videocassette units are available in some rooms.

Services available: juice bar, limousine pickup.

Phone for rates, reservations and directions.

L.A. Waterworks: An intriguing mixture of natural wood, green plants and skylight, with mirrors, chrome and fiberglass.

Elysium Institute: A psychotherapy session conducted by Dr. Al Freeman in the Elysium hydropool was part of a Tom Snyder *Tomorrow* show videotaped at the Institute.

#470 ELYSIUM INSTITUTE
814 Robinson Rd. (213) 455-1000
☐ Topanga, CA 90290

A ten-acre clothing-optional growth center, located in smog-free Topanga Canyon, 30 miles west of Los Angeles, Elevation: 1,000 ft. Open all year.

Gas-heated tap water, chlorine-treated is used in a large outdoor hydropool maintained at a temperature of 105°. Chlorine-treated tap water is also used in a solar-heated swimming pool. Clothing is not permitted in pools, optional elsewhere on the grounds.

This is a membership organization not open to the public for drop-in visits. Phone or write for a copy of the Elysium Journal, which describes all seminar programs and the procedure for obtaining an introductory guest pass.

Massage, sauna, tennis, volleyball, recreation room and educational/experimential workshops and seminars are available on the premises. Also a seasonal snack bar on weekends. No credit cards accepted. It is two miles to a store, cafe and service station, seven miles to a motel.

#471B SHERATON UNIVERSAL HOTEL
☐ 30 Universal City Plaza. (213) 980-1212
North Hollywood, CA 91608 Hydropool MH

#471C VALLEY TRAILER PARK
☐ on Lankershim Blvd. (213) 767-2983
North Hollywood, CA 91604 Hydropool CRV

#472 TRAVEL VILLAGE
☐ on Hwy 126 (805) 255-4222
Valencia, CA 91355 Hydropool CRV

#473 KOA - CASTAIC LAKE
☐ on Ridge Route Rd. (805) 257-3340
Castaic, CA 91310 Hydropool CRV

#474A BERMUDA INN REDUCING RESORT
☐ 43019 Sierra Hwy. (805) 942-1493
Lancaster, CA 93534 Hydropool MH

#474B THE ESSEX HOUSE
☐ 44916 10th St. W. (805) 948-0961
Lancaster, CA 93534 Hydropool MH

#474C SAND SAILER MOTOR HOTEL
☐ 43321 Sierra Hwy. (805) 948-2691
Lancaster, CA 93534 Hydropool MH

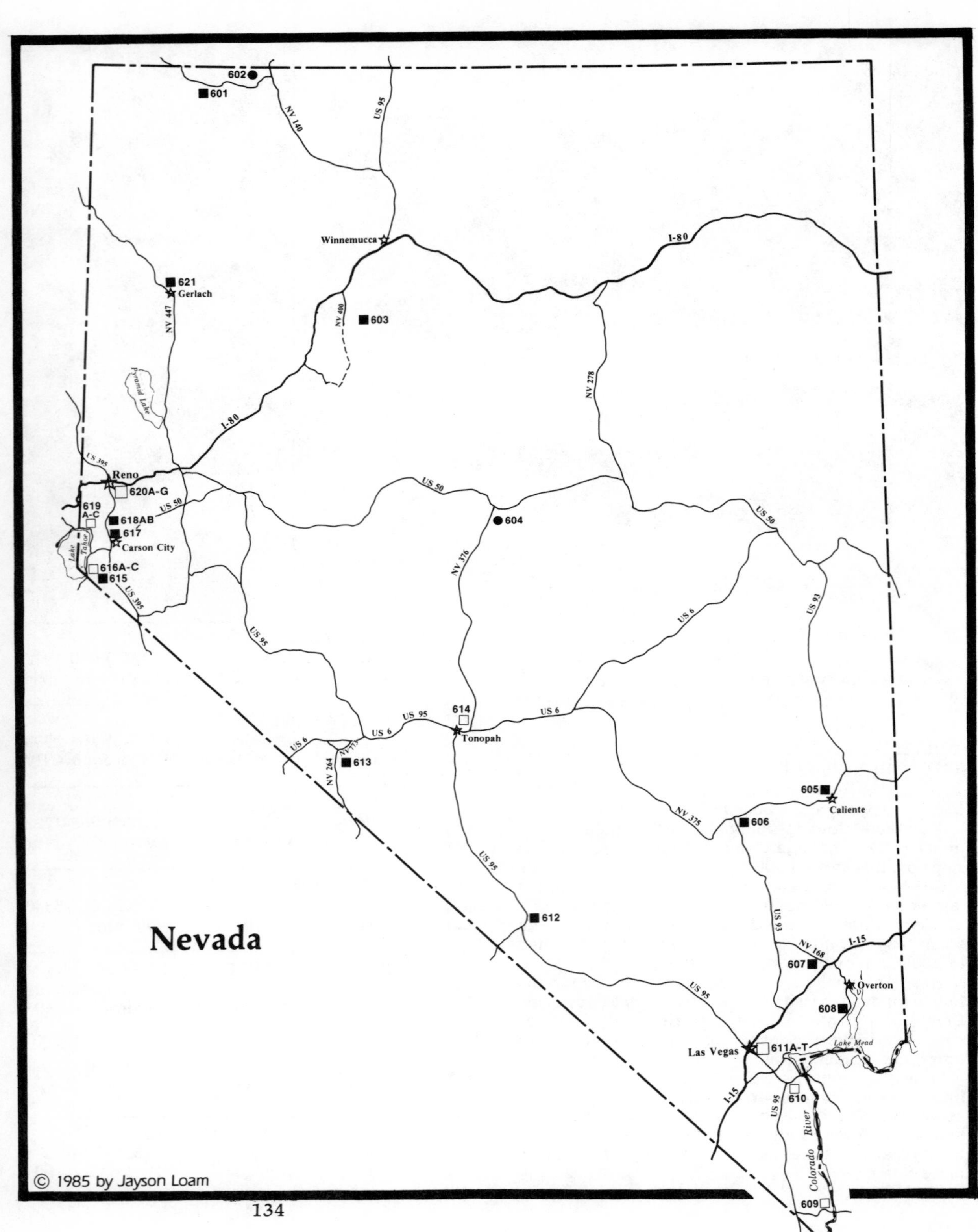
602
601
NV 140
US 95
Winnemucca
I-80
621
Gerlach
NV 447
NV 400
603
Pyramid Lake
NV 278
I-80
US 395
Reno
620A-G
US 50
619
A-C
618AB
617
Carson City
Lake Tahoe
616A-C
615
US 395
US 50
604
US 50
NV 376
US 6
US 93
US 95
614
US 95
US 6
US 6
Tonopah
US 6
NV 773
NV 264
613
605
Caliente
NV 375
606
US 95
612
US 93
Nevada
NV 168
I-15
607
Overton
US 95
608
Las Vegas
611A-T
Lake Mead
I-15
610
US 95
River
Colorado
609

MAP AND DIRECTORY SYMBOLS

- ● **Unimproved natural mineral water pool**
- ■ **Improved natural mineral water pool**
- □ Gas-heated tap or well water pool
- ——— Paved highway
- - - - Unpaved road
- ······ Hiking route

PR = Tubs or pools for rent by hour, day or treatment

MH = Rooms, cabins or dormitory spaces for rent by day, week or month

CRV = Camping or vehicle parking spaces, some with hookups, for rent by day, week, month or year

Virgin Valley Warm Springs: This is not the place for a hot soak but it is a lovely oasis surrounded by miles of wasteland.

#601 VIRGIN VALLEY WARM SPRING

in the Sheldon Wildlife Refuge

■

A charming gravel-bottom warm pond, with an old adobe bath house, in a small campground. Located in high desert foothills, near the Nevada-Oregon border. Elevation 5,100 ft. Open all year, subject to snow blockage on road.

Natural mineral water emerges up through the pond bottom, and is piped from other nearby springs, at 88°. The rate of flow maintains pond temperature at approximately 85°, depending on air temperature and wind speed. No chemical treatment is necessary. Bathing suits are required.

A continuous spring-fed shower at 88° is available in the bath house, and the campground is equipped with chemical toilets.

Directions: On NV 140, 24 miles west of Denio Junction and ten miles east of the Cedarville Road Junction, watch for a road sign, *Virgin Valley. Royal Peacock Mine.* Go south on gravel road 2.5 miles to campground.

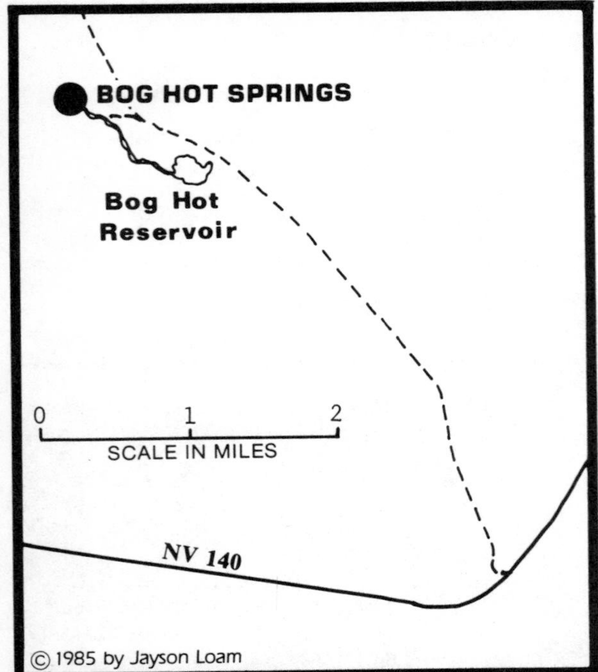

#602 BOG HOT SPRINGS (see map)

near the town of Denio

non-commercial

A large sand-bottom ditch carrying hot mineral water to an irrigation pond. Located on brush-covered flat land just below the Nevada-Oregon border. Elevation 4,300 ft. Open all year.

Natural mineral water flows out of several springs at 122°, is gathered into a single man-made channel, and gradually cools as it travels toward the reservoir. A dam with spillway pipe has been built at the point where the temperature is approximately 100°, depending on air temperature and wind speed. Around the dam, brush has been cleared away for easy access and nearby parking, but it is possible to soak in the ditch farther upstream if a warmer water temperature is desired. Clothing optional is probably the custom at this remote location.

There are no services available but there is an abundance of level space on which overnight parking is not prohibited.

It is seven miles to a restaurant, store, and service station, 18 miles to a motel and RV hookups.

Directions: From Denio Junction go west on NV 140 for 9.1 miles, then northwest 3.6 miles on a gravel road to the ditch.

#603 KYLE HOT SPRINGS

near the town of Winnemucca

non-commercial

Very funky soaking pit and steam bath built from scrap wood over a high sulphur hot spring on a barren mountainside. Elevation 4,500 ft. Open all year.

Natural mineral water flows out of the ground at 106° into a covered soaking pit. High sulphur content give the water a milky appearance and some sulphur dioxide odor. Another small shack has been built over a nearby steam vent, providing a limited steam bath effect. Clothing optional is probably the custom at this remote location.

There are no services available, but there is a limited amount of level space on which overnight parking is not prohibited. It is 18 miles to a store, restaurant and service station.

Directions: From Interstate 80, exit in Mill City onto NV 400 and go 16 miles south. Watch for *Kyle Hot Springs* sign, then go 11.2 miles east on a gravel road to the springs.

Bog Hot Springs: On a crisp fall morning, steam creates feathery frost on the weeds.

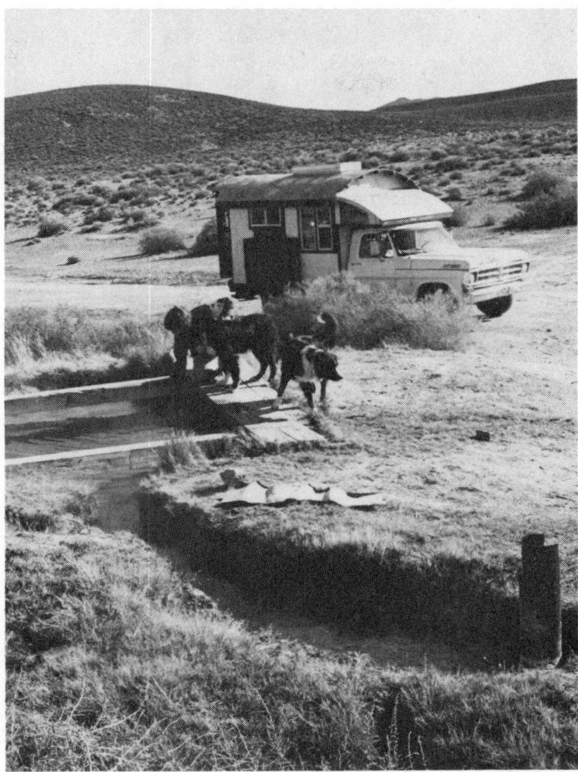

Spencer Hot Springs: The primitive control system, with a little trial and error, keeps the soaking pool comfortable

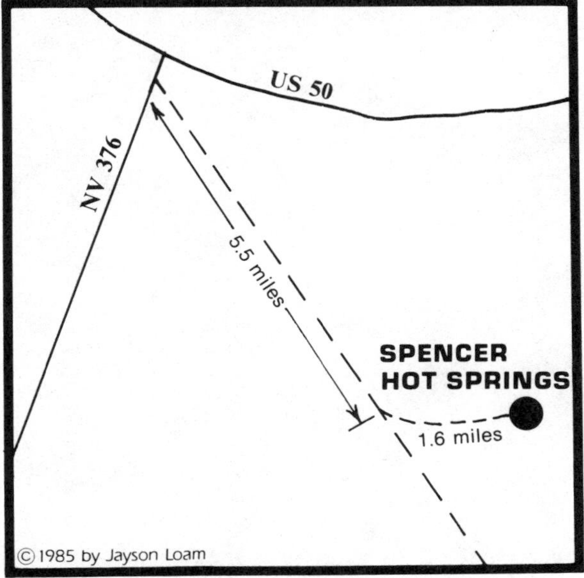

#604 SPENCER HOT SPRINGS (see map)

near the town of Austin

non- commercial

A small volunteer-built rock-and-sand soaking pool near a hot main spring. Located on a knoll overlooking barren desert foothills. Elevation 5,700 ft. Open all year.

Natural mineral water flows out of a spring at 122°, then through a shallow channel down the slope of the knoll. Volunteers have dug a small soaking pool next to this channel, and control the temperature in the pool by admitting only as much of the hotter water as is desired by those in the pool. Clothing optional is probably the custom at this remote location.

There are no services available. A man-made swimming pool was bulldozed and filled several years ago after an injury lawsuit against the Bureau of Land Management was filed and won. There is a limited amount of level space on which overnight parking is not prohibited.

Directions: From the intersection of US 50 and NV 376, go 100 yards south on NV 376, then go 5.5 miles southeast on a gravel road. Bear left on a dirt road which leads up to the hot-spring knoll.

#605 CALIENTE HOT SPRINGS MOTEL

Box 325 **(702) 726-3777**
Caliente, NV 89008 **MH**

Primarily a motel, with some hot-water facilities. Located on the edge of Caliente, 150 miles north of Las Vegas on US 93. Elevation 4,400 ft. Open all year.

Natural mineral water flows from a spring at 115° and is piped to swimming and soaking pools. An outdoor swimming pool (open May to October) uses chlorine-treated mineral water and averages 85°. There are three indoor family-size tiled soaking pools, in which hot mineral water and cold tap water may be mixed as desired by the customer. No chemical treatment is necessary because soaking pools are drained, cleaned and refilled after each use.

Bathing suits are required in the swimming pool, which is available only to registered guests in the motel. Soaking pools may be rented by the public on an hourly basis.

Rooms and RV spaces are available on the premises, and a hot mineral-water soak is included in the room rent. Visa and MasterCard are accepted. A restaurant, store and service station are within six blocks.

Directions: From the center of Caliente go ½ mile north on US 93. Watch for signs and entrance road on east side of highway.

#606 HUNT'S ASH SPRINGS

Box 11 **(702) 725-3362**
Ash Springs, NV 89017

A picture-postcard "Ye Olde Swimming Hole" filled with 86° natural mineral water, surrounded by barren desert foothills. Located 105 miles north of Las Vegas on US 93. Elevation 4,000 ft. Open all year, 24 hours.

Natural mineral water flows out of springs on the resort property and on adjoining BLM land at a temperature of 91°. The combined flow follows natural, tree-lined channels which include one very large gravel-botton swimming hole. The rate of flow is so large that no chemical treatment of the water is necessary. Bathing suits are required.

Facilities on the premises include picnic tables, restaurant, store, service station, overnight camping and RV hookups. Visa, MasterCard and Chevron credit cards accepted.

Directions: From the intersection of US 93 and NV 375 go five miles south on US 93 to location on east side of highway.

This primitive sign at *Hunt's Ash Springs* has inspired many parents to join their children with a whoop, holler and splash.

Hunt's Ash Springs: The gravel bottom is visible through the constantly-flowing crystal-clear warm mineral water.

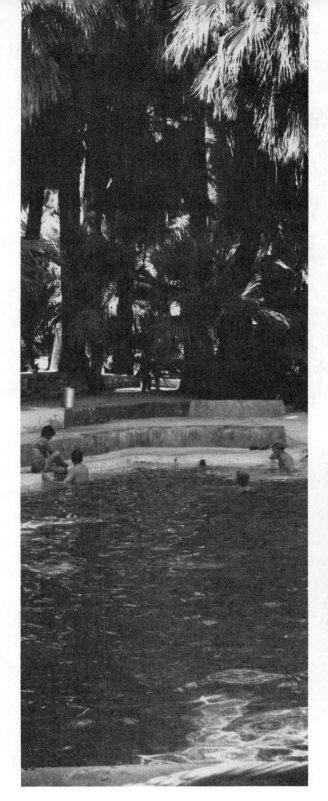

#607 WARM SPRINGS RESORT

(702) 865-2780

Moapa, NV 89925 **PR + CRV**

A large RV oasis in the desert, with acres of grass and dozens of palm trees, blessed with a warm-water flow of 3,000,000 gallons per day. Located just off I-15, 50 miles north of Las Vegas. Elevation 1,800 ft. Open all year.

Natural mineral water flows out of several springs at 90° and runs through the grounds in a series of gravel-bottom pools and tree-lined channels. A large outdoor swimming pool uses mineral water on a flow-through basis, maintaining a temperature near 90°. The outdoor hydropool uses mineral water heated to approximately 101°, and is chlorine-treated. Bathing suits are required in both pools.

Facilities include a club house and men's and women's locker rooms. Pool use is available on a day rate basis. RV hookups and camping spaces are available only to members of a coast-to-coast campers' organization. Prospective members may arrange a two-day trial visit. Phone first for a confirmed trial-visit reservation. No credit cards are accepted.

There are no services available on the premises. It is nine miles to a store, restaurant, service station, etc.

Directions: From I-15 take NV 168 north for seven miles, then follow signs two miles west to resort.

Warm Springs Resort: This always-warm swimming pool is too large to ever get crowded, even when the park is full.

This tiled hydrojet pool, and the surrounding acres of shaded grass, makes *Warm Springs Resort* a popular destination.

#608 ROGERS WARM SPRING

■ **near the town of Overton non-commercial**

A refreshing warm pond and shady picnic oasis on the barren north shore of Lake Mead, in the Lake Mead National Recreation Area. Elevation 1,600 ft. Open all year.

Natural mineral water flows directly up through a gravel bottom into a 100-foot-diameter pool at approximately 90°, and at a sufficient rate to maintain the entire three-foot-deep pool at approximately 85°. Hundreds of gallons per minute flow over a cement and rock spillway in a series of small waterfalls. Bathing suits would be advisable at this location in the daytime.

There are no services available, and overnight parking (after 10 PM) is prohibited. It is ten miles to a store, restaurant and service station and five miles to a campground.

Directions: From the intersection of US 93 and NV 147 in the city of Henderson, go northeast on Lake Mead Drive. At the intersection with Northshore Road (NV 167) follow Northshore Road northeast toward Overton. Rogers Warm Springs is four miles beyond the Echo Bay Marina turnoff.

Rogers Warm Spring: An ideal place to go for a picnic and turn the kids loose for a few hours, to explore the rocks and splash everywhere in the shallow pool.

#609 EDGEWATER MOTEL & CASINO

□ P.O. Box 642 (702) 298-2453
Laughlin, NV 89046 Hydropool MH

#610 NEVADA INN

□ 1009 Nevada Hwy. (702) 293-2044
Boulder City, NV 89005 Hydropool MH

#611A SPRING FEVER

□ 3434 Boulder Hwy. (702) 457-5044
Las Vegas, NV 89121 PR

Modern rent-a-tub establishment located near downtown Las Vegas. Elevation 2,500 ft. Open all year. 24 hours.

Pools for rent to the public, using gas-heated tap water, treated with chlorine.

20 private rooms, rented by the hour. Water temperature 94-98° in the summer, 100°-102° in the winter. Sauna and toilet included in each room.

Special features: No reservations. First come, first served.

Service available: juice bar.

Credit cards accepted: Visa and MasterCard.

Phone for rates, reservations and directions.

#611B AMBASSADOR INN
☐ 377 Flamingo Road (702) 733-7777
Las Vegas, NV 89109 Hydropool MH

#611C DESERT INN AND COUNTRY CLUB
☐ 3145 Las Vegas Blvd. (702) 733-4444
Las Vegas, NV 89109 Hydropool MH

#611D MGM GRAND HOTEL
☐ 3645 Las Vegas Blvd. (702) 739-4111
Las Vegas, NV 89109 Health Club MH

#611E ROYAL PALMS MOTEL
☐ 3660 S. Las Vegas Blvd. (702) 735-4321
Las Vegas, NV 89109 Health Club MH

#611F SAHARA HOTEL
☐ 2535 S. Las Vegas Blvd. (702) 735-2111
Las Vegas, NV 89109 Health Club MH

#611G LAS VEGAS HILTON
☐ P.O. Box 15087 (702) 735-5111
Las Vegas, NV 89114 Health Club MH

#611H DUNES HOTEL
☐ 3650 S. Las Vegas Blvd. (702) 737-4110
Las Vegas, NV 89109 Health Club MH

#611I IMPERIAL PALACE
☐ 3535 S. Las Vegas Blvd. (702) 731-3311
Las Vegas, NV 89109 Hydropool MH

#611J CAESAR'S PALACE
☐ 3570 S. Las Vegas Blvd. (702) 731-7110
Las Vegas, NV 89109 Health Club MH

#611L UNION PLAZA HOTEL AND CASINO
☐ 1 Main St. (702) 386-2110
Las Vegas, NV 89101 Health Spa MH

#611M SANDS HOTEL
☐ 3355 S. Las Vegas Blvd. (702) 733-5000
Las Vegas, NV 89109 Health Club MH

#611N RIVIERA HOTEL
☐ 2901 S. Las Vegas Blvd. (702) 734-5110
Las Vegas, NV 89109 Health Club MH

#611O TROPICANA TRAVELODGE
☐ 3111 W. Tropicana (702) 798-1111
Las Vegas, NV 89103 Hydropool MH

#611P GOLDEN NUGGET HOTEL
☐ P.O. Box 610 (702) 385-7111
Las Vegas, NV 89101 Hydropool MH

#611Q FRONTIER HOTEL
☐ 3120 S. Las Vegas Blvd. (702) 734-0110
Las Vegas, NV 89109 Hydropool MH

#611R CIRCUSLAND RV PARK
☐ on S. Las Vegas Blvd. (702) 734-0410
Las Vegas, NV 89109 Hydropool CRV

#611S RIVIERA TRAVEL TRAILER PARK
☐ on Palm Street. (702) 457-8700
Las Vegas, NV 89104 Hydropool CRV

#611T SILVER NUGGET CASINO AND RV PARK
☐ on S. Las Vegas Blvd. (702) 649-4133
Las Vegas, NV 89101 Hyrdopool CRV

#612 BAILEY'S HOT SPRINGS

■ **Box 387** **(702) 553-2395**
Beatty, NV 89003 **PR + CRV**

Primarily a restaurant, bar and RV park, with three large indoor hot mineral water soaking pools. Located in high desert country just east of Death Valley National Monument. Elevation 2,900 ft. Open all year.

Natural mineral water emerges from a capped artesian well at 160°, then is piped into three large gravel-bottom indoor soaking pools, which used to be railroad water reservoirs. Flow rates are controlled to maintain three different temperatures in the three pools; approximately 101°, 105° and 108°. The rate of flow is sufficient to permit customers to use soap and shampoo in the pools and no chemical treatment is necessary.

A restaurant, bar, overnight camping and RV hookups are available on the premises. Visa and MasterCard are accepted. It is six miles to a store and service station.

Directions: From the only traffic signal in Beatty go three miles north on US 95. Watch for large sign on east side of road.

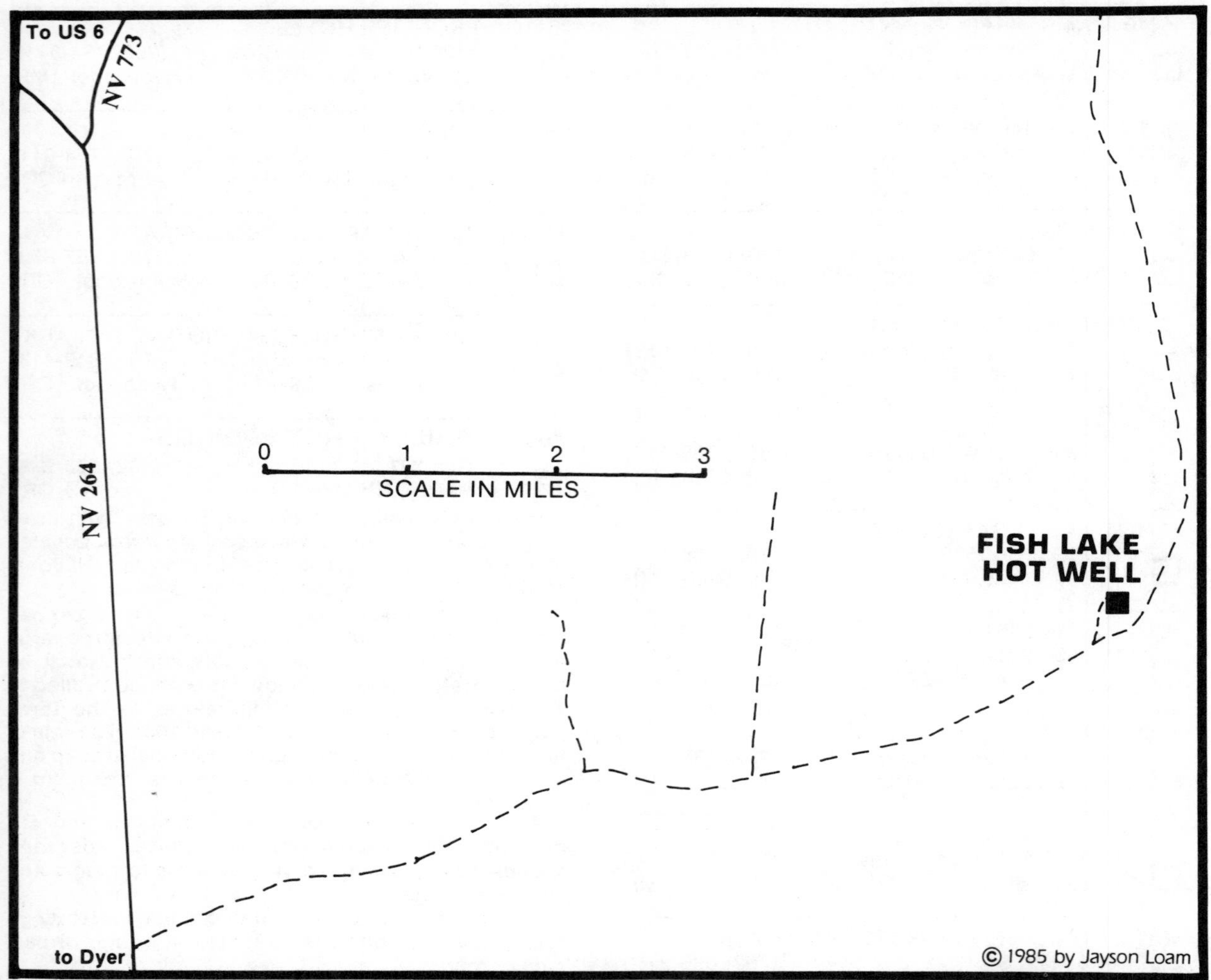

#613 FISH LAKE HOT WELL

■ **near the town of Dyer** **(see map)**
non-commercial

An inviting cement-lined soaking pool on the edge of a truly remote barren desert wash. Located approximately half way between Reno and Las Vegas in Fish Lake Valley. Elevation 4,800. Open all year.

Natural mineral water emerges from a well casing at 105°, and at a rate of more than 50 gallons per minute. The casing is surrounded by a six foot by six foot cement sump which maintains a water depth of four feet above a gravel bottom. The overflow goes to a nearby shallow pond as a water supply for cattle. Wood pallets have been placed around the cement pool to prevent cattle damage. Clothing optional is probably the custom at this remote location.

There are no services, but there is an abundance of level space where overnight parking is not prohibited. Despite the fact that it is possible to drive within a few feet of the pool it has been kept surprisingly clear of cans and broken glass. Please help keep it clean.

Directions: From the junction of NV 264 and NV 773, go 5.7 miles south on NV 264, and watch for sign *Middle Creek Trail Canyon.* Go east on gravel road 7.0 miles to fork then bear left for 0.1 mile to spring. The gravel road is subject to flash-flood damage, so should not be attempted at night.

Source maps: USGS *Davis Mountain* and *Rhyolite Ridge* (well not shown on map).

#614 BEST WESTERN HI-DESERT IN

□ P.O. Box 351 (702) 482-3511
Tonopah, NV 89049 Hydropool MH

#615 WALLEY'S HOT SPRING RESORT

■ **Box 109** **(702) 782-8155**
Genoa, NV 89411 **PR MH**

A self-styled "upscale destination resort" which attempts to present a nineteenth century resort image while carefully avoiding any appearance of being "funky". Located 50 miles south of Reno at the foot of the Sierra. Elevation, 4,700 ft. Open all year.

Natural mineral water from the original springs bubbles up through the sandy bottom of a large hot pond at 110°, gradually cooling to less than 100° at the overflow spillway. This pond is posted with NO SWIMMING signs. Natural mineral water also flows from several wells at temperatures up to 160° and is then piped to the bath house and to six outdoor cement pools where temperatures are maintained from 96° to 104°. The cement swimming pool uses chlorine-treated creek water and averages 80°. Bathing suits are required in the outdoor pools but are not proper dress in the dining rooms.

The main building is a two-story health club, with separate men's and women's sections each containing a sauna, steam bath and weight training equipment. Massage is also available in each section. Facilities include rooms, dining rooms, bars and meeting rooms. Visa, MasterCard and American Express are accepted. It is seven miles to a store, service station and RV hookups.

Directions: From Minden, on US 395, go 1/2 mile north to Muller Lane, turn west and go three miles to Foothill Road, then 1/2 mile north to resort.

#616A HARRAH'S TAHOE HOTEL
□ P.O. Box 8 (702) 586-6605
Stateline, NV 89449 Health Spa MH

#616B DEL WEBB'S SAHARA TAHOE MOTEL
□ P.O. Box C (702) 588-6211
Stateline, NV 89449 Hydropool MH

#616C CAESAR'S TAHOE
□ P.O. Box 5800 (702) 588-3515
Statleline, NV 89449 Health Club MH

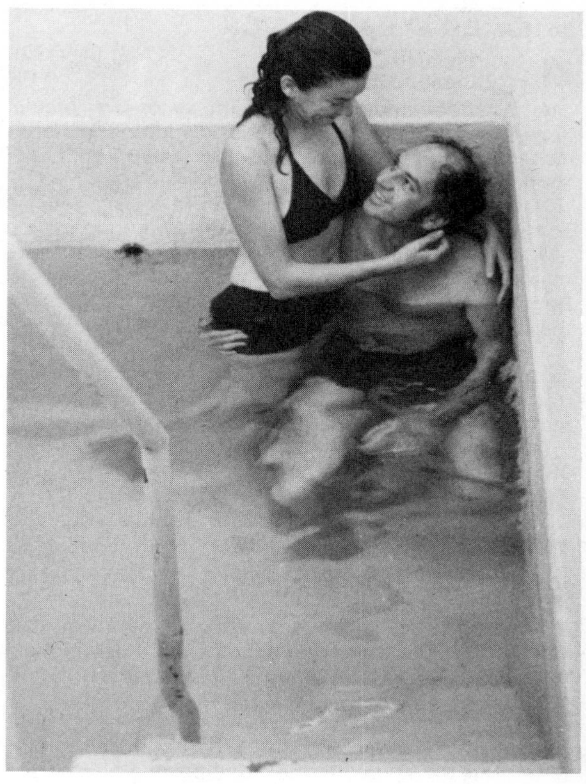

▲ *Carson Hot Springs:* These unjetted soaking pools are not fancy, but their generous size does permit bathing with a friend.

#617 CARSON HOT SPRINGS

■ **1500 Hot Springs Road** **(702) 882-9863**
Carson City, NV 89701 **PR + CRV**

Older hot springs resort with swimming pool and nine large private rooms, each containing a sunken tub large enough for eight persons. Located in the northeast outskirts of Carson City. Elevation 4,300 ft. Open all year.

Natural mineral water flows out of the the ground at 126°. Air spray and evaporative cooling is used to lower this water temperature when pools are drained and refilled during each week. No chemical or city water is added. The outdoor swimming-pool temperature is maintained at 98° in the summer and 102° in the winter. Individual room pool temperatures can be controlled as desired, from 95° to 110°.

Bathing suits are required in the swimming pool, optional in the private rooms.

Massage, restaurant and no-hookup RV parking are available on the premises. No credit cards are accepted. It is one mile to a store and service station.

Directions: From US 395, in the north end of Carson City, go east on Hot Springs Road one mile to resort.

#618A BOWERS MANSION

■ **4001 US 395 North** **(702) 849-1825**
Carson City, NV 89701 **PR**

A Washoe County Park, with extensive picnic, playground and parking facilities, in addition to a large modern swimming pool. Elevation 4,500 ft. Open Memorial Day to Labor Day.

Natural mineral water, pumped from wells at 116°, is combined with cold well water as needed. The swimming pool and children's wading pool are maintained at 80°. Both pools are treated with chlorine. Bathing suits are required. There is no charge for using the facilities.

There are no services available on the premises. Tours of the mansion are conducted from Mother's Day to the end of October. It is four miles to a restaurant, motel, store, service station and RV hookups.

Directions: Go ten miles north of Carson City on US 395. Watch for signs and turn west on side road 1/2 mile to location.

#618B STEAMBOAT SPRINGS

■ **16020 So. Virginia Ave.** **(702) 853-6600**
Reno, NV 89511 **PR**

The oldest spa in Nevada; same family ownership since 1904. The primary emphasis is on healing and medicinal services. Elevation 4,500 feet. Open all year, daytime hours only.

Natural mineral water flows out of the ground in the form of boiling water and is cooled in a series of holding tanks. It is then piped to the bath house. A one-person tub and single bed are in each of eight private treatment rooms, supervised by a registered nurse. In private rooms bathing suits are optional for women; men are issued bikinis.

Facials, mud body packs, blanket wraps and massage are available on the premises. No credit cards are accepted. It is two miles to a restaurant, motel, store and service station, four miles to RV hookups.

Directions: Go ten miles south of Reno on US 395 and look for signs and a large steam plume on the east side of the highway.

#619A COEUR DU LAC
□ P.O. Box 7107 (702) 831-3318
Incline Village, NV 89450 Hydropool MH

#619B HYATT LAKE TAHOE AT INCLINE VILLAGE
□ P.O. Box 3239 (702) 831-1111
Incline Village, NV 89450 Health Club MH

#619C ALL SEASONS RESORT
□ 807 Alder St. (702) 831-2311
Incline Village, NV 89450 Hydropool MH

Steamboat Springs: Historic equipment and buildings (above) are appropriate for traditional health treatment (below).

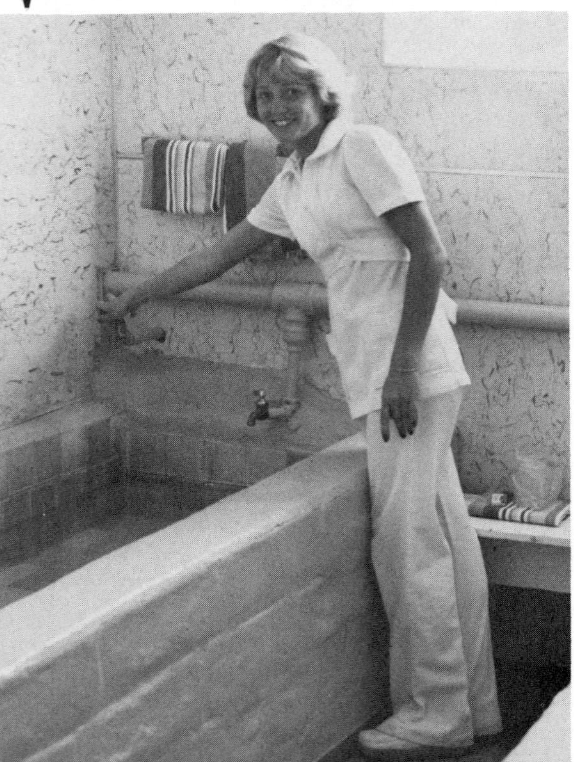

#620A GRAND CENTRAL SAUNA & HOT TUB CO.

☐ 285 S. Wells (702) 323-8827
Reno, NV PR

One of a chain of urban locations, established by Grand Central, a pioneer in the private room rent-a-tub business.

Pools for rent to the public, using gas-heated tap water treated with chlorine.

20 private rooms, rented by the hour. Water temperature 100°. Sauna included.

Services available: juice bar.

Credit cards accepted: Visa and MasterCard.

Phone for rates, reservations and directions.

#620B GRAND MOTOR LODGE
☐ 2050 Market St. (702) 786-2500
Reno, NV 89502 Hydropool MH

#620C MGM GRAND — RENO
☐ 2500 East Second St. (702) 789-2000
Reno, NV 89595 Health Club MH

#620D HARRAH'S RENO HOTEL
☐ P.O. Box 10 (702) 786-3232
Reno, NV 89504 Health Club MH

#620E BEST WESTERN AIRPORT PLAZA
☐ 1981 Terminal Way (702) 348-6370
Reno, NV 89502 Hydropool MH

#620F ELDORADO HOTEL CASINO
☐ P.O. Box 3399 (702) 786-5700
Reno, NV 89505 Hydropool MH

#620G KOA — RENO/SPARKS
☐ on Newport Lane (702) 323-1447
Reno, NV 89506 Hydropool CRV

#621 GERLACH HOT SPRINGS

■ **in the town of Gerlach (702) 557-2220**

Newly constructed large soaking pool intended to replace a popular, but dangerous, old free-flowing very hot spring. Located on the edge of Gerlach, surrounded by desert foothills. Elevation 3,700 ft. Open all year.

Natural mineral water at boiling temperature is piped from a capped artesian well to an adjoining cement-lined soaking pool and to a mud bath. Water temperature in the soaking pool is maintained at approximately 100° by adding cold tap water as needed, providing a flow-through process needing no chemical tretment. Bathing suits are required.

Men's and women's locker rooms are available on the premises, as are overnight camping spaces. No credit cards are accepted. There is a motel, restaurant, store and service station within six blocks.

Directions: From the old train station in Gerlach, go ½ mile north on NV 447 to location on east side of highway.

Gerlach Hot Springs: Local citizens formed an improvement district and raised funds to build this modern facility to replace a funky old mud-bottom pool which was fed by scalding water in open ditches.

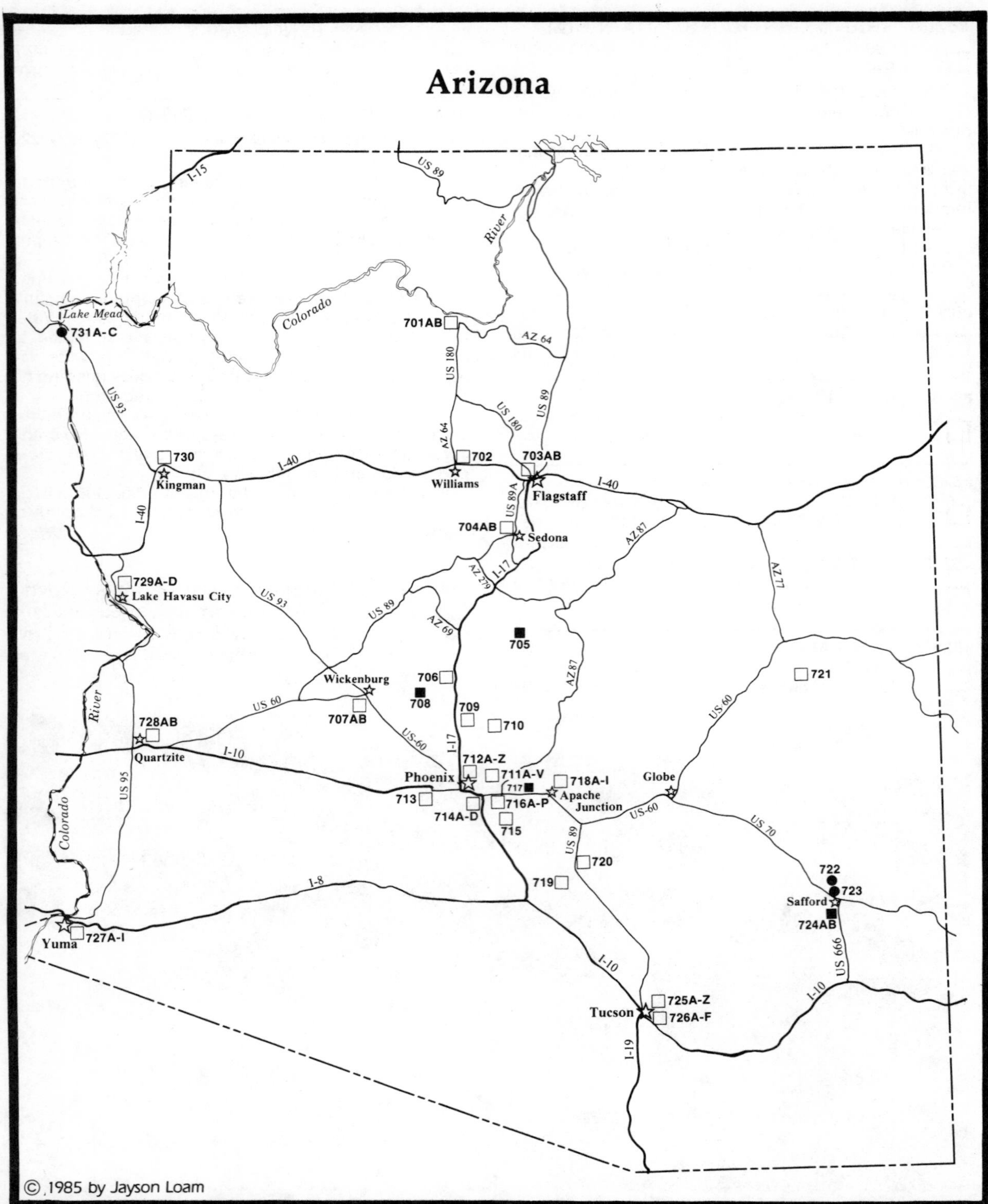
Arizona
I-15
US 89
River
Colorado
Lake Mead
731A-C
701AB
AZ 64
US 180
US 93
US 89
US 180
AZ 64
730
702
703AB
I-40
I-40
Kingman
Williams
Flagstaff
US 89A
I-40
704AB
Sedona
AZ 87
729A-D
Lake Havasu City
AZ 279
I-17
AZ 77
US 93
US 89
AZ 69
705
706
708
Wickenburg
707AB
AZ 87
721
River
728AB
US 60
709
710
US 60
Quartzite
I-10
US-60
I-17
712A-Z
711A-V
Phoenix
717
718A-I
Globe
713
714A-D
716A-P
Apache Junction
US-60
715
US 95
Colorado
US 89
US 70
720
719
722
723
I-8
Safford
724AB
Yuma
727A-I
I-10
US 666
I-10
725A-Z
Tucson
726A-F
I-19
©, 1985 by Jayson Loam

MAP AND DIRECTORY SYMBOLS

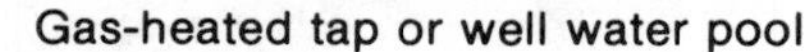

● **Unimproved natural mineral water pool** — Paved highway

■ **Improved natural mineral water pool** — Unpaved road

□ Gas-heated tap or well water pool — Hiking route

PR = Tubs or pools for rent by hour, day or treatment

MH = Rooms, cabins or dormitory spaces for rent by day, week or month

CRV = Camping or vehicle parking spaces, some with hookups, for rent by day, week, month or year

---

#701A □ QUALITY INN RED FEATHER
P.O. Box 520 (602) 638-2673
Grand Canyon Village, AZ 86023
Hydropool MH

#701B □ CANYON SQUIRE INN
P.O. Box 130 (602) 638-2681
Grand Canyon Village, AZ 86023
Hydropool MH

#702 □ KOA - GRAND CANYON - WILLIAMS
on Hwy 64 (602) 635-2307
Williams, AZ 86046 Hydropool CRV

#703A □ FLAGSTAFF TRAVELODGE EAST
2285 Bulter Ave. (602) 774-1821
Flagstaff, AZ 86001 Hydropool MH

#703B □ FLAGSTAFF TRAVELODGE UNIVERSITY
801 W. Hwy 66 (602) 774-3381
Flagstaff, AZ 86001 Hydropool MH

#704A □ BEST WESTERN RONDEE MOTEL
P.O. Box 1021 (602) 282-7131
Sedona, AZ 86336 Hydropool MH

#704B □ POCO DIABLO RESORT
P.O. Box 1709 (602) 282-7333
Sedona, AZ 86336 Hydropool MH

Verde Hot Springs: Geothermal bubbles are part of the atmosphere in the main soaking pool, built right over a spring.

The road to *Verde Hot Springs* is also too steep and winding for trailers or RV rigs with a long turning radius.

#705 VERDE HOT SPRINGS (see map)

near the town of Camp Verde

non-commercial

The surprisingly clean remains of an historic resort which burned down years ago. Located on the west bank of the Verde River, in a beautiful high desert canyon. Elevation 2,800 ft. Open all year, subject to river level and bad-weather road hazards.

Natural mineral water flows out of several riverbank springs at 104° into small indoor cement soaking pools. A larger outdoor cement pool is built over another spring and averages a temperature of 98°. Twenty feet below, at low water level, are several more springs which feed volunteer-built rock-and-sand pools. The apparent local custom is clothing optional. Conscientious visitors have done a superb job of packing out all trash. Please respect this tradition.

There are no services available on the premises, and it is more than 20 miles to the nearest store, service station, etc. There is an unofficial camping area on the east bank of the river, which must be forded to reach the springs. Check with the ranger station in Camp Verde regarding road conditions and river level before attempting to reach this site.

Source maps: *Coconino National Forest.* USGS *Verde Hot Springs.*

Verde Hot Springs: This beautiful setting is one of the reasons *Verde* gets rather crowded on week-ends and holidays.

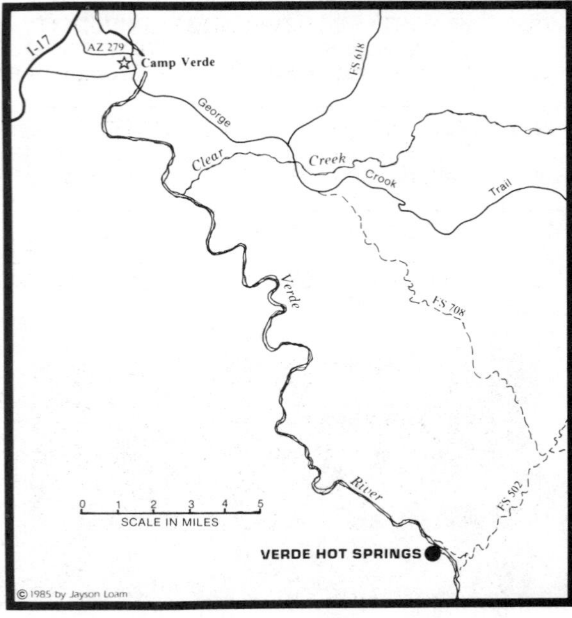

#706 KOA — BLACK CANYON CITY
□ on I-17 frontage road (602) 374-5318
Black Canyon City, AZ 85234 Hydropool
CRV

#707A WESTPARK
□ on US 60 (602) 684-2210
Wickenburg, AZ 85358 Hydropool CRV

#707B WICKENBURG INN TENNIS AND GUEST RANCH
□ P.O. Box P (602) 684-7811
Wickenburg, AZ 85358 In-room hydropools
MH

#708 CASTLE HOT SPRINGS

■ near Lake Pleasant (602) 388-2239

An historic resort, closed for remodeling after several years operating as a department of the University of Arizona. The new owners plan to develop a major commercial resort after clearing up zoning and use-permit problems.

Telephone for current information on construction progress, and on a scheduled date for re-opening.

#709 SHRANGRI LA RESORT
□ Box 4343 New River Rte. (602) 995-9553
Phoenix, AZ 85029 MH + CRV

Primarily a membership naturist resort, located in a scenic high desert valley 30 miles north of Phoenix. Elevation 1,900 ft. Open all year.

Gas-heated well water, chlorine-treated, is used in all pools. A large, shaded fiberglass hot pool is maintained at 104°. The adjoining swimming pool averages 75° to 80°. Bathing suits are prohibited in both pools, and clothing is optional everywhere else on the grounds.

Facilities include a large club house, volleyball court, sauna and steamroom. Lodge rooms, camping spaces and RV hookups are also available.

A seasonal snack shack is open on most weekends. No credit cards are accepted. It is three miles to a restaurant and five miles to a store and service station.

Being a membership club, Shangri La is not open to the public on a drop-in basis. However, a limited number of guest passes may be issued to qualified visitors. Write or telephone well in advance to make arrangements to visit and to obtain directions.

Shangri La Resort: This hydropool is covered to protect it from the desert sun.

710 CAREFREE INN RESORT
☐ Mule Train Rd. (602) 488-3551
Carefree, AZ 85337 Hydropool MH

#711A SUNBURST HOTEL
☐ 4925 N. Scottsdale Rd. (602) 945-7666
Scottsdale, AZ 85251 Hydropool MH

#711B QUALITY INN TOWER
☐ *7233 E. Shoeman Lane* (602) 947-8301
Scottsdale, AZ 85251 Hydropool MH

#711C DOUBLETREE INN — SCOTTSDALE MALL
☐ 7353 Indian School Rd. (602) 994-9203
Scottsdale, AZ 85251 Hydropool MH

#711D RED LION INN
☐ 4949 E. Lincoln Dr. (602) 952-0420
Scottsdale, AZ 85253 Hydropool MH

#711E SHERATON SCOTTSDALE INN
☐ 7200 N. Scottsdale Rd. (602) 948-5000
Scottsdale, AZ 85253 Hydropool MH

#711F MARRIOTT'S CAMELBACK INN
☐ 5402 E. Lincoln Dr. (602) 948-1700
Scottsdale, AZ 85252 Hydropool MH

#711G THE REGISTRY RESORT
☐ 7171 N. Scottsdale Rd. (602) 991-3800
Scottsdale, AZ 85253 Hydropool MH

#711H SCOTTSDALE CONFERENCE CENTER
☐ 7700 E. McCormick Pkwy. (602) 991-9000
Scottsdale, AZ 85258 Health Club MH

#711I THE INN AT MCCORMICK RANCH
☐ 7401 S. Scottsdale Rd. (602) 948-5050
Scottsdale, AZ 85253 Hydropool MH

#711J JOHN GARDINER'S TENNIS RANCH
☐ 5700 E. McDonald Dr. (602) 948-2100
Scottsdale, AZ 85253 Hydropool MH

#711K HOSPITALITY INN SCOTTSDALE
☐ 409 N. Scottsdale Rd. (602) 949-5115
Scottsdale, AZ 85257 Hydropool MH

#711L MOUNTAIN SHADOWS RESORT
☐ 5641 E. Lincoln Dr. (602) 945-7111
Scottsdale, AZ 85253 Hydropool MH

#711N RAMADA SCOTTSDALE SAFARI RESORT
☐ 4611 N. Scottsdale Rd. (602) 945-0721
Scottsdale, AZ 85251 Hydropool MH

#711M QUALITY INN SCOTTSDALE INNSUITES
☐ 1400 N. 77th St. (602) 941-1202
Scottsdale, AZ 85257 Hydropool MH

#711O RAMADA VALLEY HO RESORT HOTEL
☐ 6850 Main St. (602) 945-6321
Scottsdale, AZ 85251 Hydropool MH

#711P SCOTTSDALE GRANADA ROYALE HOMETEL
☐ 5001 N. Scottsdale Rd. (602) 949-1414
Scottsdale, AZ 85252 Hydropool MH

#711Q SCOTTSDALE HILTON
☐ 6333 N. Scottsdale Rd. (602) 948-7750
Scottsdale, AZ 85253 Hydropool MH

#711R DOUBLETREE INN — FASHION SQUARE
☐ 4710 N. Scottsdale Rd. (602) 947-5411
Scottsdale, AZ 85251 Hydropool MH

#711S FIFTH AVENUE TRAVELODGE
☐ 6935 5th Ave. (602) 994-9461
Scottsdale, AZ 85251 Hydropool MH

#711T SCOTTSDALE QUALITY INN SUITES
☐ 1400 N. 77th St. (602)941-1202
Scottsdale, AZ 85257 Hydropool MH

#711U SCOTTSDALE ROADRUNNER TRAVEL TRAILER RESORT
☐ on 92nd St. (602) 945-0787
Scottsdale, AZ 85260 Hydropool CRV

#711V HERMOSA INN
☐ 5532 N. Palo Cristi Rd. (602) 955-8614
Paradise Valley, AZ 85253 Hydropool MH

#712A TUBBIE'S
☐ 24 West Camelback Rd. (602) 263-6055
Phoenix, AZ 85013 PR

Basic private room rent-a-tub facility, located in a shopping center near downtown Phoenix.

Pools for rent to the public, using gas heated tap water, treated with chlorine.

Six private rooms, rented by the hour, each containing a fiberglass hot pool and a changing room. Water temperature 100-105°, will adjust on request.

Special features: one party room with sauna, large enough for 12 persons.

Services available: massage.

Credit cards accepted: MasterCard, Visa, American Express.

Phone for rates, reservations and directions.

#712B SHERATON GREENWAY INN
☐ 2510 West Greenway Rd. (602) 993-0800
Phoenix, AZ 85023 Hydropool MH

#712C QUALITY INN — WEST
☐ 2420 W. Thomas Rd. (602) 257-0801
Phoenix, AZ 85015 Hydropool MH

#712D THE POINTE RESORT
☐ 7677 N. 16th St. (602) 997-2626
Phoenix, AZ 85020 Health Spa MH

#712E HYATT REGENCY — PHOENIX
☐ 2nd St. & Adams (602) 257-1110
Phoenix, AZ 85004 Hydropool MH

#712F DOUBLETREE INN
☐ 212 W. Osborn Rd. (602) 248-0222
Phoenix, AZ 85013 Hydropool MH

#712G ARIZONA BILTMORE
☐ P.O. Box 2290 (602) 955-6600
Phoenix, AZ 85002 Health Club MH

#712H KACHINA INN
☐ 1102 N. Central Ave. (602) 258-6341
Phoenix, AZ 85004 Hydropool MH

#712I KON TIKI PASSPORT INN
☐ 24th St. & Van Buren (602) 224-9361
Phoenix, AZ 85006 Hydropool MH

#712J BEST WESTERN COUNTRY VILLAGE
☐ 2425 S. 24th St. (602) 273-7251
Phoenix, AZ 85034 Hydropool MH

#712K RODEWAY INN — METROCENTER
☐ 10402 N. Canyon Hwy. (602) 943-2371
Phoenix, AZ 85021 Hydropool MH

#712L CAMELBACK SAHARA HOTEL
☐ 502 W. Camelback Rd. (602) 264-9290
Phoenix, AZ 85013 Hydropool MH

#712M ARIZONA RANCH HOUSE INN
☐ 5600 N. Central Ave. (602) 279-3221
Phoenix, AZ 85012 Hydropool MH

#712N GRANADA ROYALE HOMETEL
GRAND AVE.
☐ 3210 Grand Ave. (602) 279-3211
Phoenix, AZ 85017 Hydropool MH

#712O HOLIDAY INN & HOLIDOME
METROCENTER
☐ 2532 W. Peoria Ave. (602) 943-2341
Phoenix, AZ 85029 Hydropool MH

#712P LA QUINTA MOTOR INN
☐ 2725 N. Black Canyon Hwy. (602) 258-6271
Phoenix, AZ 85009 Hydropool MH

#712Q MAINE CHANCE
☐ 5830 Jean Ave. (602) 947-6365
Phoenix, AZ 85018 Hydropool MH

#712R PHOENIX HILTON
☐ P.O. Box 1000 (602) 257-1525
Phoenix, AZ 85001 Health Club MH

#712S POINTE TAPATIO
☐ 1111 N. 7th St. (602) 866-7500
Phoenix, AZ 85020 Health Spa MH

#712T HOTEL WESTCOURT
☐ 10220 N. Metro Pkwy East (602) 944-2616
Phoenix, AZ 85021 Hydropool MH

#712U RODEWAY INN — AIRPORT
☐ 1202 S. 24th St. (602) 273-1211
Phoenix, AZ 85034 Hydropool MH

#712V SHERATON AIRPORT INN
☐ 2901 E. Sky Harbor Blvd. (602) 275-3634
Phoenix, AZ 85034 Hydropool MH

#712W TRAVELODGE CONVENTION HOTEL
☐ 3333 E. Van Buren St. (602) 244-8244
Phoenix, AZ 85008 Hydropool MH

#712X CASA FIESTA TRAVEL TRAILER RESORT
☐ on Baseline Rd. (602) 839-1052
Phoenix, AZ 85040 Hydropool CRV

#712Y DESERT SHADOWS TRAVEL
TRAILER RESORT
☐ on 29th Ave. (602) 869-8178
Phoenix, AZ 85009 Hydropool CRV

#712Z ROYAL PALM MOBILE HOME PARK
☐ on Dunlap Ave. (602) 943-5833
Phoenix, AZ 85020 Hydropool CRV

#713	BEST WESTERN CROSSROADS INN 1770 N. Dysart Rd. Goodyear, AZ 85338	(602) 932-9191 Hydropool MH	☐
#714A	FIESTA INN 2100 S. Priest St. Tempe, AZ 85282	(602) 967-1441 Hydropool MH	☐
#714B	VAGABOND MOTOR HOTEL 1221 E. Apache Blvd. Tempe, AZ 85281	(602) 968-7793 Hydropool MH	☐
#714C	GRANADA ROYALE HOMETEL 1635 N. Scottsdale Rd. Tempe, AZ 85281	(602) 947-3711 Hydropool MH	☐
#714D	CASA FIESTA TRAVEL TRAILER RESORT on Baseline Road Tempe, AZ 85283	(602) 839-1052 Hydropool CRV	☐
#715	CASAS DEL CAMPO on Knox Rd. Chandler, AZ 85224	(602) 963-9747 Hydropool CRV	☐
#716A	BEST WESTERN MESA INN 1625 E. Main St. Mesa, AZ 85204	(602) 964-8000 Hydropool MH	☐
#716B	QUALITY INN — ROYAL 951 W. Main St. Mesa, AZ 85201	(602) 833-1231 Hydropool MH	☐
#716C	APACHE WELLS TRAVEL TRAILER RESORT on McKellips Rd. Mesa, AZ 85201	(602) 832-4324 Hydropool CRV	☐
#716D	AZTEC TRAVEL TRAILER RESORT on US 60/80/89 Mesa, AZ 85201	(602) 832-2700 Hydropool CRV	☐
#716E	CASA FIESTA TRAVEL TRAILER RESORT on Baseline Rd. Mesa, AZ 85202	(602) 839-1052 Hydropool CRV	☐
#716F	FIESTA TRAVEL TRAILER PARK on University Dr. Mesa, AZ 85201	(602) 832-6490 Hydropool CRV	☐
#716G	GOOD LIFE TRAVEL TRAILER RESORT on US 60/80/89 Mesa, AZ 85201	(602) 832-4990 Hydropool CRV	☐
#716H	GREEN ACRES TRAILER PARK on US 60/80/89 Mesa, AZ 85201	(602) 964-5058 Hydropool CRV	☐
#716I	MESA REGAL RV RESORT on US 60/80/89 Mesa, AZ 85201	(602) 830-2821 Hydropool CRV	☐
#716J	GRANGEWOOD SHADOWS TRAVEL TRAILER RESORT on University Dr. Mesa, AZ 85201	(602) 832-9080 Hydropool CRV	☐
#716K	PALM GARDENS MOBILE MANOR on US 60/80/89 Mesa, AZ 85201	(602) 832-0290 Hydropool CRV	☐
#716L	PARK PLACE TRAVEL TRAILER RESORT on Recker Rd. Mesa, AZ 85206	(602) 830-1080 Hydropool CRV	☐
#716M	TOWERPOINT RESORT on US 60/80/89 Mesa, AZ 85201	(602) 832-4996 Hydropool CRV	☐
#716N	TRAILER VILLAGE on US 60/80/89 Mesa, AZ 85201	(602) 832-1770 Hydropool CRV	☐
#716O	VAL VISTA VILLAGE TRAVEL TRAILER on Val Vista Dr. Mesa, AZ 85204	(602) 832-2547 Hydropool CRV	☐
#716P	VENTURE OUT AT MESA on US 60/80/89 Mesa, AZ 85201	(602) 832-0200 Hydropool CRV	☐

Buckhorn Mineral Wells: Traditional service and equipment at Buckhorn includes the use of historic tub-edge hydrojet machines.

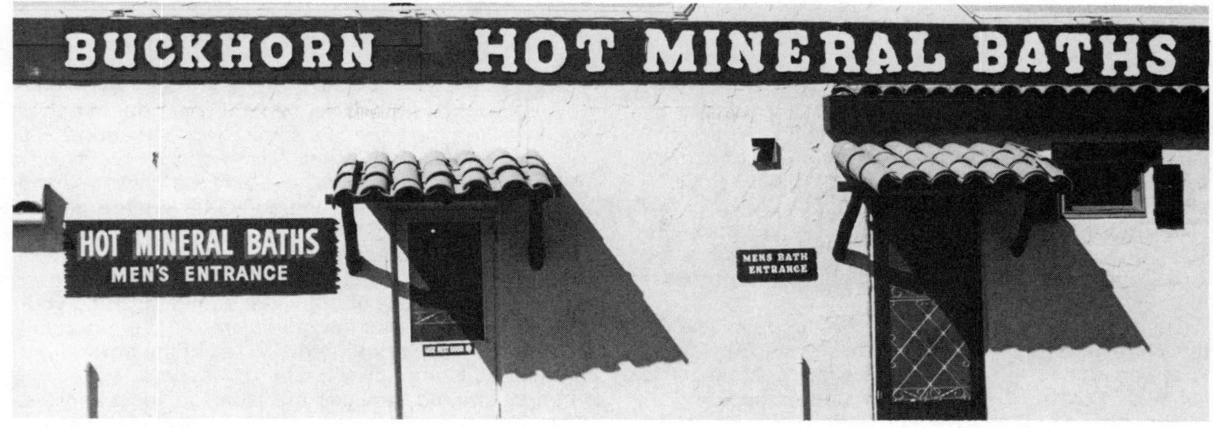

Buckhorn Mineral Wells: The traditional strict separation of men's and women's sections includes separate entrances.

#717 BUCKHORN MINERAL WELLS

■ **5900 Main St.** **(602) 832-1111**
Mesa, AZ 85205 **PR + MH**

An historic older motel-spa which still offers many traditional hot mineral-water treatment services. Elevation 1,200 ft. Open all year.

Natural mineral water is pumped from two wells at 130° and 140°, then run through a cooling tower. Facilities include separate men's and women's departments, each containing 12 small individual rooms with cement tub. A whirlpool pump is mounted on the side of each tub. The temperature of tub water may be varied by controlling the proportions of hot and cold water admitted. Tubs are drained, cleaned and refilled after each use, so no chemical treatment is required.

Massage, sweat-wrap therapy and motel rooms are available on the premises. Stores and restaurants are located across the street. Service stations and RV spaces are available within one-half mile.

No credit cards are accepted. Phone for information about rates, reservations and directions.

#718A THE RESORT AT GOLD CANYON RANCH
☐ 6210 S. Kings Ranch Rd. (602) 982-9090
Apache Junction, AZ 85220 MH
In-room hydropools

#718B HAPPY DAYS TRAVEL TRAILER PARK
☐ on Meridian Rd. (602) 982-4369
Apache Junction, AZ 85220 Hydropool CRV

#718C CAREFREE MANOR TRAVEL TRAILER RESORT
☐ on Delaware Dr. (602) 982-4008
Apache Junction, AZ 85220 Hydropool CRV

#718D COUNTRYSIDE TRAVEL TRAILER RESORT
☐ on Idaho Rd. (602) 982-1537
Apache Junction, AZ 85220 Hydropool CRV

#718E GOLDEN ACRES MOBILE MANOR
☐ on Delaware Rd. (602) 982-4049
Apache Junction, AZ 85220 Hydropool CRV

#718F IRONWOOD MOBILE COURT
☐ on Ironwood Rd. (602) 982-3413
Apache Junction, AZ 85220 Hydropool CRV

#718G LOST DUTCHMAN TRAVEL TRAILER RESORT
☐ on North Plaza Drive (602) 982-4173
Apache Junction, AZ 85220 Hydropool CRV

#718H ROCK SHADOWS TRAVEL TRAILER RESORT
☐ on Idaho Rd. (602) 982-0450
Apache Junction, AZ 85220 Hydropool CRV

#718I SIERRA DEL SAGUARO
☐ on Southern Ave. (602) 982-2444
Apache Junction, AZ 85220 Hydropool CRV

#719 HO HO KAM MOBILE VILLAGE
☐ on Hwy 87/287 (602) 723-3697
Coolidge, AZ 85228 Hydropool CRV

#720 CALIENTE CASA DEL SOL
☐ on US 89 (602) 868-5520
Florence, AZ 85232 Hydropool CRV

#721 SUNRISE LODGE
☐ P.O. Box 217 (602) 334-2144
McNary, AZ 85930 Hydropool MH

#722 WATSON WASH HOT WELL

Near the town of Safford **(see map)**
non-commercial

A delightful little sand-bottom pool surrounded by willows in a primitive setting. It is also a favorite party spot for local youths, so it is slightly tainted with broken bottles and other party trash. Elevation 3,000 ft. Open all year, subject to flash floods.

Natural mineral water flows out of a well casing at 102°, directly into a volunteer-built shallow pool large enough for four people. Clothing optional is probably the custom at this remote location.

There are no services available on the premises. On the plateau above the wash there is unlimited level space on which overnight parking is not prohibited. It is six miles to a store, cafe, service station, etc.

Directions: From US 70 in Safford, go north on Eighth Ave. across the river to the highway Y. Bear left on River Road for 4.7 miles, then turn right on a rough gravel road for 1.0 mile to the bluff directly above the hot well in the wash.

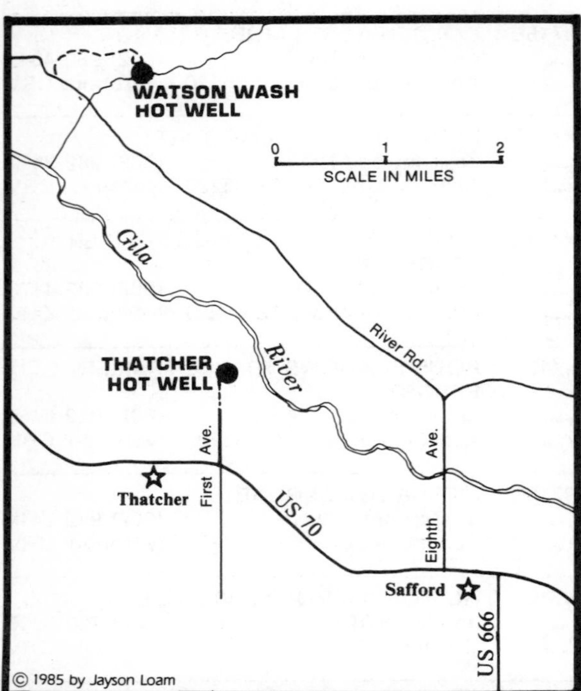

#723 THATCHER HOT WELL

Near the town of Thatcher **(see map)**
non-commercial

A substantial flow of hot mineral water out of a river bank well on the edge of a small town. Elevation 2,900 ft. Open all year, subject to flash floods.

Natural mineral water flows out of a large well casing at 112°, then runs across mud flats toward the current channel occupied by the Gila River. Volunteers dig shallow soaking pools in the mud adjoining the flow of 112° water, controlling the pool water temperature by limiting the amount of hot water admitted. Bring your own shovel; the volunteer pools are very temporary. It is possible to drive within five yards of the hot well, so bathing suits are advisable in the daytime.

There are no services available on the premises. There is a limited amount of adjoining space on which overnight parking is not prohibited. It is one mile to a store, cafe, service station, etc.

Watson Wash Hot Well: Volunteers don't waste time on a fancy pool because each year's flash floods would sweep it away.

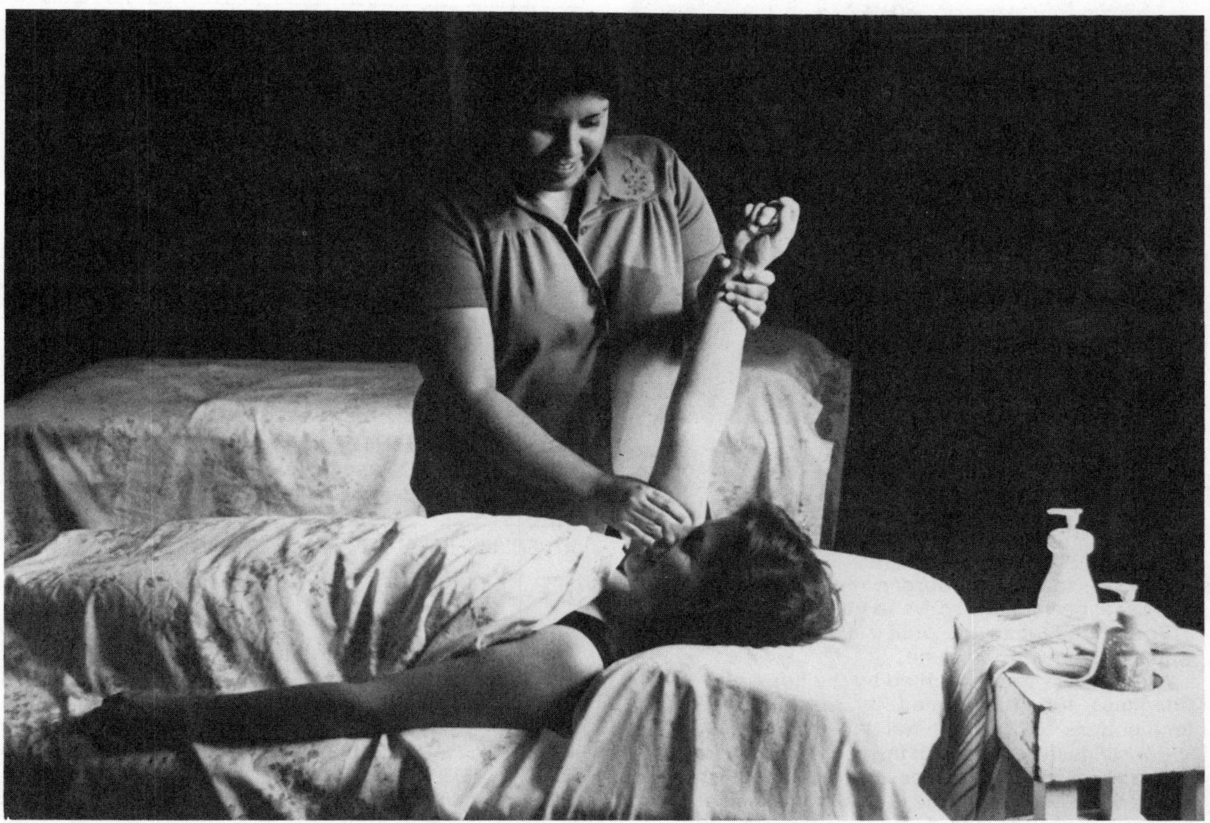

Lebanon Hot Mineral Baths: A free hot-pool soak comes with each therapy service, but private pool use may also be rented.

#724A LEBANON HOT MINERAL BATHS

Rte. 2, Box 1003-1 **(602) 428-3299**
Safford, AZ 85546 **PR + CRV**

Therapy-oriented bath house and RV park located in the suburbs south of Safford. Elevation 3,000 ft. Open all year.

Natural mineral water flows out of an artesian well at 108° and is piped to private-room soaking tubs. There are four tiled sunken tubs, each six feet by six feet. They are drained, cleaned and refilled after each customer, so no chemical treatment of the water is necessary.

Reflexology, therapy massage and sweat wrap are available on the premises. The facilities include RV hook-up spaces. It is six miles to a store, restaurant, service station, etc. No credit cards are accepted. Phone for rates and reservations.

Directions: From the intersection of US 70 and US 666 in Safford, go 4.8 miles south on US 666, then turn right one mile on paved road to Lebanon Hot Mineral Baths.

#724B KACHINA MINERAL SPRINGS SPA

Rte. 2, Box 987 **(602) 428-7212**
Safford, AZ 85546 **PR + CRV**

Therapy-oriented bath house and RV park, located in the suburbs south of Safford. Elevation 3,000 ft. Open all year.

Natural mineral water flows out of an artesian well at 108° and is piped into private-room soaking tubs. There are four tiled sunken tubs, each four feet by six feet. They are drained, cleaned and refilled after each customer, so no chemical water treatment is necessary.

Reflexology, therapy massage and sweat wrap are available on the premises. The facilities include RV hookup spaces. It is six miles to a store, restaurant, services station, etc. No credit cards are accepted. Phone for rates and reservations.

Directions: From the intersection of US 70 and US 666 in Safford, go six miles south on US 666, then follow signs west for ¼ mile.

Oasis Hot Tubs: Deluxe comfort at its best.

#725A **OASIS HOT TUBS**
☐ 2834 E. Grant Rd. (602) 795-8827
Tucson, AZ 85716 PR

A clean, spacious suburban rent-a-tub facility, with several especially attractive extras.

Pools for rent to the public, using gas-heated tap water treated with bromine.

Nine private rooms, rented by the hour, each with a fiberglass tub surrounded by colorful tile. Water temperature 100° - 102°, will vary on request.

Special features: Each of the two largest rooms has a sauna, bathroom, fireplace and sliding glass doors onto an enclosed sun patio. Some of the smaller rooms have skylights and one or more of these extras.

Services available: juice bar.

Credit cards accepted: Visa and MasterCard.

Phone for rates, reservations and directions.

#725B HACIENDA DEL SOL
☐ N. Hacienda Del Sol Rd. (602) 299-1501
Tucson, AZ 85718 Hydropool MH

#725C GRANADA ROYALE HOMETEL
☐ 5335 E. Broadway (602) 745-2700
Tucson, AZ 85711 Hydropool MH

#725D DOUBLETREE INN
☐ 445 S. Alvernon Way (602) 881-4200
Tucson, AZ 85711 Hydropool MH

#725E SANTA RITA INN
☐ 109 S. Scott Ave. (602) 791-7581
Tucson, AZ 85701 Hydropool MH

#725F RANCHO DEL RIO
☐ 2800 N. Sabino Cyn Rd. (602) 298-2351
Tucson, AZ 85715 Hydropool MH

#725G SPANISH TRAIL INN
☐ 7 S. 4th Ave. (602) 624-4461
Tucson, AZ 85713 Hydropool MH

#725H SMUGGLER'S INN
☐ 6350 E. Speedway (602) 296-3292
Tucson, AZ 85710 Hydropool MH

#725I AMBASSADOR INN
☐ 4425 E. 22nd St. (602) 745-1777
Tucson, AZ 85711 Hydropool MH

#725J SUNDANCER RESORT
☐ 4110 Sweetwater Dr. (602) 743-0411
Tucson, AZ 85705 Hydropool MH

#725K PLAZA INTERNATIONAL HOTEL
☐ 1900 E. Speedway (602) 327-7341
Tucson, AZ 85719 Hydropool MH

#725L SHERATON—PUEBLO INN
☐ 350 S. Freeway (602) 622-6611
Tucson, AZ 85705 Hydropool MH

#725M WESTWARD LOOK RESORT
☐ 245 E. Ina Rd. (602) 297-1151
Tucson, AZ 85704 Hydropool MH

#725N BRAVE BULL RANCH RESORT
☐ P.O. Box 335 (602) 791-7880
Tucson, AZ 85704 Hydropool MH

#725O CANYON RANCH SPA
☐ 8600 E. Rockcliff Rd. (602) 749-9000
Tucson, AZ 85715 Hydropool MH

#725P HOWARD JOHNSON MOTOR LODGE
☐ 1025 E. Benson Hwy. (602) 623-7792
Tucson, AZ 85713 Hydropool MH

#725Q QUALITY INN—TANQUE VERDE
☐ 7007 E. Tanque Verde (602) 298-2300
Tucson, AZ 85711 Hydropool MH

#725R SHERATON TUCSON EL CONQUISTADOR
☐ 1000 N. Oracle Rd. (602) 742-6116
Tucson, AZ 85704 Health Club MH

#725S WHITE STALLION RANCH
☐ Rte. 28 Box 567 (602) 297-0252
Tucson, AZ 85743 Hydropool MH

#725T BEST WESTERN AIRPORT INN
☐ 7060 S. Tucson Blvd. (602) 746-0271
Tucson, AZ 85706 Hydropool MH

#725U GRANADA ROYALE HOMETEL
7051 S. Tucson Blvd. (602) 573-0700
Tucson, AZ 85706 Hydropool MH

#725V HOLIDAY INN—AIRPORT
4550 S. Palo Verde Blvd. (602) 746-1161
Tucson, AZ 85714 Hydropool MH

#725W BEST WESTERN AZTEC INN
102 N. Alvernon Way (602) 795-0330
Tucson, AZ 85711 Health Club MH

#725X BEST WESTERN GHOST RANCH LODGE
801 W. Miracle Mile (602) 791-7565
Tucson, AZ 85703 Hydropool MH

#725Y BEST WESTERN INNSUITES
6201 N. Oracle Rd. (602) 297-8111
Tucson, AZ 85704 Hydropool MH

#725Z BEST WESTERN SANDMAN INN
3020 S. 6th Ave. (602) 623-5881
Tucson, AZ 85713 Hydropool MH

#726A CRAZY HORSE CAMPGROUND & RV PARK
on Craycroft Rd. (602) 889-0157
Tucson, AZ 85711 Hydropool CRV

#726B EL FRONTIER TRAVEL TRAILER RESORT
on Flowing Wells Road (602) 887-6369
Tucson, AZ 85705 Hydropool CRV

#726C FAR HORIZONS TRAILER VILLAGE
on Pantano Rd. (602) 296-1234
Tucson, AZ 85710 Hydropool CRV

#726D PRINCE OF TUCSON
on I-10 frontage road (602) 887-3501
Tucson, AZ 85701 Hydropool CRV

#726E RINCON COUNTRY TRAILER VILLAGE
on Escalante Rd. (602) 886-8431
Tucson, AZ 85730 Hydropool CRV

#726F THE SOUTH FORTY RV PARK
on Orange Grove Rd. (602) 297-2501
Tucson, AZ 85704 Hydropool CRV

#727A ROYAL INN
2941 4th Ave. (602) 344-0550
Yuma, AZ 85364 Hydropool MH

#727B STARDUST HOTEL
2350 S. 4th Ave. (602) 783-8861
Yuma, AZ 85364 Hydropool MH

#727C DESERT HOLIDAY TRAVEL TRAILER RANCH
on 4th Ave. (602) 344-4680
Yuma, AZ 85364 Hydropool CRV

#727D FOOTHILL VILLAGE RV PARK
on I-8 frontage road (602) 342-1030
Yuma, AZ 85364 Hydropool CRV

#727E FRIENDLY ACRES TRAILER PARK
on 8th St. (602) 783-8414
Yuma, AZ 85364 Hydropool CRV

#727F SPRING GARDEN TRAILER PARK
on 8th St. (602) 783-1526
Yuma, AZ 85364 Hydropool CRV

#727G YUMA MESA RV PARK
on I-8 business loop (602) 344-3369
Yuma, AZ 85364 Hydropool CRV

#727H YUMA — VENTURE
on I-8 frontage road (602) 342-9592
Yuma, AZ 85364 Hydropool CRV

#727I SUNI-SANDS TRAVEL TRAILER PARK
on I-8 business loop (602) 726-5941
Yuma, AZ 85364 Hydropool CRV

#728A ROCKING EH MOBILE RESORT
on I-10 business loop (602) 927-6321
Quartzite, AZ 85346 Hydropool CRV

#728B TYSON MOBILE & RV PARK
on I-10 business loop (602) 927-6480
Quartzite, AZ 85346 Hydropool CRV

#729A LAKE HAVASU TRAVEL TRAILER PARK
on Beachcomber Blvd. (602) 855-2322
Lake Havasu City, AZ 86403 Hydropool CRV

#729B KOA — LONDON BRIDGE
on London Bridge Blvd. (602) 855-3422
Lake Havasu City, AZ 86403 Hydropool CRV

#729C CRAZY HORSE CAMPGROUNDS
on Beachcomber Blvd. (602) 855-2127
Lake Havasu City, AZ 86403 Hydropool CRV

#729D HOLIDAY INN
271 S. Lake Havasu Ave. (602) 855-1111
Lake Havasu City, AZ 86403 Hydropool MH

#730 BEST WESTERN KINGS INN MOTEL
2930 Andy Devine Dr. (602) 753-6101
Lake Havasu City, AZ 86403 Hydropool MH

THREE HOT SPRINGS NEAR HOOVER DAM

Over many centuries flash floods have carved spectacular canyons leading to the Colorado River. In three of these canyons downstream from Hoover Dam, natural mineral water flows out of rocky side walls at temperatures above 105°. then gradually cools as it tumbles over a series of waterfalls between sandy-bottom pools. The water is sparkling clear, with no odor and a pleasant taste. Elevation 800 ft. Open all year except during flash floods.

Land routes to these hot springs range from difficult to impossible, requiring a minimum of several hours of strenuous hiking and scrambling. Information and safety instructions can be obtained at the Visitors Center maintained by Lake Mead National Recreation Area, three miles east of Boulder City on US 93.

If reached by boat from the Colorado River, all three hot springs can be visited in a single day. Fully equipped outboard-powered boats may be rented at Willow Beach Resort, eight to ten miles downstream from the springs. Willow Beach also has an excellent ramp for launching your own boat, a restaurant, a store, a motel and an RV park, The access road to Willow Beach connects with US 93, 13 miles south of Hoover Dam, on the Arizona side of the river.

Overnight camping, including campfires, is permitted at all times, but you will need to bring your own firewood.

731A GOLD STRIKE HOT SPRINGS

near Hoover Dam **(see map)**

non-commercial

The beach at the bottom of this canyon is within sight of a warning cable stretched across the river just below the dam. Hot-spring water is lukewarm as it flows into the river, but the stream temperature is higher and the waterfalls are more difficult as you travel up the canyon. Space for overnight camping is limited.

Gold Strike Hot Springs: All of this flow is geothermal water, still warmer than 90° in this lower canyon cascade.

Arizona (Ringbolt) Hot Springs: This ladder provides the only access to the upper canyon.

Boy Scout Hot Springs: Sheer rock walls make upper canyon travel challenging.

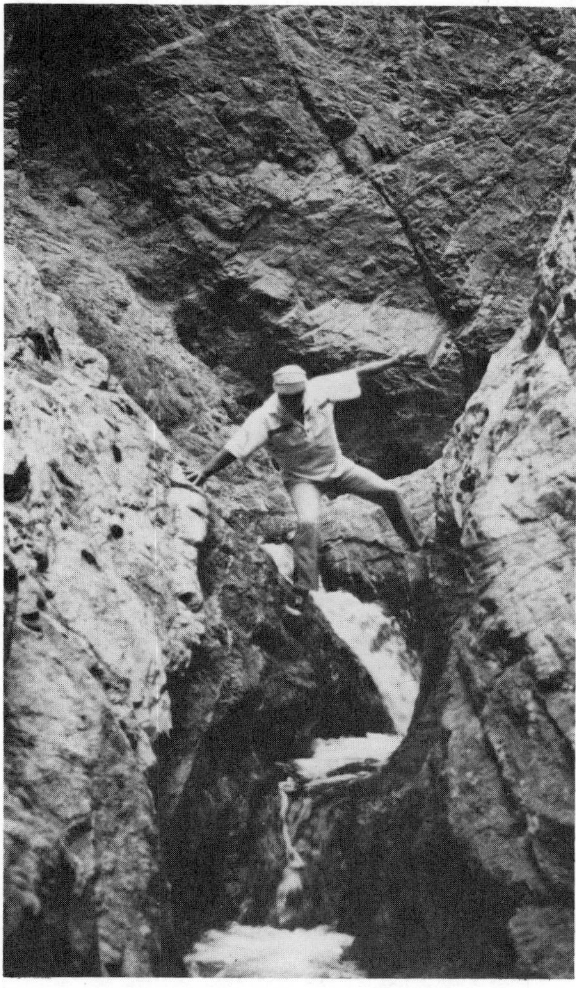

731B BOY SCOUT HOT SPRINGS

near Hoover Dam **(see map)**
non-commercial

A large cave can be seen in the riverbank just upstream from this canyon. The hot-spring water flow disappears under the canyon sand a hundred yards from the river, so there is no visible runoff at the landing beach. Temperatures in the lower pools and waterfalls are over 90°, and they increase as you travel up the canyon. Some hazardous climbing past waterfalls is required to reach several upper pools. In the wide lower canyon there is plenty of room for a large group to set up camp.

731C ARIZONA (RINGBOLT) HOT SPRINGS

near Hoover Dam **(see map)**
non-commercial

This is the most popular of the three hot springs because it is downstream from Ringbolt Rapids, a turbulent stretch of river too difficult for canoes and kayaks. A warning buoy can be seen on a large submerged rock near the beach at the bottom of this canyon.

The rangers have installed a metal ladder at the main waterfall in this canyon, so it is not difficult to reach the source pools, where water temperature is 106°, This water cools to 95° by the time it goes over the 25-foot waterfall.

The flow disappears under the canyon sand several hundred yards away from the river so there is a large amount of space available for overnight camping.

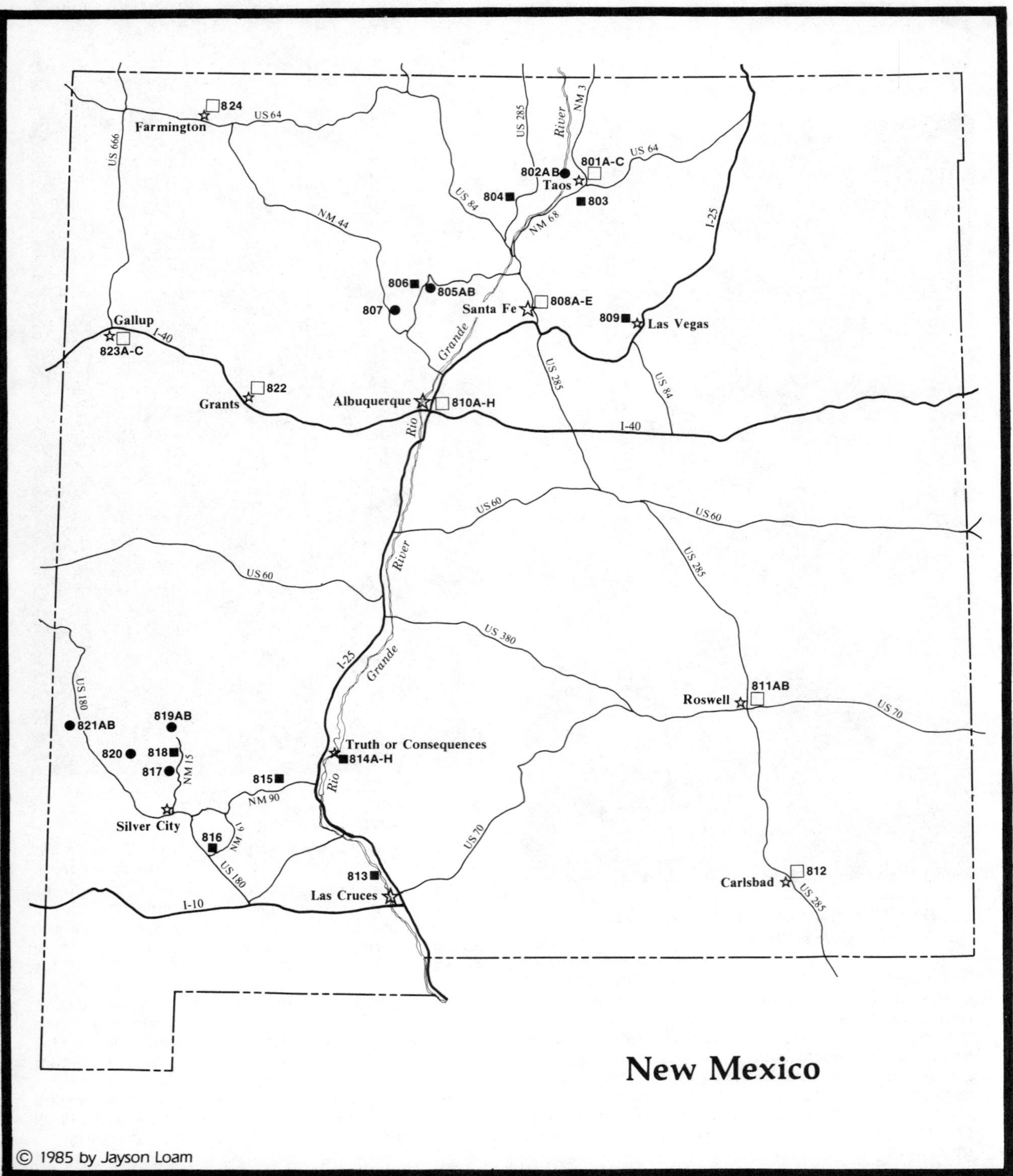

Farmington
824
US 64
US 666
US 285
River
NM 3
802AB
801A-C
US 64
Taos
804
803
US 84
NM 44
NM 68
I-25
806
805AB
807
Santa Fe
808A-E
809
Las Vegas
Gallup
I-40
823A-C
Grande
US 285
US 84
822
Grants
Albuquerque
810A-H
Rio
I-40
US 60
US 60
US 285
US 60
River
US 380
I-25
Grande
US 180
811AB
Roswell
US 70
821AB
819AB
820
818
817
NM 15
Truth or Consequences
814A-H
815
NM 90
Rio
Silver City
816
NM 61
US 70
US 180
813
Las Cruces
I-10
812
Carlsbad
US 285
New Mexico

MAP AND DIRECTORY SYMBOLS

● **Unimproved natural mineral water pool**
■ **Improved natural mineral water pool**
□ Gas-heated tap or well water pool

——— Paved highway
- - - Unpaved road
• • • • Hiking route

PR = Tubs or pools for rent by hour, day or treatment
MH = Rooms, cabins or dormitory spaces for rent by day, week or month
CRV = Camping or vehicle parking spaces, some with hookups, for rent by day, week, month or year

▲ *Black Rock Hot Springs:* Jagged rocks look somewhat forbidding, but this crystal-clear pool has a lovely soft sandy bottom.

#801A □ TENNIS RANCH OF TAOS
P.O. Drawer BBB (505) 776-2211
Taos, NM 87571 Hydropool MH

#801B □ EDELWEISS HOTEL
P.O. Box 931 (505) 776-2301
Taos, NM 87571 Hydropool MH

#801C □ INNSBRUCK LODGE
(505) 776-2313
Taos Ski Valley, NM 87571 Hydropool MH

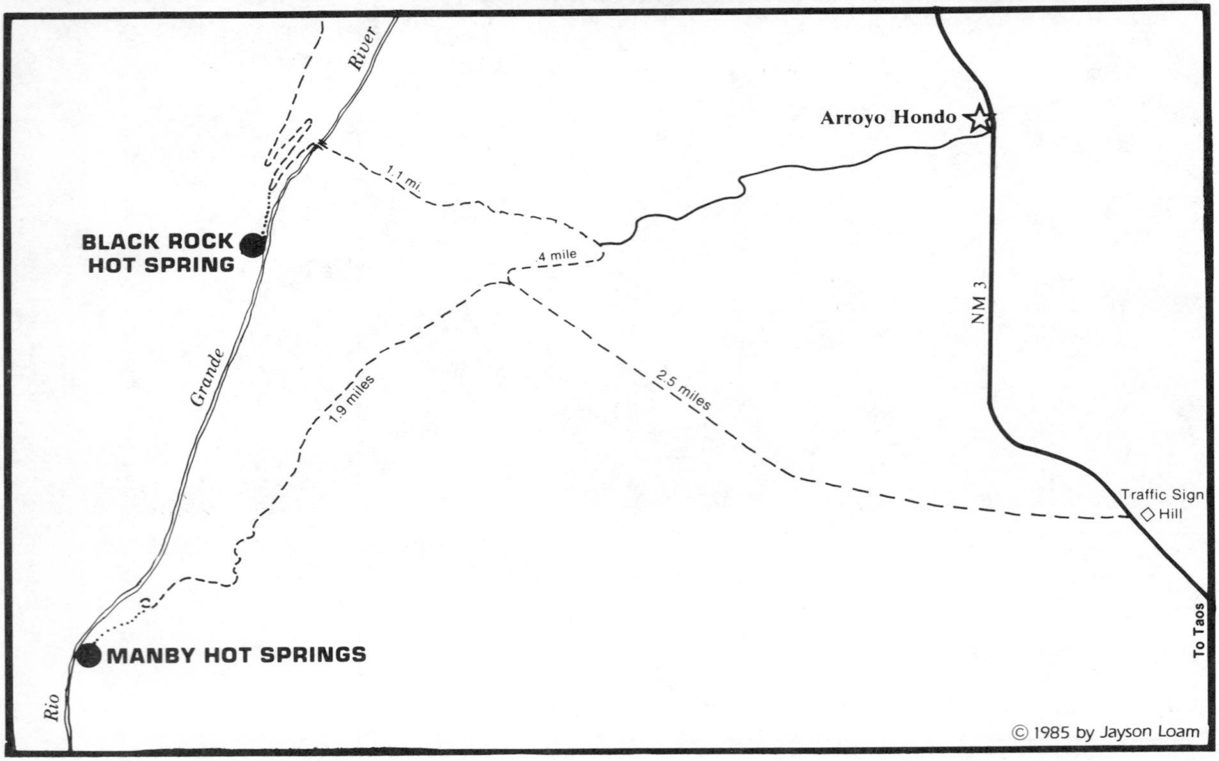

River
Arroyo Hondo
1.1 mi.
BLACK ROCK
HOT SPRING
.4 mile
NM 3
Grande
1.9 miles
2.5 miles
Traffic Sign
Hill
To Taos
MANBY HOT SPRINGS
Rio
© 1985 by Jayson Loam

#802A BLACK ROCK HOT SPRINGS

near the town of Arroyo Hondo (see map)
non-commercial

Rugged but friendly sand-bottom rock pool located on the west bank of the Rio Grande Gorge, just a few feet above river level. Elevation 6,500 ft. Open all year.

Natural mineral water flows up through the bottom at a rate sufficient to maintain pool temperature at 97°, except when high water in the river floods the pool. The apparent local custom is clothing optional.

There are no services available. It is three miles to a store, cafe, service station, etc. and nine miles to RV hookups.

Directions: There is a small parking area at the end of the first switchback on the gravel road that winds up the west face of the gorge. Follow the trail downstream from that parking area.

Black Rock Hot Springs: Three steps from the geothermal pool it is possible to dive into the cool and clear Rio Grande River. Hundreds of miles downstream, in West Texas, the same river becomes warmer and browner.

#802B MANBY HOT SPRINGS (see map)

near the town of Arroyo Hondo
non- commercial

Two primitive soaking pools in the ruins of an old stagecoach stop on the east bank of the Rio Grande Gorge. Elevation 6,500 ft. Open all year.

Natural mineral water flows out of the ground at 97° directly into two rock pools large enough for five or six people. The lower pool is only slightly above low water in the river so the temperature depends on the amount of cold water seeping into the volunteer-built rock pool. The apparent local custom is clothing optional.

There are no services on the premises. There is a limited amount of nearby level space in which overnight parking is not prohibited. It is four miles to a store, cafe, service station, etc. and ten miles to RV hookups.

Directions: Follow the map to the parking area on the edge of the gorge, then hike down the grade of the old stagecoach road to the springs.

Source maps: USGS *Arroyo Hondo.*

Manby Hot Springs: From this lower pool a plunge in the river is only one step away.

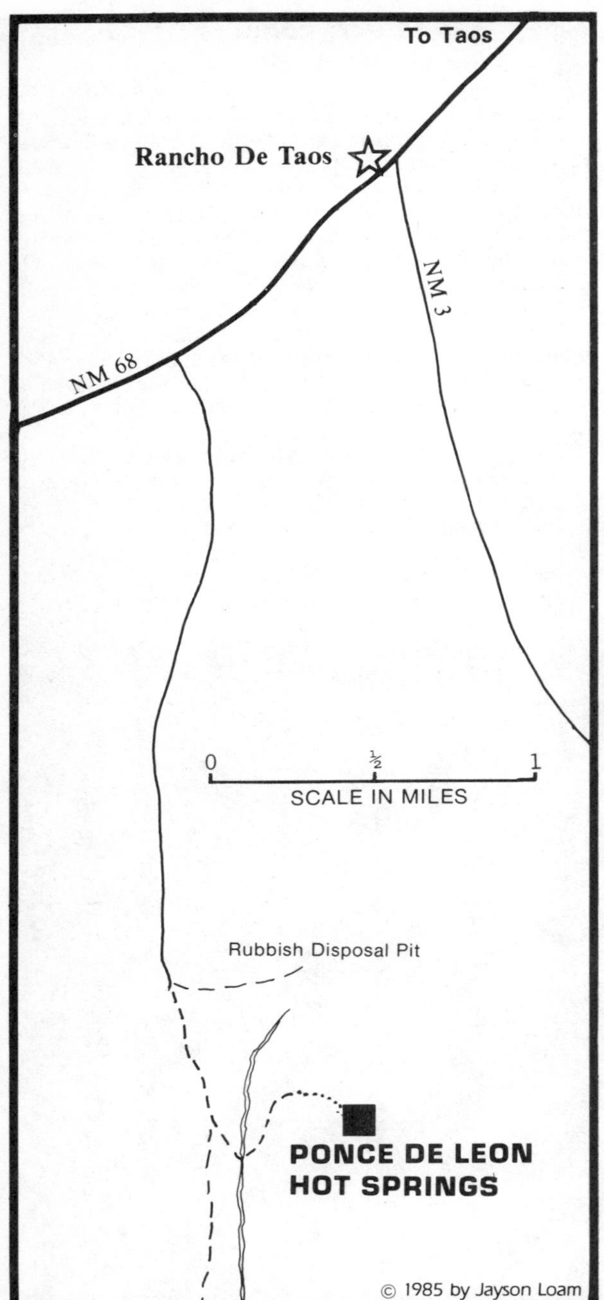

#803 PONCE DE LEON HOT SPRINGS

(see map)

near the town of Rancho de Taos

non- commercial

The dynamited and bulldozed remains of a once-elaborate resort, located in the desert foothills south of Taos. Elevation 6,900 ft. Open all year.

Natural mineral water flows out of the ground at the rate of 50 gallons per minute and at a temperature of 90°. This flow meanders through the ruins, supplying two badly littered small pools that are used by visitors willing to wade through empty beer cans and broken glass. This appears to be a heavy-duty party place, so clothing is advisable, day and night.

There are no services available, and very limited parking space. It is three miles to a store, cafe, service station, etc. and six miles to RV hookups.

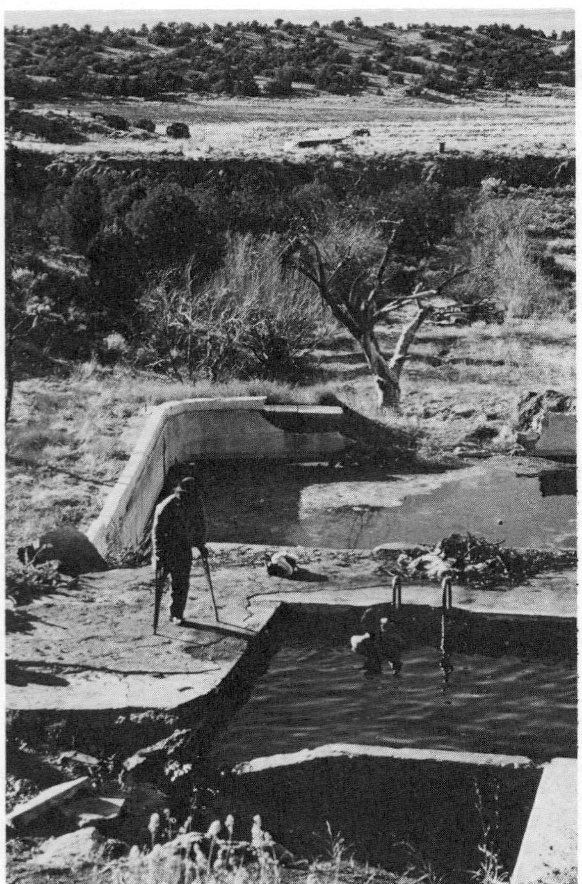

Ponce De Leon Hot Springs: The farther wall of the main swimming pool was blown out to discourage use, especially at night.

#804 OJO CALIENTE RESORT

Box 468 **(505) 583-2233**
Ojo Caliente, NM 87549 **PR + MH + CRV**

An older resort and bath house, located in the foothills of Carson National Forest, 46 miles north of Santa Fe. Elevation 6,300 ft. Open all year.

Natural mineral water flows out of five different springs with different temperatures and different mineral contents. The outdoor swimming pool (open May through September) averages 75°. There are separate men's and women's bath houses, each containing a large soaking pool at 113° and individual tubs with temperatures controllable up to 105°. Bathing suits required in swimming pool but not in bath house.

Massage, sweat wrap, dining room (April through October), store, cabins, rooms, RV hookups, campground and picnic area available on the premises. MasterCard and Visa accepted. It is 25 miles to a public bus, and pick-up service is available for registered guests—phone for details.

Directions: From Santa Fe go 46 miles north on US 285. Watch for signs.

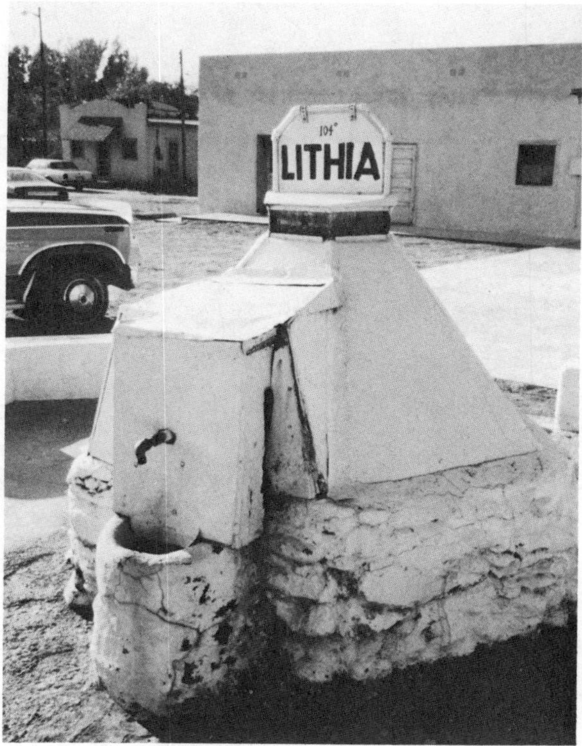

Ojo Caliente Resort: Water with different mineral content comes out of several springs on the grounds.

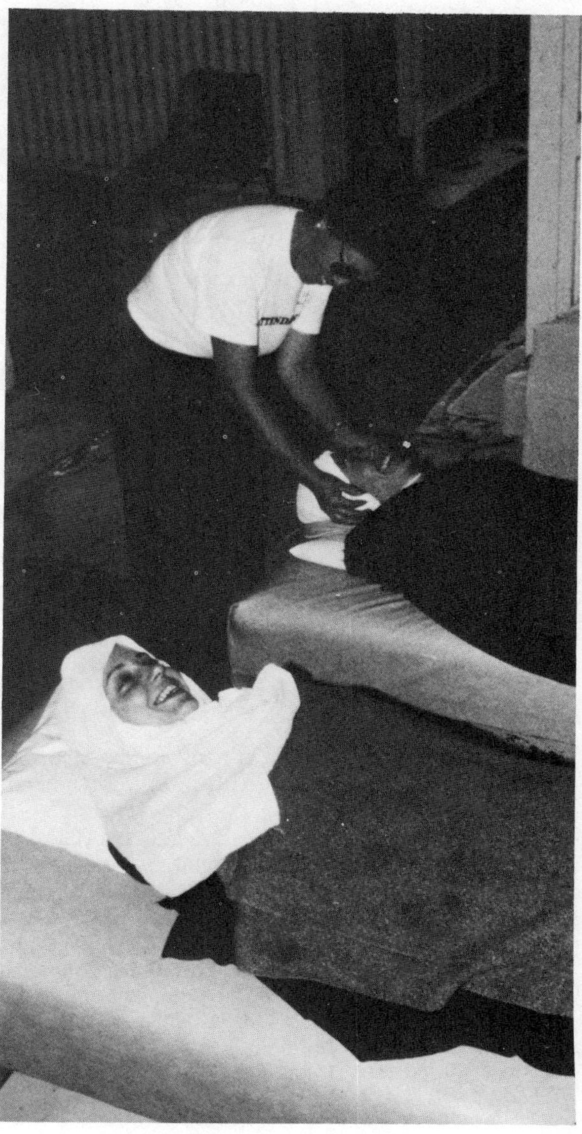

One of the goals of the *Ojo Caliente* staff is to keep customers comfortable while they are tightly wound in a sweat wrap.

Spence Hot Spring: A truly spectacular hot spring blessed with a setting to match.

#805A SPENCE HOT SPRING (see map)

near the town of Jemez Springs

non-commercial

A unique sand-bottom pool on a steep hillside, with a spectacular view of surrounding mountains. Located in the Santa Fe National Forest on the east side of the Jemez River. Elevation 6,600 ft. Open all year.

Natural mineral water (106°) flows up through the sandy bottom into a rock-bordered pool large enough for ten people. The rate of flow-through is enough to keep the pool clean and averaging 104°. Several years ago the spring had a posted Forest Service rule requiring bathing suits on Thursday, Friday and Saturday, with suits optional on Sunday, Monday, Tuesday and Wednesday. Now the apparent local custom is clothing optional every day.

There are no services available. It is seven miles to a store, motel and service station.

Directions: From the town of Jemez Springs, go seven miles north on NM 4, to a large parking area on the east side of the highway. The trail includes a log spanning the Jemez River, and a steep slope up to the springs. Warning—some cars have been broken into while in this parking area.

Source map: *Santa Fe National Forest.*

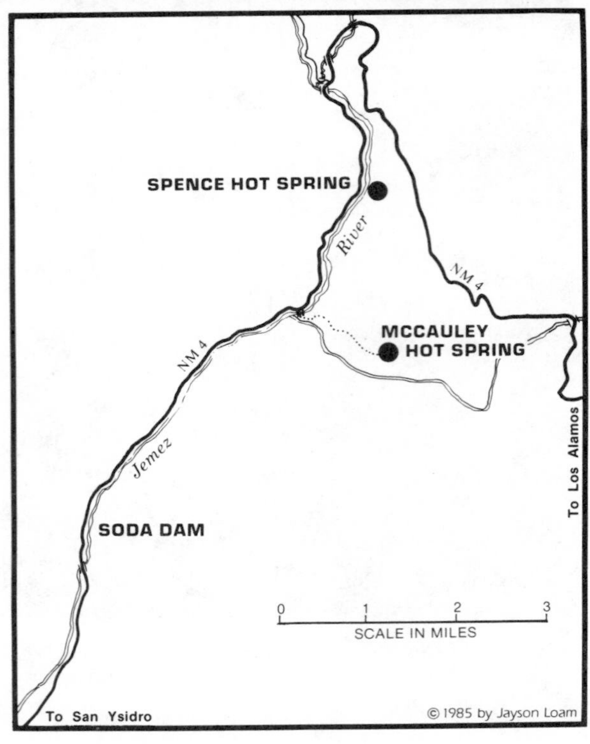

Builders of the *Spence Hot Spring* pool were able to stabilize a steep slope with no visible use of concrete.

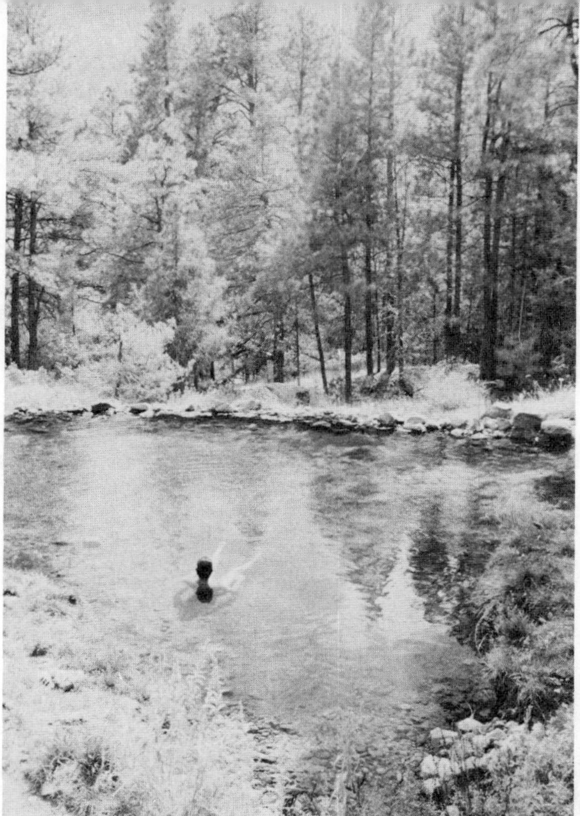

McCauley Hot Springs: This graceful pool is a legacy from the good old CCC.

#805B MCCAULEY HOT SPRING (see map)

near the town of Jemez Springs

non-commercial

Very large warm pool in a gorgeous mountain clearing. Elevation 7,300 ft. Open approximately mid-April through October.

Natural mineral water flows out of the ground at 90° directly into a two-foot-deep pond, 40 feet in diameter. The rate of flow is sufficient to hold the temperature at approximately 85°. The apparent local custom is clothing optional.

There are no services available. However, the guppies and neon tetras that live in the pool will entertain you by nibbling on your body hair. It is six miles to a store, cafe, service station, etc. and 17 miles to RV hookups.

Directions: From Jemez Springs, go 5.2 miles north on NM 4 to Battleship Rock picnic area. From the firepit gazebo hike 1¼ miles up USFS trail #137 to spring and campsite. This trail is moderately strenuous, especially at this altitude.

Source map: USGS *Jemez Springs*.

#806 JEMEZ SPRINGS BATH HOUSE AND MOTEL

Box 8 **(505) 829-3854**
Jemez Springs, NM 87205 **PR + MH**

A four-unit motel with primitive riverbank hot pools, plus an older traditional bath house, both operated by the adjoining Bodhi Mandala Zen Center. Located in the town of Jemez Springs. Elevation 6,200 ft. Open all year subject to weather conditions. Phone for current information.

Natural mineral water flows out of the ground at 169°, then into four rock-and-sand soaking pools, where it is mixed with river water to achieve the desired soaking temperature. Use of the pools is reserved for registered motel guests only. Clothing is optional in the pools and in the river.

Natural mineral water from a city-owned spring is piped to the city-owned bath house, which has four private rooms, each containing a one-person bath tub. The hot mineral water is mixed with tap water in the tub to provide the desired soaking temperature.

Massage and therapeutic reflexology are available on the premises. It is one block to a store, cafe and service station. Phone for rates, reservations and directions.

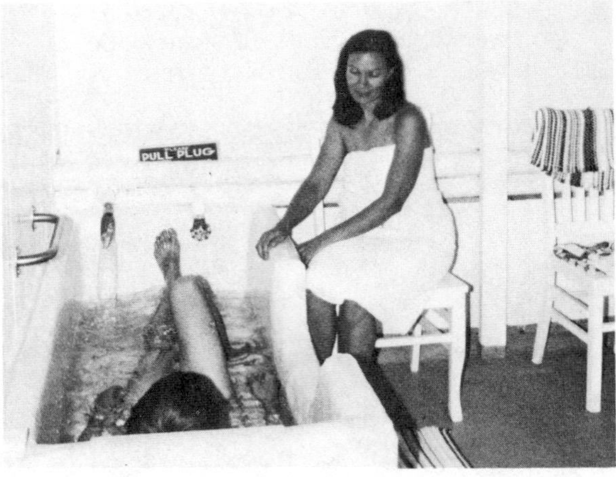

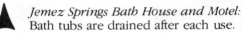

Jemez Springs Bath House and Motel: Bath tubs are drained after each use.

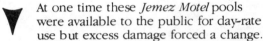

At one time these *Jemez Motel* pools were available to the public for day-rate use but excess damage forced a change.

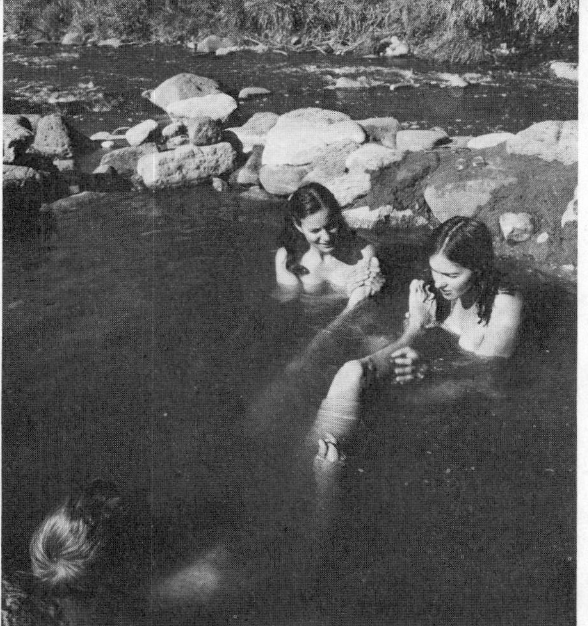

#807 HOLY GHOST WARM SPRINGS

near the town of San Ysidro

non-commercial

Ruins of an old burned-out resort, now reduced to a few primitive soaking pools, surrounded by colorful rock formations. Elevation 6,000 ft. Open all year.

Natural mineral water flows out of a large spring at 129°, then through a ditch to an arroyo where volunteers have carved several pools in the tufa formations. Pool water temperature is controlled by admitting limited amounts of the hotter water flowing by. The apparent local custom is clothing optional.

There are no services available on the premises. There is a limited amount of level space on which overnight parking is not prohibited. It is twelve miles to a store, cafe, service station, and RV hookups.

Directions: From the junction of NM 4 and NM 44 in San Ysidro, go 11.8 miles north on NM 44 to a small asphalt parking area on the east side of the highway. Walk 100 yards east past ruins to the hot springs.

Source map: USGS *Holy Ghost Spring.*

If you want your primitive skinnydipping hot spring to be within a few steps of your room, these *Jemez Motel* pools are for you.

Holy Ghost Warm Springs: These pools were carved from the soft mineral deposits left when the mineral water evaporated.

Ten Thousand Waves: This is the kind of service and atmosphere which is giving new rent-a-tub places a very good name.

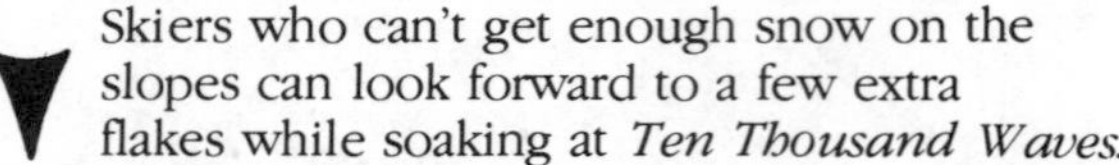

Skiers who can't get enough snow on the slopes can look forward to a few extra flakes while soaking at *Ten Thousand Waves.*

#808A TEN THOUSAND WAVES

☐ P.O. Box 6138 (505) 982-9304
Santa Fe, NM 87502 PR

An intriguing blend of American technology and Japanese hot-tub traditions, located on Ski Basin Road northeast of Santa Fe.

Pools for rent to the public, using gas-heated tap water, treated with ultraviolet light and hydrogen peroxide.

Seven private enclosures, rented by the hour. Water temperature: 104 - 106°. A sauna is available in one enclosure.

One enclosed communal wood tub, large enough for 14 people. Water temperature: 104 - 106°.

Special features: kimono, sandals, shampoo and hair dryers provided. Private lockers are available in men's and women's dressing rooms.

Bathing suits: optional everywhere except at front desk.

Services available: massage, juice bar.

Credit cards accepted: Visa and MasterCard.

Phone for rates, reservations and directions.

The creative use of wood and greenery creates a primitive atmosphere around the pools of *Ten Thousand Waves.*

#808B BISHOP'S LODGE

☐ P.O. Box 2367 (505) 983-6377
Santa Fe, NM 87501 Hydropool MH

#808C SANTA FE INN

☐ 3011 Cerrillos Rd. (505) 471-1211
Santa Fe, NM 87501 Hydropool MH

#808D BEST WESTERN LAMPLIGHTER MOTEL

☐ 2405 Cerrillos Rd. (505) 471-8000
Santa Fe, NM 87501 Hydropool MH

#808E KOA — RANCHERO DE SANTA FE

☐ on I-25 frontage road (505) 983-3482
Santa Fe, NM 87501 Hydropool CRV

Montezuma Hot Springs: This is a rare example of an abandoned resort being salvaged by the work of volunteers.

#809 MONTEZUMA HOT SPRINGS

■ **near the town of Las Vegas non-commercial**

The once-abandoned ruins of a major turn-of-the-century hot-springs resort bath house, with indoor and outdoor soaking pools, now cleaned up with public cooperation and open to the public without charge. Located on NM 65, at the mouth of a mountain canyon, just below the main buildings newly occupied by United World College, a project of the Armand Hammer Foundation. Elevation 7,700 ft. Open all year.

Natural mineral water flows out of several springs (94° to 113°) into nine old-fashioned cement soaking pits (four outdoor, five in a battered bath house), resulting in a wide range of temperature choices. Volunteer work by students and public-spirited citizens will probably result in further improvement. The apparent local custom is bathing suits during the day and clothing optional at night.

There are no services available on the premises. It is six miles to a store, cafe, service station, etc.

Directions: From the town of Las Vegas, go six miles northwest on NM 65. The hot-spring area is on the right side of the road below the group of large college buildings.

#810A BEST WESTERN FOUR SEASONS MOTOR INN
☐ 3500 Carlisle Blvd. (505) 888-3311
Albuquerque, NM 87110 Hydropool MH

#810B HILTON INN — ALBUQUERQUE
☐ 1901 University Blvd. NE (505) 884-2500
Albuquerque, NM 87125 Hydropool MH

#810C ROYAL MOTOR HOTEL
☐ 4119 Central Ave. (505) 265-3585
Albuquerque, NM 87108 Hydropool MH

#810D BEST WESTERN AIRPORT INN
☐ 2400 Yale Blvd. SE (505) 242-7022
Albuquerque, NM 87106 Hydropool MH

#810E SHERATON — OLD TOWN INN
☐ 800 Rio Grande Blvd. NW (505) 843-6300
Albuquerque, NM 87104 Hydropool MH

#810F BEST WESTERN CLASSIC HOTEL
☐ 6815 Menaul Blvd. NE (505) 881-0000
Albuquerque, NM 87110 Hydropool MH

#810G BEST WESTERN AMERICAN MOTOR INN
☐ 12999 Central Ave. NE (505) 298-7426
Albuquerque, NM 87123 Hydropool MH

#810H ALBUQUERQUE MARRIOTT HOTEL
☐ 2101 Lousiana Blvd. NE (505) 881-6800
Albuquerque, NM 87110 Hydropool MH

#811A TRAVELODGE CONVENTION CENTER
☐ 2101 N. Main St. (505) 623-6050
Roswell, NM 88201 Hydropool MH

#811B BEST WESTERN SALLY PORT INN
☐ 2000 N. Main St. (505) 622-6430
Roswell, NM 88201 Hydropool MH

#812 RODEWAY INN
☐ 3804 National Parks Hwy (505) 887-5535
Carlsbad, NM 88220 Hydropool MH

#813 RADIUM SPRINGS

■ **Radium Springs, NM 88054**

An older health resort closed during litigation between the owners and the state. It is probable that some form of commercial resort will reopen eventually, and that the local office of the Dona Ana County Sheriff will know when that happens.

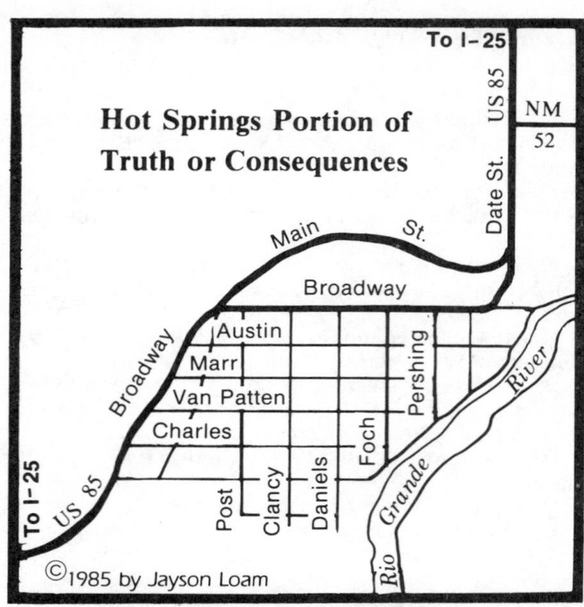

Marshall Apartments and Baths: Most of the bath house buildings date back to before the city of Hot Springs changed its name to Truth or Consequences.

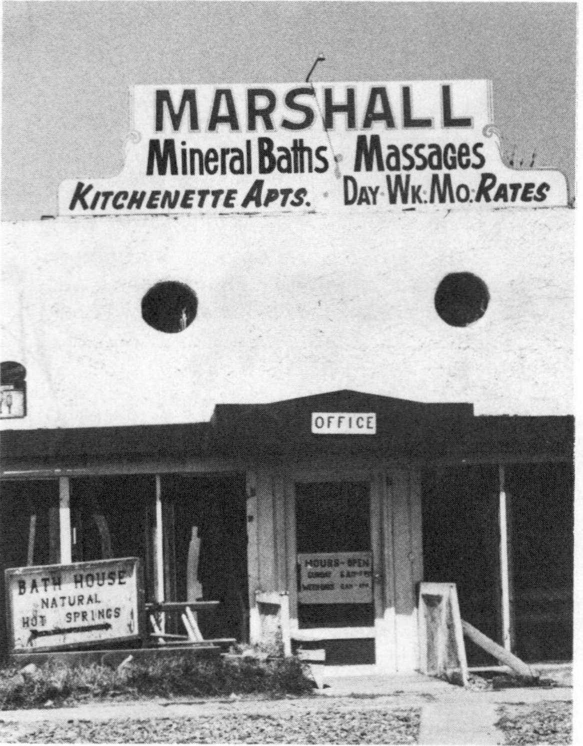

THE CITY OF TRUTH OR CONSEQUENCES

There are eight natural mineral-water establishments located in the hot-springs area of Truth or Consequences (see adjoining map). Take either of 2 exits from I-25. The city is on the Rio Grande River, below ElephantButte Dam. Elevation 4,300 ft. Open all year. Cafe, store, service station and RV hookups are within four blocks.

#814A DAVE'S CLOVERLEAF BATHS
■ 207 S. Daniels (505) 894-6303
Truth or Consequences, NM 87901 PR

Primarily a therapy and health facility, owned and operated by a physical therapist and naturopathic doctor.

Six private rooms, each containing a sunken pool and table. Temperature of pool controllable up to 108°.

Massage, acupressure, reflexology, diathermy and corrective physical therapy are available on the premises. No credit cards accepted.

#814B ROYCE LODGE AND BATHS
■ 720 Broadway (505) 894-3619
Truth or Consequences, NM 87901 PR + MH

Therapy-oriented bath house and hotel.

Three private rooms, each equipped with a sunken tub and massage table. Water temperature in tub controllable up to 110°.

Massage and reflexology therapy available on the premises, conducted by two doctors of naturopathy. MasterCard and Visa accepted.

#814C CHARLES MOTEL AND BATH HOUSE
■ 701 Broadway (505) 894-7154
Truth or Consequences, NM 87901 PR + MH

Older bath house and motel with some new units.

Indoor separate men's and women's sections, each equipped with a sauna, steam bath and four individual tubs with controllable water temperatures up to 110°.

Massage available on the premises. MasterCard and Visa accepted.

#814D BLACKSTONE APARTMENT & BATH HOUSE
■ 508 Austin (505) 894-6303
Truth or Consequences, NM 87901 PR + MH

Older bath house and motel units converted to apartments, now rented by the week or month.

Four private rooms, each containing a sunken tub and table. Water temperature in tubs is controllable up to 110°.

Massage and sweat wrap are available on the premises. No credit cards accepted.

#814E MARSHALL APARTMENTS AND BATHS
■ 213 S. Pershing (505) 894-3343
Truth or Consequences, NM 87901 PR + MH

Older bath house and motel units converted to apartments, now rented by the week or month.

Four private rooms with large pools, each with a gravel bottom and direct flow-through of unchlorinated hot mineral water. Temperatures range from 106° to 112°.

Massage available on the premises. No credit cards accepted.

#814F BROOKS APARTMENTS AND BATH HOUSE
■ 611 Marr (505) 894-3431
Truth or Consequences, NM 87901 PR + MH

Older bath house and motel units converted to apartments, now rented by the week or month.

Three private rooms, each containing a sunken tub and table. Water temperature in tubs is controllable up to 110°.

No credit cards accepted.

#814G TEXAS MOTEL
■ 409 Broadway (no phone)
Truth or Consequences, NM 87901 PR + MH

Older motel with bath house.

Three private rooms, each containing a sunken tub and table. Water temperature controllable up to 110°.

No credit cards accepted.

#814H ARTESIAN BATH HOUSE AND TRAILER PARK
■ 312 Marr (505) 894-2684
Truth or Consequences, NM 87901 PR + CRV

Older bath house and trailer park.

Nine private rooms, each containing a table and soaking pool, six single size and three double size. Water temperature controllable up to 110°.

RV hookups available on the premises. No credit cards accepted.

#815 HILLSBORO WARM SPRING

■ **near the town of Hillsboro**

non- commercial

Primarily a cattle-watering tank, frequently used by humans for soaking. Elevation 5,800 ft. Open all year. (Note: the BLM access road is open to the public. There are two closed but unlocked cattle gates which must be carefully reclosed after you drive through.)

Natural mineral water flows out of the ground at 94°, directly into a ten-foot-by-fifteen-foot-by-four-foot-deep concrete reservoir, where the water temperature is approximately 88°. The reservoir is fenced to keep cattle from falling in, but there are plenty of cow pies and flies under the nearby cottonwood trees. The remote location indicates the probability of a clothing optional custom, but that should be checked with anyone present when you arrive.

There are no services available, and it is four miles to a store, cafe, service station, etc. There is abundant level space on which overnight parking is not prohibited.

Source map: USGS *Hillsboro* (Note: the spring is marked "tank").

Hillsboro Warm Springs: Sometimes fences can be confusing. The rancher who leases this land from the BLM has the right to build fences to control his stock, *and* the public has access to this warm spring.

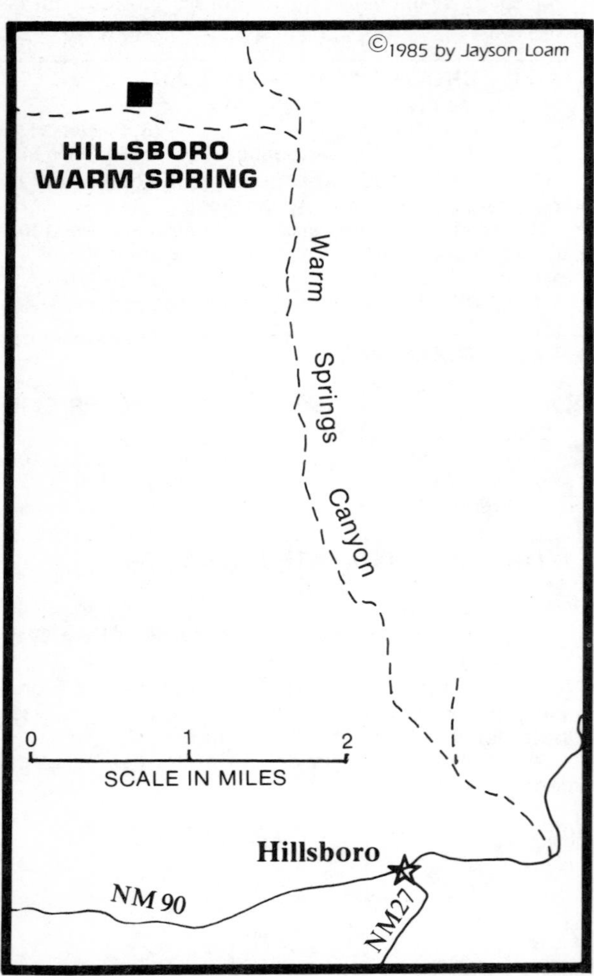

Faywood Hot Spring: There is a possibility that this location may become part of City of Rocks State Park. Watch for signs.

#816 FAYWOOD HOT SPRINGS (see map)

near the City of Rocks State Park

Enjoyable rock-and-mortar soaking pools on a desert knoll owned by a copper company. Administrative controversy has been going on for years, and may affect access, or use charges, at any time., Elevation 5,000 ft. Open all year.

Natural mineral water flows out of the ground at 129° and is piped to troughs serving four large three-foot-deep pools. The mineral water averages 115° when it reaches the pools, so pool water temperature is regulated by diverting the inflow whenever desired. During a recent period of regulated use, bathing suits were required in three of the pools, with clothing optional in the fourth. It would be advisable to ask everyone present about any current rules or customs.

There are no services available on the premises, and overnight parking might or might not be permitted. It is three miles to a campground, five miles to a store, motel, etc. and 10 miles to RV hookups.

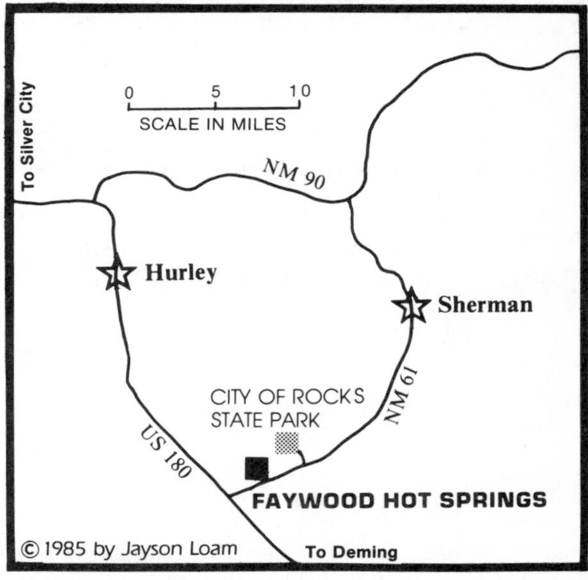

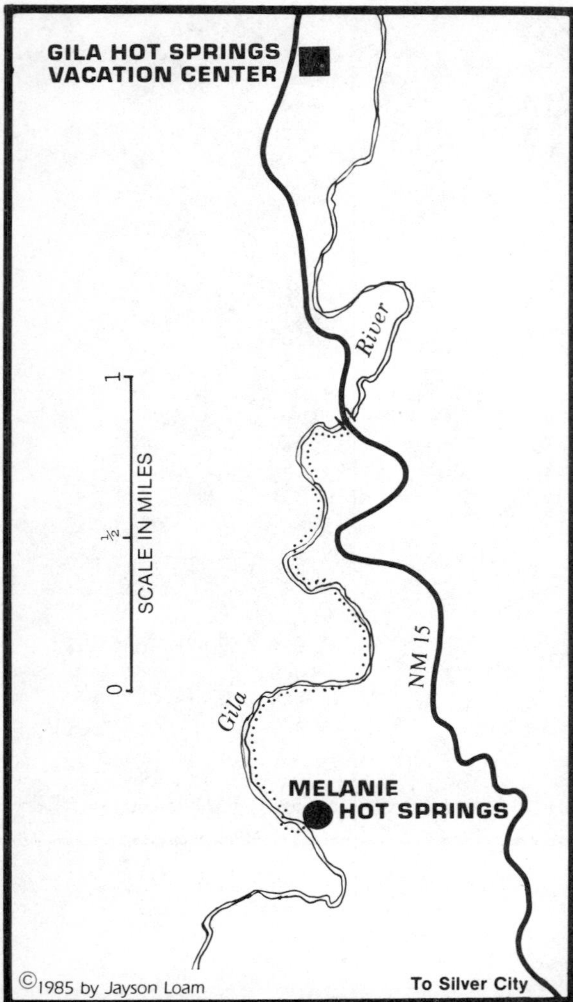

Melanie Hot Springs: The hike to and from this location would be a superb one-day trip, with picnic lunch, if only a volunteer would build a nice soaking pool to collect the hot-spring water.

#817 MELANIE HOT SPRINGS (see map)

near the town of Silver City

non-commercial

A group of wilderness hot springs which have soaking-pool potential, but which presently flow directly into the Gila River. Elevation 5,200 ft. Accessible only during low water in the river. Wilderness permit required.

Natural mineral water flows out of many rock fissures at 102° and runs across a steep slope before dropping directly into the river. With a shovel, a hand axe and some plastic sheeting, volunteers could build some small soaking pools on a ledge 20 feet above the river. Clothing optional is probably the custom at this remote location.

There are no services, but there is a tree-shaded campsite nearby. Vehicle overnight camping is available in Forks Campground where the 1½-mile trail to this hot spring starts. Most services are available at the Gila Hot Springs Vacation Center, three miles away.

Prepare to ford the river eight times in each direction. Parts of the unmaintained trail are not suitable for children. The last crossing, at the springs, is deeper than the other seven.

Source maps: *Gila National Forest.* USGS *Gila Hot Springs.*

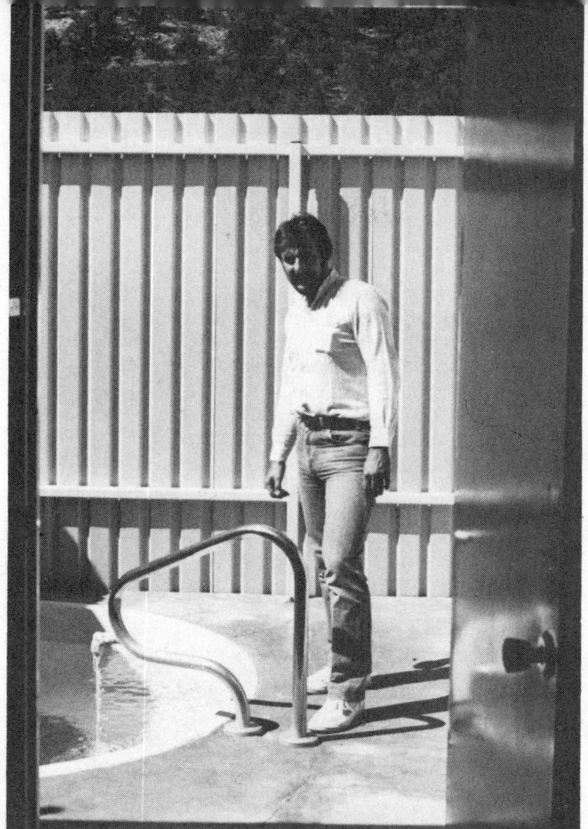

#818 GILA HOT SPRINGS VACATION CENTER (see map)

Gila Hot Springs, Rte. 11 **(505) 534-9551**
Silver City, NM 88061 **MH + CRV**

An all-year vacation resort located in the middle of the Gila National Forest. Elevation 5,000 ft. Open all year.

Natural mineral water flows out of springs on the east bank of the Gila River at 150° and is piped under the river to the Vacation Center, where it is used in an enclosed fiberglass hydropool, available only to registered guests. Pool water temperature is maintained at 90° in the summer and 100° in the winter. Clothing is optional within the pool enclosure.

Store, snack bar, cabins, RV hookups, laundromat, showers, trailer rental, service station, campground and picnic area are available on the premises. No credit cards are accepted.

Gila Hot Springs Vacation Center: Five years ago this location had plans to build a series of natural stone soaking pools overlooking the Gila River. To date the only pool is this fiberglass jet pool, closely surrounded by sterile blue plastic fence panels. There is no wilderness visible while soaking in hot-spring water.

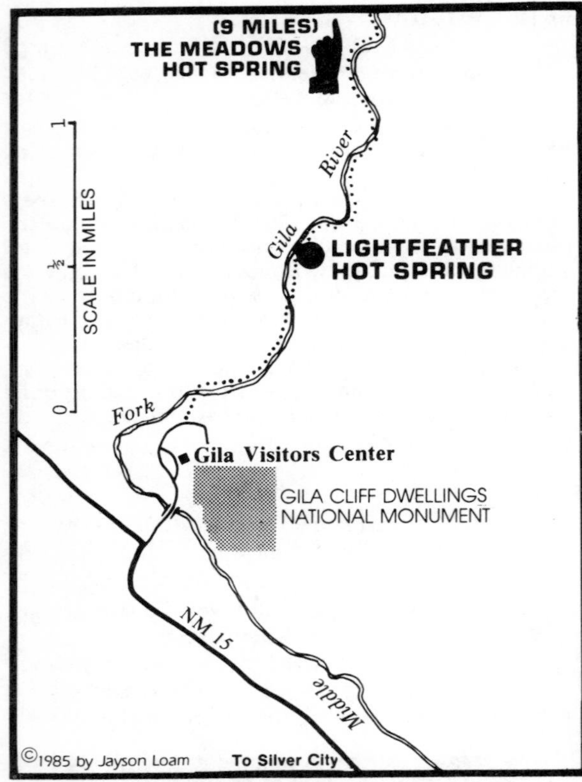

#819A LIGHTFEATHER HOT SPRING

near the Gila Visitors Center **(see map)**
non-commercial

A primitive rock-and-sand soaking pool on the Middle Fork of the Gila River, ½ mile from the Gila Visitors Center. Elevation 5,800 ft. Open all year, subject to high water in the river, which must be forded twice.

Natural mineral water flows out of the spring at 150°, directly into a large rock-and-sand pool, where the water gradually cools as it flows to the other end. Bathing suits are probably advisable during the daytime at this location.

There are no services available. It is four miles to a store, cafe, service station and RV hookups.

Lightfeather Hot Springs: The scalding hot water from the springs tends to form a shoulder-burning top layer, while leaving bone-chilling cold water on the bottom.

#819B THE MEADOWS HOT SPRING

near the Gila Visitors Center **(see map)**
non-commercial

A remote unimproved hot spring on a tree-and-fern covered hillside in the Gila Wilderness, on the Middle Fork on the Gila River. Elevation 6,200 ft. Accessible only during low water level in the river.

Natural mineral water flows out of a spring at 92° and cascades directly into a log-and-rock-dam pool large enough to hold 10 people. The apparent local custom is clothing optional.

There are no services available. The nine-mile hike from Lightfeather Hot Spring requires fording the river 42 times, so come prepared to camp overnight. All services are on the south side of Lightfeather Hot Spring.

A wilderness permit is required before entering this area. While obtaining your permit from the ranger at the Gila Visitors Center, check on the adequacy of your provisions and on the level of the water in the river.

Source maps: Gila National Forest. USGS *Woodland Park.* (Note: This hot spring is not shown on either map.)

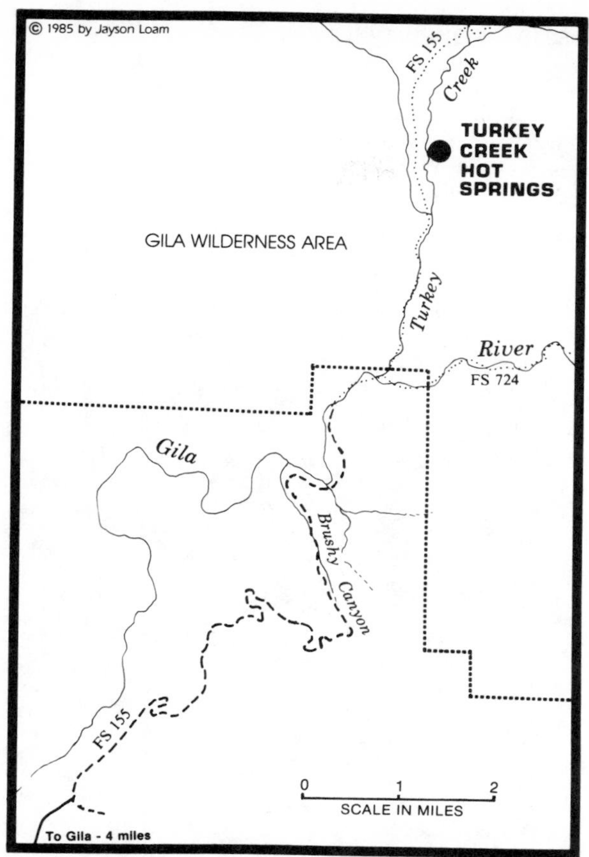

#820 TURKEY CREEK HOT SPRINGS

near the town of Cliff **(see map)**

non-commercial

Several truly primitive hot springs accessible only via a challenging and rewarding hike into the Gila Wilderness. Elevation 5,200 ft. Not accessible during high water flow in the Gila River.

Natural mineral water (approximately 160°) flows out of many rock fractures along the bottom of Turkey Creek Canyon, combining with creek water in several volunteer-built soaking pools. Temperatures are regulated by controlling the relative amounts of hot and cold water entering a pool. The apparent local custom is clothing optional.

There are no services available, but there are a limited number of overnight camping spots near the hot springs. Visitors have done an excellent job of packing out all their trash; please do your part to maintain this tradition. A store, cafe, service station, etc. are 17 miles away.

From the end of the jeep road, Wilderness Trail #724 crosses the Gila River several times before reaching a junction with Wilderness Trail #155, which starts up Turkey Creek Canyon. Approximately two miles from that junction, #155 begins to climb up onto a ridge separating Turkey Creek from Skeleton Canyon. Do not follow #155 up onto that ridge. Instead, stay in the bottom of Turkey Creek Canyon, even though there is often no visible trail. Another half mile will bring you to the first of the springs.

Source maps: Gila National Forest. Gila Wilderness and Black Range Primitive Area. USGS *Canyon Hill*. (Note: Turkey Creek Hot Springs does not appear on any of these maps.)

Turkey Creek Hot Springs: This is not a place to meditate in silence. However, if you are soothed by the sounds of a waterfall while soaking, this could be worth your time.

#821A SAN FRANCISCO HOT SPRINGS

● **near the town of Pleasanton** **(see map)**
non-commercial

Several primitive hot springs along the east bank of the San Francisco River in the Gila National Forest. Elevation 4,600 ft. Open all year.

Natural mineral water flows out of the ground at 108° and flows into a series of volunteer-built rock-and-mud pools on the riverbank. The parking area for this popular hot-spring site is only ten yards away, but the apparent local custom is clothing optional in the pools and adjoining river.

There are no services available, and overnight parking and camping are prohibited. It is five miles to a store, cafe, service station etc., seven miles to a campground, and 52 miles to RV hookups.

Directions: Watch for San Francisco Hot Springs signs on US 180, two miles south of Pleasanton; turn off onto gravel road leading to parking area.

#821B BUBBLES HOT SPRINGS (see map)

● **near the town of Pleasanton**
non-commercial

One of the truly great unimproved hot springs, in terms of size, water temperature, location and scenery. Elevation 4,600 ft. Open all year except during high water in the river.

Several years ago a major flood scoured out a 50-by-100-foot pool under a spectacular cliff, deposited a giant sand bar in front of the pool, and dropped the normal river flow into a channel 100 yards away. Natural mineral water now flows up through the sandy pool bottom at 106°, maintaining the entire five-foot-deep pool at 102°. The pool even skims and cleans itself by flowing out over a small volunteer-built dam. The apparent local custom is clothing optional.

There are no services available. See the previous listing for the distance to services.

Directions: From the parking area at San Francisco Hot Springs, hike downstream approximately ½ mile, crossing the river three times.

Source map: USGS *Wilson Mountain.*

#822 ☐ BEST WESTERN — THE INN
P.O. Drawer T (505) 287-7901
Grants, NM 87020 Hydropool MH

#823A ☐ TRAVELODGE
1709 W. Hwy 66 (505) 863-9301
Gallup, NM 87301 Hydropool MH

#823B ☐ RODEWAY INN
2003 W. Hwy 66 (505) 863-9385
Gallup, NM 87301 Hydropool MH

#823C ☐ BEST WESTERN — THE INN
309 W. Hwy 66 (505) 722-2221
Gallup, NM 87301 Hydropool MH

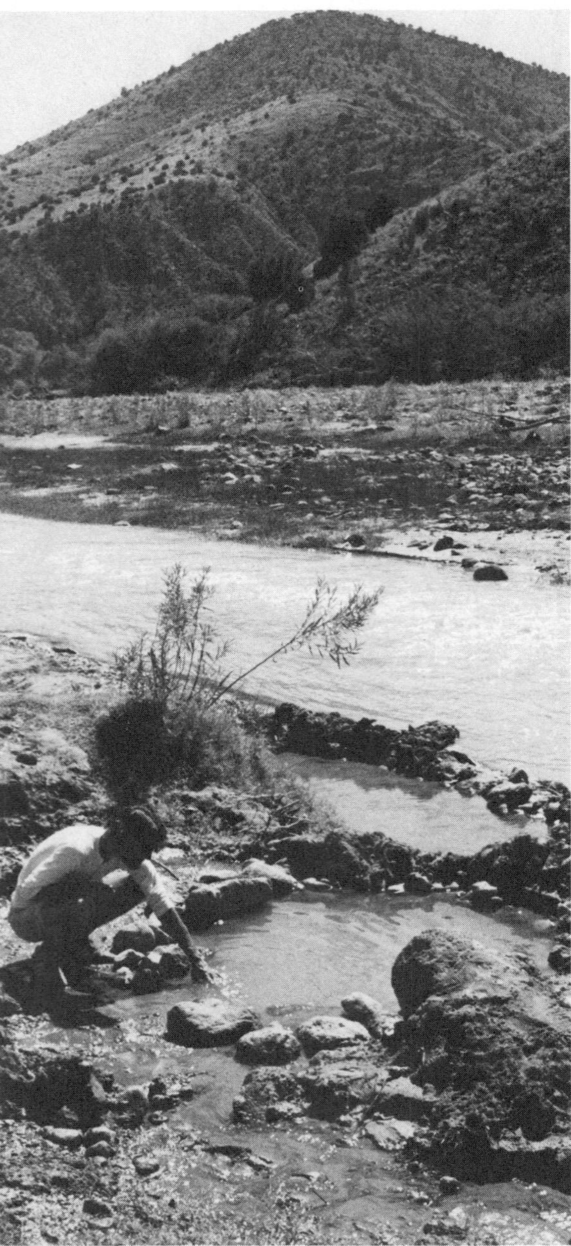

#824 BEST WESTERN — THE INN
700 Scott Ave. (505) 327-5221
Farmington, NM 87401 Hydropool MH

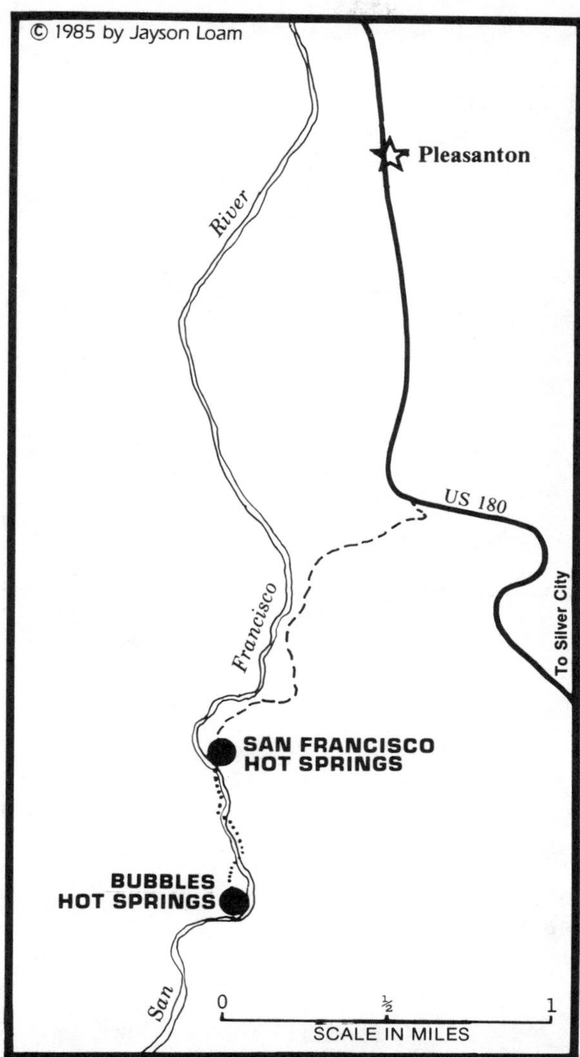

San Francisco Hot Springs: These are truly expendable volunteer-built pools. Each spring flood wipes them all out and deposits a fresh batch of rocks and mud.

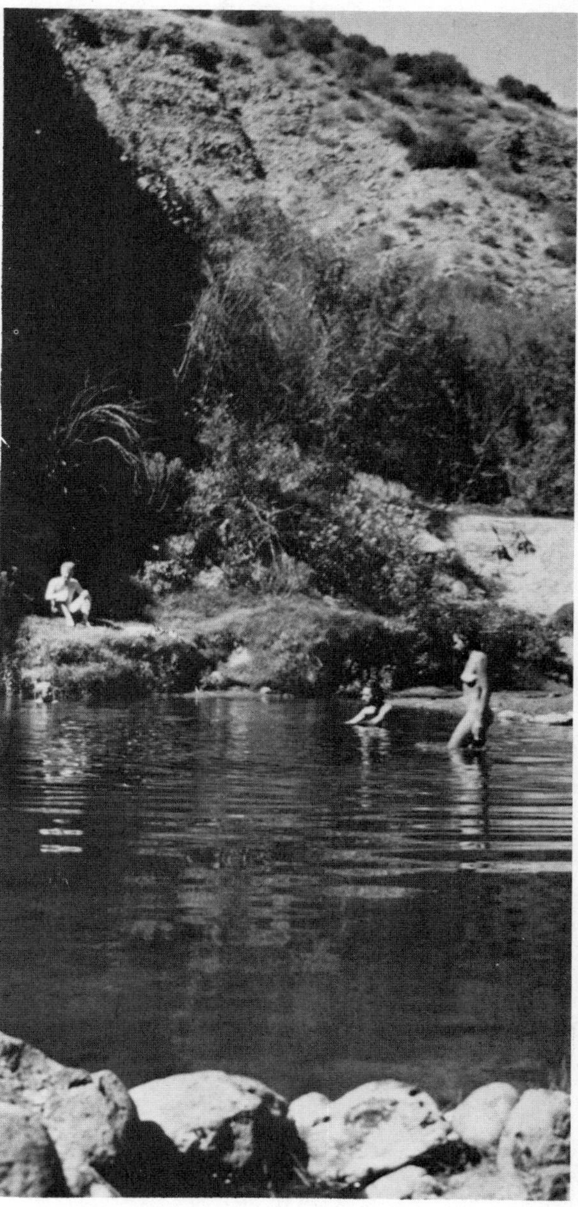

▲ *Bubbles Hot Springs:* This giant pool at the foot of a sheer rock cliff qualifies for the description "dramatic tranquility."

Far West Texas

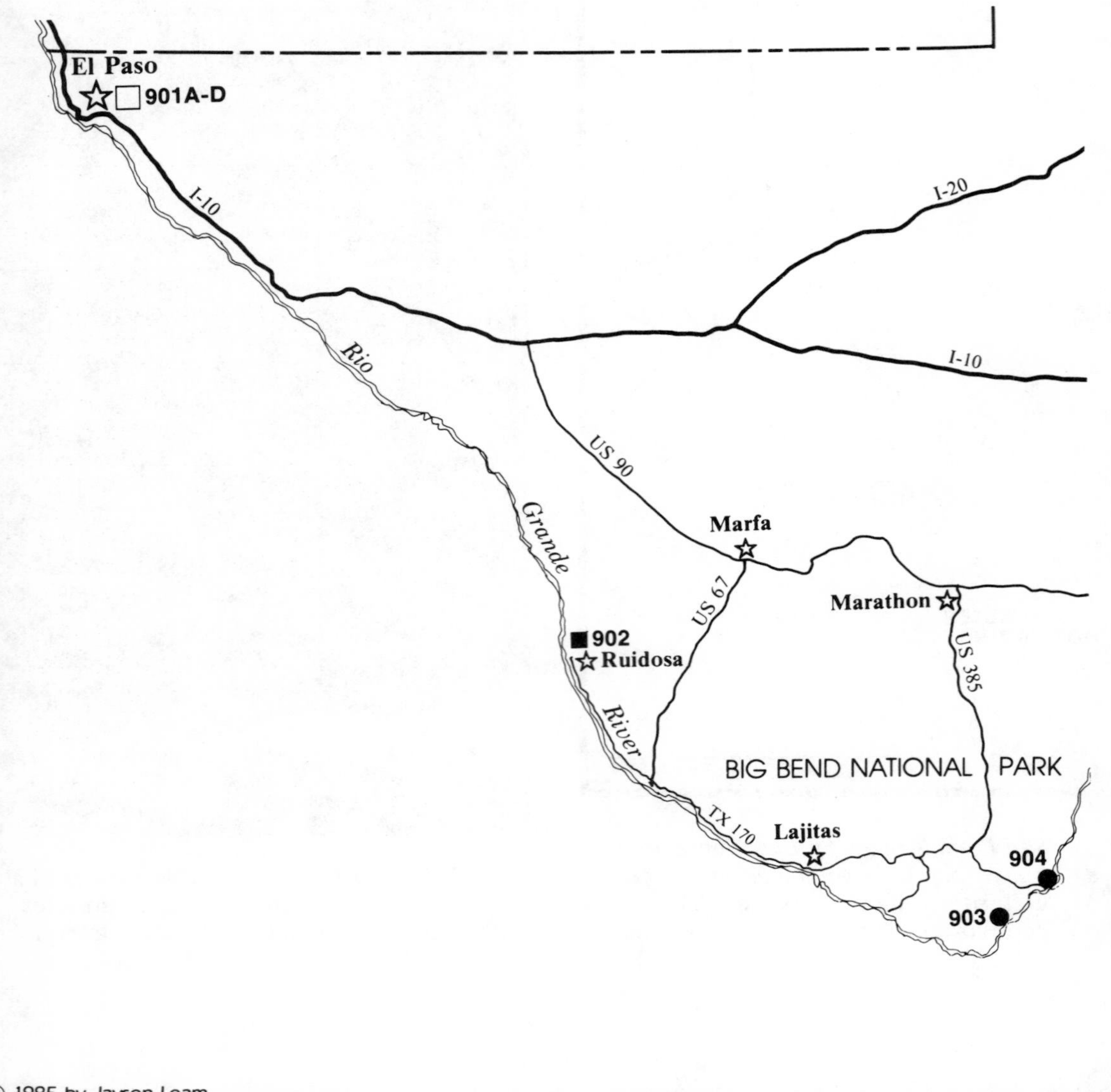

MAP AND DIRECTORY SYMBOLS

● **Unimproved natural mineral water pool**
■ **Improved natural mineral water pool**
□ Gas-heated tap or well water pool

——— Paved highway
- - - Unpaved road
.... Hiking route

PR = Tubs or pools for rent by hour, day or treatment
MH = Rooms, cabins or dormitory spaces for rent by day, week or month
CRV = Camping or vehicle parking spaces, some with hookups, for rent by day, week, month or year

Kingston Hot Springs: There are no fancy hydrojets, air blower bubbles or spray mists in this no-frills Texas hot bath.

#901A EXECUTIVE INN — EL PASO
□ 500 Executive Center Blvd. (915) 532-8981
El Paso, TX 79902 Hydropool MH

#901B GRANADA ROYALE HOMETEL
□ 6100 Gateway East (915) 779-6222
El Paso, TX 79905 Hydropool MH

#901C EL PASO MARRIOTT HOTEL
□ Airways Blvd. & Montana Ave. (915) 779-3300
El Paso, TX 79949 Hydropool MH

#901D MISSION RV PARK
□ on I-10 business loop (915) 859-1133
El Paso, TX 79901 Hydropool CRV

#902 KINGSTON HOT SPRINGS
■ **Box 22, Ruidosa Route (915) 358-4416**
Marfa, TX 79843 PR + MH + CRV

Older commercial resort in a verdant canyon surrounded by miles of barren, rugged desert. Elevation 3,600 ft. Open all year.

Natural mineral water flows out of a spring at 118° and is piped to individual soaking tubs in four small private rooms. Tub temperature is adjustable by adding cold water as needed.

Motel rooms, overnight camping and RV spaces are available on the premises. It is 15 miles to a service station and 45 miles to a restaurant.

Directions: From the town of Presidio go 60 miles northwest on TX 170 to Ruidosa. Follow signs seven miles to Kingston Hot Springs.

Boquillas Hot Springs: More than two million gallons of this mineral water flows out every day, from "fossil water" deposited deep underground at least 20,000 years ago. In this century the Rio Grande has flooded more than 20 ft. above the level seen here.

#903 WILDERNESS HOT SPRING AND RIVER RAFTING ALONG THE RIO GRANDE IN TEXAS

More than a dozen primitive hot springs are scattered along both banks of the Rio Grande River in the Big Bend National Park area. There are also many rapids (up to Class IV) to be run. Trips can be arranged for from one day up to ten days, depending on the part of the river selected. Telephone either of the following numbers for more information.

The Rio Grande Guides Association: (915) 371-2489

National Park Service: (915) 477-2251.

#904 BOQUILLAS HOT SPRING

near the town of Lajitas, Texas

non-commercial

Historic masonry hot pool in the ruins of an old resort on the banks of the Rio Grande River. Located near the Rio Grande Village Campground in Big Bend National Park. Elevation 1,800 ft. Open all year.

Natural mineral water flows out of the ground at 105°, into a large, shallow soaking pool a few feet above river level. Bathing suits are advisable during the daytime at this location.

There are no services on the premises. It is six miles to a store, service station, overnight camping and RV hookups, 28 miles to a motel and restaurant.

Directions: From Big Bend National Park Headquarters drive 16 miles toward Rio Grande Village Campground. Turn right at Hot Spring sign; drive two miles on dirt road to end and walk ¼ mile downriver to hot spring.

Source map: *Big Bend National Park*.

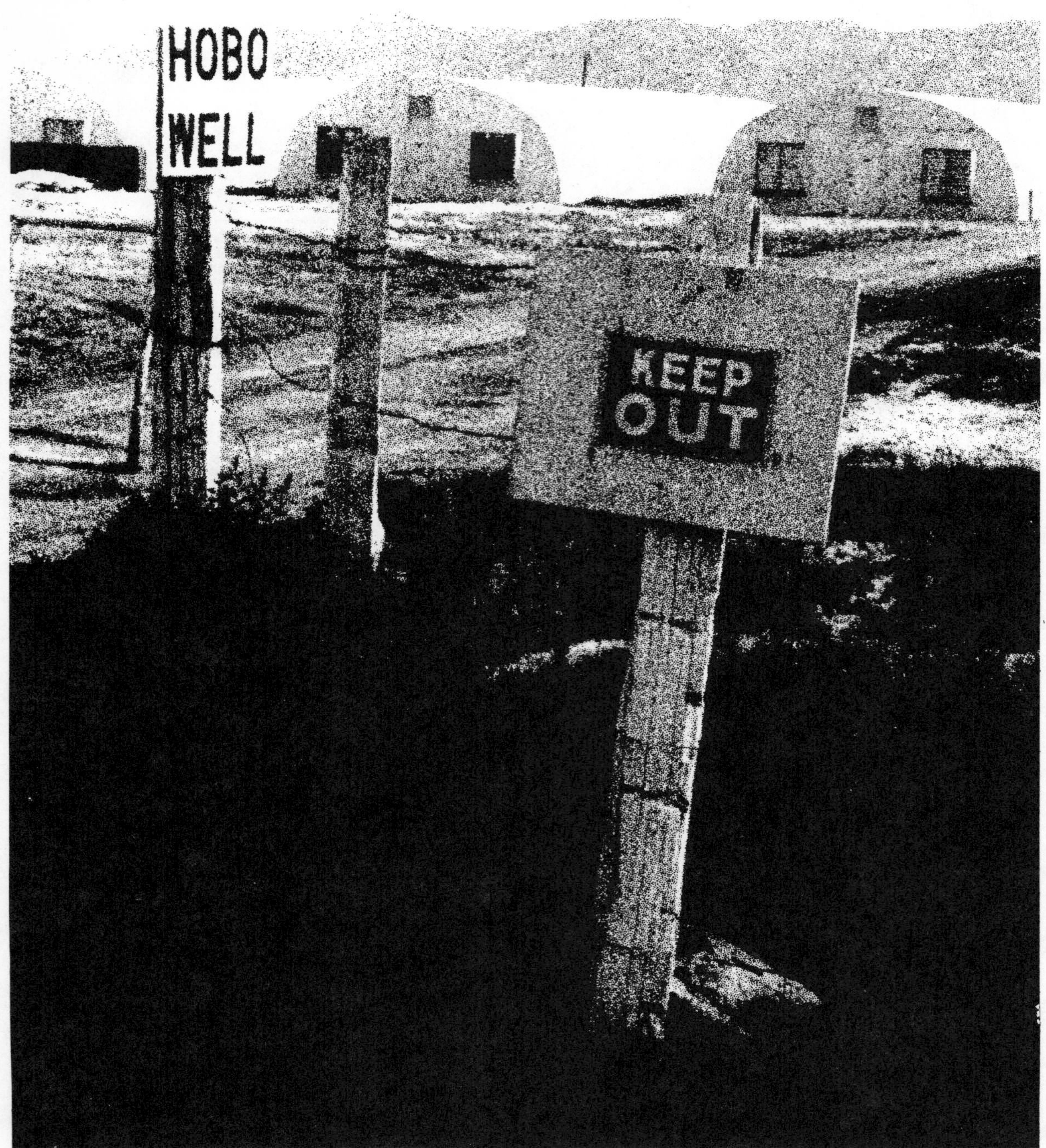
HOBO
WELL
KEEP
OUT

Alphabetical Master Index of Mineral Water Locations

This index is designed to help you locate a hot spring or resort listing when you start with the location name. Turn to the page given for that name and look for the location number. If you then want to know where it is, turn to the key map given and look for the location number on that map.

This index also includes several dozen locations labeled NUBP (Not Usable By the Public), with no further location information. On the basis of my research I have determined that a NUBP location is not operational, is not legally accessible by the public or is no longer in existence. Space does not permit including all NUBP locations in this index, but I chose some examples to convey the fact that I do not simply overlook them. The photographs in this section illustrate the NUBP status of several such locations.

During the early stages of my research I tried to determine the history of all commercial sites, especially those which had been open to the public at one time. However, I learned that some places had been defunct for so many years that no one clearly remembered what happened. If I asked four different people, I got four different answers, none of them verifiable. Eventualy, I concluded that the only significant fact, for the purpose of this book, was that a specific site was no longer usable, regardless of the reason. I decided to let the historians speculate about what happened at those places where we *can't* go, and concentrated on what is presently happening at the places where we *can* go.

If you deem yourself to be adventurous you should also know about another hot spring author, Eric D. Irving, who takes a dim view of all commercial mineral water operations. He, and his correspondents, prefer to concentrate on "freebie" soaking opportunities, without worrying about little technicalities such as permission. As a result, his publications contain a few of the locations labeled NUBP in my publications. For more information send $1.00 with your name and address to:

Eric D. Irving
Doodly-Squat Press
P.O. Box 480740
Los Angeles, Ca 90048

You will at least receive a catalog of his publications, but I do not accept any responsibility for the accuracy of the material, nor for what you choose to do with the information.

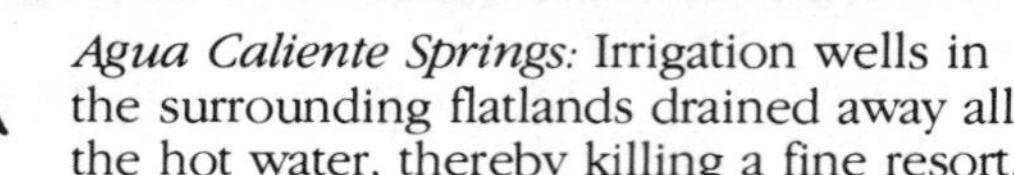
Agua Caliente Springs: Irrigation wells in the surrounding flatlands drained away all the hot water, thereby killing a fine resort.

Howard Hot Springs: This big old resort no longer meets health and safety codes.

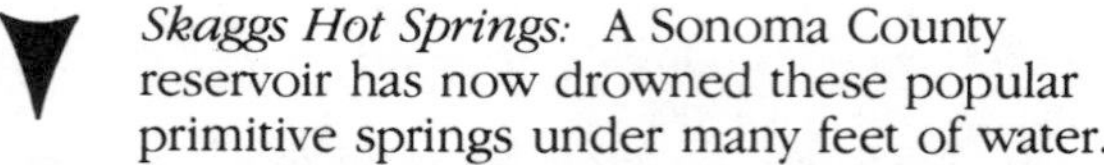
Skaggs Hot Springs: A Sonoma County reservoir has now drowned these popular primitive springs under many feet of water.

Name	Page Number	Area Key Map	Location Number
CACTUS LODGE	110	SC	#440G
CACTUS SPRINGS LODGE	110	SC	#440H
CALIENTE HOT SPRINGS MOTEL	137	NV	#605
CALIFORNIA HOT SPRINGS	63	CC	#220
CALISTOGA HOT SPRINGS	39	NC	#121B
CALISTOGA SPA	40	NC	#121E
CAMPBELL HOT SPRINGS	34	NC	#113
CARAVAN MOTEL	110	SC	#440I
CARSON HOT SPRINGS	143	NV	#617
CASTLE HOT SPRINGS	149	AZ	#708
CHARLES MOTEL AND BATH HOUSE	173	NM	814C
CLIFTON HOT SPRINGS	NUBP	AZ	
COFER HOT SPRINGS	NUBP	AZ	
CORKHILL RV AND MOBILE HOME PARK	114	SC	#442B
COSO HOT SPRINGS	NUBP	SC	
CRABTREE HOT SPRINGS	NUBP	NC	
DAVE'S CLOVERLEAF BATHS	173	NM	#814A
DEEP CREEK HOT SPRINGS	120	SC	#448
DELONEGHA HOT SPRINGS	65	CC	#223
DERRY WARM SPRINGS	NUBP	NM	
DESERT HOT SPRINGS SPA	110	SC	#440K
DESERT HOT SPRINGS TRAILER PARK	114	SC	#442C
DESERT VIEW ADULT MOBILE PARK	115	SC	#442E
DIRTY SOCK HOT SPRING	63	CC	#219
DRAKESBAD GUEST RANCH	32	NC	#109
DR. WILKINSON'S HOT SPRINGS	39	NC	#121D
EAGLE CREEK HOT SPRINGS	NUBP	AZ	
EAST CARSON RIVER HOT SPRINGS	49	CC	#201
EDEN HOT SPRINGS	NUBP	SC	
ELIAS' HIDE-A-WAY	94	SC	#403C
EL MYRA LODGE	111	SC	#440L
ESALEN INSTITUTE	81	CC	#262
FAYWOOD HOT SPRINGS	175	NM	#816
FISH CREEK HOT SPRING	60	CC	#214
FISH LAKE HOT WELL	142	NV	#613
FOUNTAIN OF YOUTH SPA	96	SC	#411A
FURNACE CREEK INN	91	SC	#401A
FURNACE CREEK RANCH	92	SC	#401B
GERLACH HOT SPRINGS	145	NV	#621
GILA HOT SPRINGS VACATION CENTER	177	NM	#818
GILLARD HOT SPRINGS	NUBP	AZ	
GILMAN HOT SPRINGS	NUBP	SC	
GLEN HOT SPRING	29	NC	#101
GLEN IVY HOT SPRINGS	122	SC	#452
GOLDEN HAVEN HOT SPRINGS	41	NC	#121G
GOLDEN LANTERN MOBILE VILLAGE	115	SC	#442F
GOLD STRIKE HOT SPRINGS	158	AZ	#731A
GRAPEVINE SPRINGS	NUBP	SC	
GROVER HOT SPRINGS	50	CC	#202
HAN'S MOTEL AND MINERAL SPA	125	SC	#454
HARBIN HOT SPRINGS	42	NC	#126
HIDEAWAY COTTAGES	41	NC	#121H
HIGHLAND SERVICE	95	SC	#408
HIGHLINE SOUTH HOT WELL	95	SC	#407
HILLSBORO WARM SPRING	174	NM	#815
HOLMES HOT SPRINGS MOBILE PARK	115	SC	#442G
HOLY GHOST WARM SPRINGS	169	NM	#807
HOOKERS HOT SPRINGS	NUBP	AZ	
HOT CREEK	54	CC	#208
HOWARD SPRINGS	NUBP	NC	
HUNT HOT SPRINGS	NUBP	NC	
HUNT'S ASH SPRINGS	138	NV	#606
IMPERIAL SEA VIEW HOT SPRINGS SPA	98	SC	#411C
INDIAN HOT SPRINGS	NUPB	AZ	
JACUMBA HOT SPRINGS HEALTH SPA	102	SC	#420
JEMEZ SPRINGS BATH HOUSE AND MOTEL	168	NM	#806
JO-RAY MOTEL	125	SC	#454
JORDAN HOT SPRINGS	61	CC	#217
KACHINA MINERAL SPRINGS SPA	155	AZ	#724B
KEANE WONDER SPRINGS	NUPB	SC	
KELLOG HOT SPRINGS	NUPB	NC	
KEOUGH HOT DITCH	58	CC	#212
KEOUGH HOT SPRINGS	59	CC	#213
KERN HOT SPRING	61	CC	#216
KINGSTON HOT SPRINGS	183	TX	#902
KISMET LODGE	111	SC	#440S
KYLE HOT SPRINGS	136	NV	#603
LAKE CITY HOT SPRINGS	NUPB	NC	
LAKEVIEW HOT SPRINGS	NUPB	SC	
LARK SPA	99	SC	#411D
LAS CRUCES HOT SPRINGS	84	CC	#271
LAS PRIMAVERAS MOTEL & SPA	111	SC	#440T
LA VIDA MINERAL SPRINGS	128	SC	#462
LEBANON HOT MINERAL BATHS	155	AZ	#724A
LEONARD'S HOT SPRING	29	NC	#102
LE SPA FRANCAIS	38	NC	#121A
LIDO PALMS SPA MOTEL	111	SC	#440U
LIGHTFEATHER HOT SPRINGS	178	NM	#819A
LINDA VISTA LODGE	112	SC	#440V
LORANE MANOR SPA	112	SC	#440W
MA-HA-YAH LODGE	112	SC	#440X
MANBY HOT SPRINGS	163	NM	#802B
MARY ANN MANOR	112	SC	#440Y

GEOTHERMAL POWER PLANT

Owner... MAMMOTH PACIFIC

A Joint Venture of Pacific Energy Resources, Inc. (a Pacific Lighting Corporation Subsidiary) and Mammoth Binary Power Company (Holt Geothermal Company General Partner).

Operator.. MAMMOTH BINARY POWER COMPANY

Lessor... MAGMA ENERGY, INC.

Engineering. THE BEN HOLT CO. PASADENA, CA.

Construction. KENNEBEC CONSTRUCTION COMPANY (a Holt Subsidiary)

Capacity... 7,000 KW

Completion.. AUGUST, 1984

▲ *Casa Diablo Hot Springs:* This well-fenced and posted project has been erected around these still bubbling and steaming springs.

◀ *Kellog Hot Spring:* Decreasing northeast California population and overage pools shut down this resort decades ago.

▼ *Scovern Hot Spring:* A high water table and no sewer system make commercial development of this site impractical.